LEARNING, POLICY MAKING, AND MARKET REFORMS

In the 1980s and 1990s, market reforms swept the world. It is widely believed that the reformist wave can be partly explained in terms of the lessons learned from policy failures of the past. Although this interpretation of events is well established, it has never been empirically proved. *Learning, Policy Making, and Market Reforms* is the first study that tests the impact of policy learning on economic policy choices across time and space. The study supports the popular explanation that, on average, governments around the world adopted privatization and trade liberalization, and sustained open capital accounts, as a result of learning from the experience of others.

Covadonga Meseguer has a Ph.D. in political science and is a member of the Juan March Institute for Advanced Study in the Social Sciences, Madrid, Spain. She has been a Fulbright Fellow at New York University; a Jean Monnet Fellow at the European University Institute, Florence; a Visiting Fellow at the Helen Kellogg Institute for International Studies, University of Notre Dame, Indiana; and a Visiting Professor at the Universitat Pompeu Fabra, Barcelona. Dr. Meseguer has written on globalization, the internationalization of policies, and Latin American political economy. Her work has been published in the *Annals of the American Academy of Social and Political Sciences*, the *Journal of Public Policy, Rationality and Society*, and the *European Journal of Political Economy*. Dr. Meseguer is currently a researcher at the Center for Research and Teaching in Economics (CIDE), Mexico City, and Visiting Professor at the Barcelona Institute for International Studies (IBEI), Barcelona.

Learning, Policy Making, and Market Reforms

COVADONGA MESEGUER

Center for Research and Teaching in Economics (CIDE),
Mexico City

Shaftesbury Road, Cambridge CB2 8EA, United Kingdom

One Liberty Plaza, 20th Floor, New York, NY 10006, USA

477 Williamstown Road, Port Melbourne, VIC 3207, Australia

314–321, 3rd Floor, Plot 3, Splendor Forum, Jasola District Centre, New Delhi – 110025, India

103 Penang Road, #05–06/07, Visioncrest Commercial, Singapore 238467

Cambridge University Press is part of Cambridge University Press & Assessment, a department of the University of Cambridge.

We share the University's mission to contribute to society through the pursuit of education, learning and research at the highest international levels of excellence.

www.cambridge.org
Information on this title: www.cambridge.org/9780521516969

© Covadonga Meseguer 2009

This publication is in copyright. Subject to statutory exception and to the provisions of relevant collective licensing agreements, no reproduction of any part may take place without the written permission of Cambridge University Press & Assessment.

First published 2009
First paperback edition 2015

A catalogue record for this publication is available from the British Library

Library of Congress Cataloging-in-Publication data
Meseguer Yebra, Covadonga.
Learning, policy making, and market reforms / Covadonga Meseguer.
p. cm.
Includes bibliographical references and index.
ISBN 978-0-521-51696-9 (hardback)
1. Privatization – Case studies. 2. Free trade – Case studies.
3. Economic policy – Case studies. 4. Social learning – Case studies. I. Title.
HD3850.M47 2009
338.9′25–dc22   2008035252

ISBN   978-0-521-51696-9   Hardback
ISBN   978-1-107-56939-3   Paperback

Cambridge University Press & Assessment has no responsibility for the persistence or accuracy of URLs for external or third-party internet websites referred to in this publication and does not guarantee that any content on such websites is, or will remain, accurate or appropriate.

Contents

List of Figures and Tables	*page* vii
List of Abbreviations	x
Acknowledgments	xi

1	The Question	1
	1.1. Governments, Market Reforms, and Learning	5
	1.2. Varieties of Learning	14
	1.3. Policy Convergence, Learning, and Alternative Hypotheses	22
	1.4. Plan of the Book	29
2	The Model	37
	2.1. Essentials	40
	2.2. On Posteriors	47
	2.3. Policy Choices	58
	2.4. Discussion	67
	2.5. Appendix	69
3	Learning and Development Strategies	73
	3.1. Development Strategies: A Description and Alternative Explanations	75
	3.2. Learning and Development Strategies: The Data	81
	3.3. Learning and Development Strategies: The Results	89
	3.4. Discussion	103
	3.5. Appendix	107

v

vi *Contents*

4	Learning and Privatization	111
	4.1. Explaining Privatization	113
	4.2. Learning and Privatization: The Data	121
	4.3. Learning and Privatization: The Results	125
	4.4. Discussion	137
	4.5. Appendix	140
5	Learning and Capital Account Liberalization	142
	5.1. The Political Economy of Capital Account Liberalization	145
	5.2. Learning and Capital Account Liberalization: The Data	150
	5.3. Mexico: A Narrative on Learning, Financial Liberalization, and Financial Crisis	157
	5.4. Learning and Capital Account Liberalization: The Results	163
	5.5. Discussion	177
	5.6. Appendix	179
6	Learning and IMF Agreements	181
	6.1. Explaining IMF Agreements	183
	6.2. Consequences of IMF Agreements	189
	6.3. Learning and IMF Agreements: The Data	193
	6.4. Learning and IMF Agreements: The Results	196
	6.5. Discussion	208
	6.6. Appendix	210
7	Conclusions	214
	7.1. Lessons about Learning	216
	7.2. Alternative Hypotheses	226
	7.3. What Remains to Be Learned?	231
References		241
Index		261

List of Figures and Tables

Figures

2.1.	Average Rates of Growth in Latin America (1964–1990)	*page* 48
2.2.	Observed Rates of Growth and Posterior Beliefs	51
2.3.	Costa Rica: Rate of Adaptation to Regional Information, IS	51
2.4.	Posterior Beliefs about Growth under IS and EO	52
2.5.	Costa Rica: Rate of Adaptation to New Data, Intervention	54
2.6.	Observed Rates of Growth and Posterior Beliefs (IS, Intervention)	55
2.7.	Posterior Beliefs about Growth, EO and IS (Intervention)	56
3.1.	Proportion of Countries with an Open Trade Regime, 1970–1999	85
3.2.	Average Rates of Growth and Volatility of Results, 1970–1999	87
3.3.	Predicted Probability of Adopting EO, Volatility of Results in the World	95
3.4.	Predicted Probability of Liberalizing Trade, Own Growth, by Regime Type	99
3.5.	Predicted Probability of Liberalizing Trade, Number of Others, by Regime Type	100
4.1.	Proportion of Privatizers, 1980–1997	123
4.2.	Average Rates of Growth with and without Privatization, 1980–1997	125

viii　　　　　　　　*List of Figures and Tables*

4.3.	Predicted Probability of Privatizing, World Growth, by Number of Other Countries	136
5.1.	Proportion of Countries with an Open Capital Account, 1968–1996	152
5.2.	Average Rates of Growth, Developed Countries, 1968–1996	154
5.3.	Figures (a) and (b) Average Rates of Growth with Standard Deviation, Developing and Transitional Countries, 1968–1996	155
6.1.	Average Rates of Growth and Volatility of Results, under and not under an IMF Agreement, 1960–1990	191
6.2.	Proportion of Countries under an IMF Agreement, 1960–1990	194
6.3.	Predicted Probability of Signing by Number of Countries under IMF Agreements	203
6.4.	Change in Predicted Probabilities	204
7.1.	Convergence in Policy Choices	218
7.2.	Predicted Change in the Probability of Adopting Several Market Policies	221

Tables

1.1.	Mechanisms of Policy Convergence	23
2.1.	Independent Variables and Expected Effects on Policy Decisions	66
3.1.	Features and Policy Instruments of Development Strategies	76
3.2.	Growth Rate per Region and Decade, Development Strategies	86
3.3.	Probability of Adoption of an EO Strategy, Development Strategies Database (1964–1990)	91
3.4.	Probability of Trade Liberalization, Trade Liberalization Database (1970–1999)	97
3.5.	Change in Predicted Probability of Opening (Percentage Points)	102
A3.6.	Prior Beliefs, Development Strategies	107
A3.7.	Descriptive Statistics, Development Strategies	108
A3.8.	Prior Beliefs, Trade Liberalization	108

List of Figures and Tables   ix

A3.9.	Average Rates of Growth and Variability of Results, Open and Close Trade Regimes after 1985	109
A3.10.	Descriptive Statistics, Trade Liberalization	109
A3.11.	List of Countries, Development Strategies	110
4.1.	Probability of Launching and Sustaining Privatization	131
4.2.	Changes in Predicted Probability of Privatizing	134
A4.3.	Prior Beliefs, Privatization	140
A4.4.	Descriptive Statistics, Privatization	140
A4.5.	List of Countries, Privatization	141
5.1.	Annual Rates of Growth and Volatility of Results by Capital Account Stance and by Region	154
5.2.	Probability of Launching and Sustaining an Open Capital Account	165
5.3.	Probability of Launching and Sustaining an Open Capital Account, Financial Crises	170
5.4.	Change in Predicted Probability of Launching and Sustaining an Open Capital Account (Percentage Points)	174
A5.5.	Prior Parameters, Capital Account Openness	179
A5.6.	Descriptive Statistics, Capital Account Openness	179
A5.7.	List of Countries, Capital Account Openness	180
6.1.	Average Rates of Growth by Region under and not under an Agreement	195
6.2.	Probability of Entering and Remaining under an IMF Agreement	201
6.3.	Probability of Entering and Remaining under an IMF Agreement, 1982 Shock	207
A6.4.	Prior Beliefs, IMF	210
A6.5.	Descriptive Statistics, IMF	211
A6.6.	List of Countries, IMF	212
7.1.	Summary of Results. Change in Predicted Probabilities of Adopting and Sustaining Policies (Percentage Points)	220

List of Abbreviations

BoP	Balance of Payments
CODESA	Corporación para el Desarrollo de Costa Rica
ECLAC	Economic Commission for Latin America and the Caribbean
EMU	European Monetary Union
EO	Export Orientation
ERM	Exchange Rate Mechanism
EU	European Union
FDI	Foreign Direct Investment
FDP	Freedom Democratic Party
GATT/WTO	General Agreement on Tariffs and Trade/World Trade Organization
IFIs	International Financial Institutions
IMF	International Monetary Fund
IOs	International Organizations
ISI	Import Substitution Industrialization
LDCs	Less Developed Countries
MNCs	Multinational Corporations
NAFTA	North American Free Trade Agreement
NICs	New Industrialized Countries
OECD	Organization for Economic Cooperation and Development
PLN	Partido de Liberación Nacional
PRI	Partido Revolucionario Institucional
PSD	Partido Social Demócrata (Social Democratic Party)
SOEs	State-Owned Enterprises
USAID	United States Agency for International Development
WB	World Bank

Acknowledgments

This is a book about learning from the experience of others: changing economic policy choices and adopting those that "work." It concentrates on the policy choices of developing and transitional countries and, in particular, on the change of economic paradigm that took place in the mid-1980s and 1990s and that gave a prominent role to markets – as opposed to the state – in economic development. Standard explanations of this change attribute an important role to learning from failed past experiences. Yet, this hypothesis remains untested. How much of the wave of economic policy reforms can be accounted for in terms of learning from others? Learning from normal times or learning from extraordinary times? Learning from neighbors or learning from any relevant experience, no matter how distant? And learning rationally or mindlessly imitating others? As this study shows, learning – especially from bad times – was part of the explanation of trade liberalization and privatization. But rational learning falls short of fully explaining these and other reforms surveyed in this study. If learning from the experience of others was not the only (and often not the most important) driver of liberalization, what other factors account for it? And with what consequences for the "quality" of policymaking? These are the important questions that I address in this study.

At the time of writing, and in the midst of deep financial turmoil originating in the United States, the main source of liberal economic ideas, the questions posed in this book seem both pertinent and urgent: What lessons will be learned from the crisis (and its interventionist solution), and by whom? Will the state be attributed new and more prominent roles in the belief that markets also fail? On this occasion, will learning flow from the South to the North – that is, will the United States and the developed world in general learn the lessons that developing countries so painfully learned in the late 1990s? Will the systemic financial crisis entail a break with the economic paradigm that has dominated public affairs since the mid 1980s? Finally, which lessons will developing countries learn from these events? Will those lessons imply a backlash against the pace of reforms as disappointment feeds on reform fatigue? These questions are central; yet their answers depend on the perceived existence or otherwise of a workable alternative to the current economic paradigm. In search of that alternative paradigm or a new incarnation of the existing one, the failed past experiences in development should be kept, again, carefully in mind.

This project began several years ago at the Center for Advanced Studies in the Social Sciences at the Juan March Institute, Madrid. *El Instituto* was crucial in the initial stages of my career as a researcher. It gave me the wonderful opportunity to learn social sciences in the company of talented classmates and a dedicated faculty. I appreciate the support of Professor José María Maravall, former scientific director of the Institute, who was always enthusiastic about this project. The research took me to New York University, where it grew under the wise and generous mentoring of Professor Adam Przeworski. I wish to thank Adam for the gift of having worked under his supervision and for his patience with my impatience. I hope that this book lives up to his standards of "thinking big and taking risks." Professor Kurt Weyland provided intellectual motivation and pushed me hard to think about learning. Despite defending contrasting views on policy learning, Kurt always showed great interest in my work. His studies on bounded learning and the political economy of market reforms were fantastic companions during this endeavor.

Two postdoctoral stays at the European University Institute (Florence) and at the Helen Kellogg Institute for International Studies (University of Notre Dame) gave me the opportunity to discuss my work with scholars from all over the world. I am particularly grateful to Scott Mainwaring, whose interest in this project was always a motivation for me to work on it. Most of the revisions to the original manuscript were accomplished during my stay at the Centro para la Investigación y la Docencia Económicas

Acknowledgments   xiii

(CIDE), in Mexico City. I am indebted to CIDE, and especially to the successive International Studies Division Chairs (Antonio Ortiz-Mena and Jorge Schiavon), for providing the perfect environment in which to work on my project.

My gratitude also goes to several scholars and colleagues who read parts of this volume at several stages or helped in different ways: Javier Aparicio, Carles Boix, Sarah Brooks, Gustavo del Angel, Zach Elkins, Joan Esteban, Pepe Fernández, Jen Gandhi, Jacint Jordana, Achim Kemmerling, Matt Kocher, Sebastián Lavezzolo, David Levi-Faur, Scott Mainwaring, Dulce Manzano, Susan Minushkin, Layna Mosley, Gabriel Negretto, Daniel Peña, Thomas Plümper, Clara Riba, Andrew Richards, Julio Ríos, Guillermo Rosas, Nita Rudra, Pacho Sánchez-Cuenca, Javier Santiso, Arturo Sotomayor, Piero Stanig, James Vreeland, my colleagues in the International Studies Division at CIDE, and the anonymous reviewers. The usual disclaimer applies.

I also thank my copy editor Michael James, who is mostly responsible for polishing the text; my research assistants Mariana Aparicio and Gonzalo Rivero for their enormous help; and my Cambridge University Press editor, Scott Parris, for his friendly and helpful company throughout the process.

My friend and colleague Fabrizio Gilardi has been my closest intellectual companion during these years of thinking about learning and the diffusion of policies. We have shared conferences, papers, discussions, projects, career dilemmas, and, above all, many good times. Another friend and colleague, Cecilia Martínez-Gallardo, was crucial in making my life in Mexico easy and fun. It is hard for me to think of a more generous person than Ceci. Without her good sense and her unconditional support and care, being far away from home would have been much more difficult for me.

I thank all my other friends – Rafa Sotoca, Elvira González, Sonia Velicia, Toñi Ruiz, Irene Martín, Marvin Cabrera, Nane Carneiro, Gulenay Özbek, Marga León, Mónica Gelambí, Teresa Martín, Zyab Ibáñez, and María José Roa – for being loving companions in every decision and in every destination. I thank my wonderful family: My brothers, Quino and Diego; my sisters, Mariela, Patricia, and Carmen; and my nephews, Edu and Joaquín, who always listened, helped, healed, and welcomed with joy their globetrotting sister and aunt. My parents, Carmen and Joaquín, have all my gratitude for their vision and their infinite patience with their restless daughter. They raised our big family with our education as their unequivocal priority. My life with them has been a constant lesson in honesty, effort, love, and unconditional support, and so it is to them that I dedicate this book about learning.

Para mis padres, Carmen y Joaquín.

ONE

The Question

> The task which the loss of the stable state makes imperative, for the person, for our institutions, for society as a whole is to learn about learning.
> (Schön 1973, quoted in Freeman 2006)

In much of the developing world, the 1980s and 1990s were decades of radical economic change. Whereas in the 1960s and 1970s, the prevailing model of development was based on state intervention and inward-looking policies, the 1980s and 1990s were characterized by the advocacy of market-oriented reforms. These reforms, packaged under the so-called Washington Consensus, aimed at opening up national economies and at reducing the role of the state in the economy.[1] The consensus became so broad that some described the new state of the debate on development as one of "universal convergence" (Williamson 1990, 1994; Biersteker 1995; Rodrik 1996: 9).[2]

The story of the "universal convergence" can be told along the following lines. The model of inward-oriented industrialization, epitomized by

[1] The Washington Consensus comprised ten policy prescriptions: Fiscal discipline, adjustment of public expenditure priorities, tax reform, financial liberalization, exchange rate adjustment, trade liberalization, promotion of foreign direct investment, privatization, deregulation, and support for property rights (Williamson 1990, 1994). For stylistic reasons, I refer to these measures as market reforms and neo-liberal programs.

[2] John Williamson acknowledges the existence of broad areas of disagreement in the Washington Consensus. See Williamson (1993) for a discussion. Also, note that this global trend toward market-oriented policies has not precluded differences in the timing of reforms, in their speed and intensity, and in their results. However, the aim of the present study is not to explain those differences but rather to explain why the thrust of economic policy, especially in the developing world, was so different in the 1980s than in the 1970s (Stallings 1992: 43).

1

the experience of many Latin American countries in the 1960s and 1970s, was a resounding failure. The bias against exports caused enormous balance-of-payment crises. Devaluations, inflation, and fiscal indiscipline became common. Governments borrowed massively from abroad to close the external and fiscal gaps. At the beginning of the 1980s, Mexico's debt moratorium alarmed foreign creditors, who cut off their lending. Without credit to finance chronic fiscal deficits, governments resorted to the printing press, which eventually resulted in hyperinflation and economic stagnation. Moreover, the proliferation of controls and the protection of industries and sectors were an invitation to evasion, rent seeking, and corruption (Iglesias 1992; Tommasi and Velasco 1995: 1–3; Krueger 1993, 1997).

In clear contrast, and simultaneously, Chile and the East Asian tigers (Korea, Singapore, Hong Kong, and Taiwan) achieved phenomenal rates of growth by relying on greater integration into the world economy. The hallmark of this strategy was an export-promotion policy, taken to be the quintessential illustration of the virtues of a small state. At the end of the 1980s, the collapse of Communist rule in Eastern Europe struck the final blow to the idea that state intervention was a requisite for development. By the early 1990s, even these countries had become engaged in market-oriented reforms.

These changes in the South and the East took place amid a neo-liberal revolution in the North. At the beginning of the 1980s, Conservatives in Britain and Republicans in the United States launched a campaign against the idea of "big government." The neo-liberal revolution put an end to the Keynesian consensus, which had dominated public affairs since World War II.

A widely accepted explanation of the wave of economic reform is that governments learned from contrasting experiences under alternative models of development. This learning would have entailed a change in the mapping from policies to economic outcomes, and a change in beliefs about the consequences of actions and the optimal strategies in a changing economic environment. Thus, the story goes, governments would have observed these contrasting experiences and changed their beliefs about the economic consequences of alternative economic models. Even short-sighted politicians could not have avoided the conclusion that

The Question

the old policies had failed and the new orthodoxy had produced economic success (Kahler 1990, 1992; Haggard and Kaufman 1992; Hall 1993; Haggard and Webb 1994; Biersteker 1995; Tommasi and Velasco 1995; Krueger 1997). Yet, the learning hypothesis remains untested. Hence the question: *Did governments switch to market-oriented policies as a result of a learning process?*

In order to test this explanation rigorously, one needs an operational concept of learning.[3] I shall assume that governments are rational (Bayesian) learners. This means that governments efficiently update their initial beliefs about the expected results of alternative policies with reference to information about policy outcomes in the past and elsewhere. After updating their beliefs, governments choose the policies that are expected to yield the best result in terms of economic growth.[4] Hence, the model I test is one in which politicians first learn in the light of experience and then make rational choices on the basis of what they learn. Having been exposed to the same information, governments converged in their beliefs and, hence, in their policy choices.

This approach is used to test the role of learning in the decisions in the 1980s and 1990s to liberalize the trade regime, privatize, open up the capital account, and enter into agreements with the International Monetary Fund (IMF). The book shows that rational learning partly motivated policy switches in the cases of privatization and trade liberalization. Whereas learning also mattered in the decision to open the capital account, the magnitude of the effect was very small. Rather, rational learning appeared more consequential in explaining the decision to sustain an open capital account. Learning also mattered in the decision to sign agreements with

---

[3] Although the discussion about learning has been widespread, it has focused more on definitional questions (Heclo 1974; Odell 1982; March and Olsen 1989; Sabatier and Jenkins-Smith 1993; Rose 1991, 1993; Bennett and Howlett 1992; May 1992; Pierson 1993; Levy 1994; Haas and Haas 1995; Adler and Haas 1997; Stone 1999; Freeman 2006).

[4] Note that I am assuming that governments judge the success of market reforms in terms of their potential to promote economic growth. This view is generally agreed. As Stiglitz puts it (2000: 552), "privatization and trade liberalization are not ends in themselves, but means to ends – ends such as more rapid, more sustainable, and more equitable growth and improved living standards." Krueger (2000: 64) adds, "structural reforms were necessary to promote higher, sustainable growth by improving the environment for physical and human capital accumulation."

the IMF, but in a way that suggests that IMF contracts are not routine policy making. Thus, learning from the experience of others mattered in all policy illustrations but according to different patterns and with different impacts on policy decisions. Indeed, rational learning was never the most important determinant of policy choices. Emulating others, third-party coercion and particular domestic characteristics drove policy decisions to a considerable extent as well.

Overall, governments learned. But governments not only learned. From a normative point of view, it is good news that learning was at least part of the explanation for the adoption of market reforms. This means that countries, on average, adopted the policies that, again on average, performed comparatively better. Yet, it is less reassuring to find that, on occasion, governments mindlessly imitated the policies of others rather than understanding them (when privatizing and when liberalizing trade); or that governments adopted particular policies for which neither theory nor evidence was conclusive about their superiority. This book discusses the welfare consequences of adopting policies for reasons other than rational learning. It also speculates about the prospects of the reform movement in light of the results of this study.

The introductory chapter proceeds as follows: In the next section, I review some of the narrative evidence regarding the role that learning from others' experience played in the adoption of market reforms. The narrative suggests that governments did, indeed, look at the performance of other countries and draw lessons from their experience. Following this, I discuss the literature on learning and the different approaches to the study of this concept. I show that, whereas learning is a major topic in international relations and comparative public policy, the discussion has mostly remained at a conceptual level. I claim that rational updating is a powerful tool to overcome the operationalization conundrum. Next, I discuss alternative explanations for the observed convergence of market reforms. At the very least, convergence could have been motivated by an attempt to imitate, rather than to learn from the success of others. Also, supranational and international institutions could have forced or persuaded countries to adopt these policies in their role as disseminators of norms and policy ideas. Finally, convergence could have been the result of identical but independent responses of countries confronted with the same environment. The chapter concludes with an outline of the book.

1.1. Governments, Market Reforms, and Learning

Most of the many studies on the political economy of market reforms assume that at least some reforms are desirable, and focus on the social and political factors that preclude, delay, or promote the adoption of reforms and their sustainability through time.[5]

According to such studies, the conjunction of a deep economic crisis, a new government with a strong mandate, and a coherent and autonomous economic team supported by a "visionary" leader are good predictors of the *launch* of economic reforms. Compensation to the groups who suffered as a result of the adjustment and some external financial aid are usually cited as requisites for reform *sustainability*. The way in which these and other variables operate has been extensively documented, so I do not delve into them here. Instead, I focus on governments and their preference for market reforms.

It is not at all obvious why governments interested in remaining in office may find market reforms desirable. Reforms are highly uncertain. Indeed, the only certain thing is that reforms will make most of the population worse off, at least temporarily (Przeworski 1992: 45). Given the political risks they entail, the adoption of such policies is remarkable.

For some authors, politicians' preference for adjustment is a question of "vision," "political will," or even "heroism" (Harberger 1993; Williamson 1994). Politicians who embark on reforms are heroes because they are willing to "lift their sights beyond the next election" and run high electoral risks for the common good. Obviously, this reading makes sense only if reforms are viewed as intrinsically virtuous and uncontroversial. Yet, it is a poor explanation of governments' preferences.

For other authors, governments opt for reforms for ideological reasons. As reflected in the fact that reform pioneers were right-wing military governments (for example, Chile under Pinochet in 1973–90 and Korea

---

[5] Nelson 1990a; Grindle and Thomas 1991; Frieden 1991a; Przeworski 1991; Haggard and Kaufman 1992; Waterbury 1993; Bresser, Maravall, and Przeworski 1993; Bates and Krueger 1993; Krueger 1993; Harberger 1993; Taylor 1993; Harrington 1993; Keeler 1993; Haggard and Webb 1994; Smith, Acuña, and Gamarra 1994; Nelson 1994; Geddes 1994; Williamson 1994; Tommasi and Velasco 1995; Haggard and Kaufman 1995; Rodrik 1996; Maravall 1997; Weyland 1996, 2002; Sturzenegger and Tommasi 1998; Drazen 2000; Krueger 2000; for criticisms and nuanced arguments about the desirability of reforms, see, for example, Murrell 1991; Przeworski 1992; Bresser, Maravall, and Przeworski 1993; Rodrik 1996; Stiglitz 1998, 2000.

6   *The Question*

under Park Chung Hee in 1963–79), the widespread contention is that market reforms are the natural preference of rightist governments. Some of the policy measures of the Washington Consensus were also vigorously defended by prominent rightist leaders in the North (such as Ronald Reagan in the United States in 1981–89 and Margaret Thatcher in the United Kingdom in 1979–90). Finally, domestic and foreign business groups, which are a traditional constituency of the right, frequently pressed for economic adjustment (Williamson and Haggard 1994: 570–71).

However, explanations based on ideological preferences cannot accommodate the fact that democratically elected leftist and populist governments also engaged in reforms, imposing the biggest sacrifices on their own constituencies – namely, labor and the poor. Socialists in Spain (under Felipe González, 1982–96), Labor governments in New Zealand (under David Lange, 1984–89) and Australia (under Bob Hawke, 1983–91), Peronists in Argentina (under Carlos Menem, 1989–99), and social democrats in Brazil (under Fernando H. Cardoso, 1995–2002) are just a few examples. Hence, ideological preferences seem to be a poor predictor of the decision to engage in these policies.[6]

I pursue another line of reasoning and argue that governments' preferences for market reforms were shaped by observing the experience of others, particularly by learning from policy failures and successes.

The hypothesis that crises facilitate the initiation of market reforms is very popular. However, it is also hotly debated. Dani Rodrik argues that, since there is no definition of crisis, the hypothesis that an economic crisis is a prerequisite for launching market reforms cannot be falsified. Indeed, it is a tautology: "[R]eform naturally becomes an issue only when policies are perceived not to be working. A crisis is just an extreme case of policy failure. That reform should follow crisis, then, is no more surprising than smoke following fire" (1996: 27; see also 1994). However, Drazen contends that there is something to be explained if,

---

[6] True, the literature on policy reform makes it clear that there is a social democratic approach to implementing these policies. As opposed to their rightist counterparts, leftist governments approach the reforms gradually, compensate the more vulnerable, and reach pacts with labor so that inflation is held in check while labor cooperation is rewarded with greater investment in welfare provision and education (Bresser, Maravall, and Przeworski 1993; Boix 1998).

1.1. Governments, Market Reforms, and Learning 7

to use Rodrik's metaphor, only big fires but not small or medium ones cause reforms (2000: 444–46). If this is the case, and only hyperinflation, burgeoning fiscal deficits, or exploding imbalances in external accounts cause reforms, the subsequent question is why do crises have to be deep in order to spur policy switches?

Periods of deep economic disarray and the accompanying sense of loss of control, great uncertainty, and looming catastrophe may weaken the power of vested interests that otherwise would block reforms. Also, the sense that something must be done creates space for "special politics," that is, for a temporary suspension of the regular channels by which interest groups, party politics, and legislatures influence the policy-making process (Balcerowicz, in Williamson 1994; Drazen 2000: 447).[7] In Keeler's words (1993), if politicians in power are backed up with a strong mandate, a deep economic crisis may open a macro window for reform.

Note that this mechanism, which links a deep crisis with an enhanced *capacity* for action, reveals nothing about the *content* of the response. But, if under particular circumstances, governments' autonomy increases, agents' preferences turn out to be crucial to understanding policy choices (Grindle and Thomas 1991).[8] Overall, crises create opportunities for change. State autonomy creates the capacity to implement choices. But the content of the response is, at least in part, determined by policy-relevant knowledge.

Deep crises generally prompt some diagnosis of what causes them. In this sense, the diagnostic conveys some policy content, at the very least, about what should be avoided. Kurt Weyland's account of the adoption of market-oriented reforms addresses politicians' motives for action and the content of their choices (1996, 1998, 2002). Weyland contends that market reforms can be explained in light of prospect theory (Kahneman and Tversky 1988). According to this psychological approach to decision making, individuals make risky policy choices only when

---

[7] Sometimes strong mandates and a divided opposition spontaneously give governments a lot of room for maneuver (as in Spain in 1982). At other times, this room is deliberately created by granting the executive special powers for swift action.

[8] Bates and Krueger's review of several episodes of reform concludes that "one of the most surprising findings of our case studies is the degree to which the intervention of interest groups fails to account for the initiation or lack of initiation of policy reform" (1993: 454).

confronted with the prospect of big losses. A deep crisis puts decision makers in the domain of losses. As a result, governments are willing to launch draconian adjustment measures. For instance, the adoption of market reforms followed hyperinflations in Argentina, Bolivia, Brazil, Peru, and Poland. In Chile, Ghana, Senegal, Russia, and Tanzania, reforms were adopted amid uncontrolled fiscal or external deficits and mounting shortages of goods.

In addition, according to Weyland, new governments can overcome the strong status quo bias that characterizes decision making. Because changing the course of the political economy implies admitting that the previous course of action has failed, insiders are unlikely to endorse radical shifts in policy. However, new leaders are not affected by this bias. Indeed, new leaders often adopt radical policies to signal a break with past policies viewed as failures. Alberto Fujimori in Peru (1990) implemented a drastic reform program after the failed heterodox experiments of Alan García. The same applies to Fernando Collor de Mello (1990–92) and Carlos Menem (1989) in Brazil and Argentina respectively. Finally, Frederick Chiluba in Zambia (1991) launched a program of economic reforms after the heterodox adjustment program of Kenneth Kaunda (1964–73) collapsed. Hence, on this account, the adoption of market reforms appears as a reaction to previous failed policies (see also Nelson 1990a). Whether that reaction entailed an improved understanding of the relationship between policies and outcomes is not specified.[9]

The mechanism that relates deep crises to the content of the response is, precisely, learning. Tommasi and Velasco argue that crises contribute to Bayesian learning about the "right" model of the world. A period of intense economic disarray leads to a reassessment of the mapping from policies to outcomes – in particular, to a realization of how costly some previous policies were (1995:17–18). In the same vein, Harberger asserts that politicians have particular worldviews that may contain sensible explanations for bad economic outcomes. However, "every now and then,

---

[9] The same behavior applies to the electorate. The prospect of big losses makes people acquiesce to and even support the reforms. Weyland (2002) contends that reforms continue because, as soon as adjustment yields results, the electorate is placed in the domain of gains, where individuals are risk-averse. This interpretation overlooks that fact that, quite often, reforms restore growth only after long lags, if at all.

1.1. *Governments, Market Reforms, and Learning*

something happens that does not fit the previous image – something that shakes our Bayesian faith in what we used to think" (in Tommasi and Velasco 1995: 18). A period of deep economic disarray is a good candidate for provoking that breakdown of faith.

The contention that governments' preferences for market reforms were shaped, at least in part, by the experience of policy failures and policy successes is widely endorsed by scholars and policy makers alike. For instance, in 1993, Williamson asserted:

[t]he hope that we can now develop far more consensus than would have been conceivable or appropriate in the 1950s is based ultimately on the fact that we now know much more about what types of economic policy work. At that time, it looked as though socialism was a viable alternative to a market economy; now we know that it is not. At that time, we had not discovered that pushing import substitution beyond the first ("easy") stage was vastly inferior to a policy of outward orientation that allowed nontraditional exports to develop: now we know better (p. 1331).

Maravall (1997: 168), discussing the adoption of market reforms in eastern and southern European countries in the mid- and late 1980s, holds that "some leaders sought to avoid experiments which might prove costly in political or economic terms. They were more likely to make this choice if they were particularly influenced by past experiments, whether in their own country or elsewhere." In fact, Hungarian reformer Peter Bod eloquently stated that "on the basis of my reading and limited personal experience of developments in industrialized and newly emerging industrial countries, it was quite clear to me that the process taking place in Hungary was not extraordinary in all respects. The painful restructuring, the decay of traditional industry, the market reorientation, the opening up and outward looking economic policies following autarkic periods – these were all concepts that could be amply studied in the economic histories of other countries" (in Blejer and Coricelli 1995: 99).

Nicolás Ardito-Barletta, president of Panama in 1984–85, asserted that "[T]here is a national learning process that permits society to discover, through trial-and-error, how to arrive at new social rules of the game and policies that are beneficial to the majority" (1994: 461). And he added: "the national learning process as a vehicle for economic policy change and stability is most useful when there is a national memory of

The Question

past economic policy performance. Documented records of the failures or inadequacies of past policies are powerful teaching devices to support policy changes" (1991: 286). In his analysis of the adjustment process in Indonesia, Iwan Azis stated that "certainly, a 'learning process' has taken place during the course of Indonesia's development over the last 25 years" lessons that "policy makers ... eventually grasped and digested" (1994: 410). Arriagada and Graham (1994: 282) contend that, in Chile, short-term populist strategies were discredited by "the chaos in neighboring countries, [which] made macroeconomic restraint much more politically palatable." Finally, Czech reformer Václav Klaus stated that "[o]f course we followed the experience of some other countries that reformed their economies in parallel with our own, especially those of Hungary and Poland, but I must say that what we learned from them was mainly on the negative side" (in Blejer and Coricelli 1995: 66).

As much as bad outcomes convey information about what not to do, good performance conveys information about alternative courses of action. If learning actually occurs, "the experience of many reforming countries (assuming a modicum of success) will ... be imitated by others before having to experience themselves a crisis and the associated economic pain" (Tommasi and Velasco 1995: 19). Therefore, learning from successful reform experiences could explain the adoption of reforms in countries such as Colombia (1985) that adjusted despite not experiencing a deep crisis.

To continue with the narrative illustration, Moisés Naim (1993: 46), former Venezuelan minister of trade and industry, contended that Carlos A. Pérez's vision was influenced by the governing experiences of two of his closest personal and political friends. These experiences were:

> ... the catastrophic failure of President Alan García in Peru and the successful reforms of Felipe González in Spain. Pérez was able to follow the policies and performance of these two governments very closely and his privileged vantage point allowed him to judge the consequences of the two radically different approaches.

The outstanding performance of Chile and the East Asian tigers appeared as the most important source of inspiration. Crucial to the appeal of the alternative cases was the interpretation of their success. While the crises

1.1. Governments, Market Reforms, and Learning

of the 1980s were seen as the result of too much state intervention, the Chilean and East Asian experiences were taken to be the living examples of the benefits of state withdrawal. Much has been written about whether this interpretation was actually warranted.[10] However, it became the official creed in international financial institutions (IFIs) and international policy-making circles. Apparently, domestic political elites also were influenced by these examples.

Richard Webb, governor of the Peruvian central bank between 1980 and 1985, stated that "this change in perception [in favor of market reforms] ... [had] been reinforced by a broad flow of information on the experience, policies, and opinion in other countries. The Chilean experience has been particularly influential in Peru" (1994: 373). In Williamson (1994: 51), Ross Garnaut, personal economic adviser to Bob Hawke, explained that "the success of outward-looking policies in East Asia exercised subtle and indirect influences over Australian policy discussion." And Miguel A. Rodríguez, minister of planning and president of the Venezuelan central bank, stated that "economists and policymakers in Latin America saw the per-capita income growth of the Asian countries over the past twenty years and became more and more convinced that the opening of the economy was the best way to produce a real transformation in Latin American societies" (1994: 377).[11]

Available experience seems not to have been treated in an indiscriminate manner. As Robinson (1998) suggests, the informative value of particular experiences increases with historical, cultural, and institutional similarities. Psychological accounts of learning also show that proximity to the source of information makes some experiences more relevant than others (Hacking 1988; Kyburg 1988; Weyland 2005, 2007).

---

[10] To give a telling example, Rodrik shows that, of the ten measures endorsed by the Washington Consensus, South Korea followed five and Taiwan, about six. Interestingly, "neither country significantly liberalized its import regime until the 1980s. Both countries interfered in the investment decisions of private enterprises. And far from privatizing public enterprises, both countries actually increased their reliance on such enterprises during the crucial decade of the 1960s" (1996: 18).

[11] In his study on economic reforms in South Asia, T. N. Srinivasan (2000: 100) asserted that "the rapid growth of East Asia and China, on the one hand, and the collapse of the Soviet Union and Communist countries of Eastern Europe on the other, clearly indicated to South Asian policy makers that their development strategy had failed and economic reforms had to be undertaken."

12   *The Question*

For example, Enrique Iglesias, former president of the Inter-American Development Bank, contended that "the ideas developed in the North during the Reagan–Thatcher era were very important in Latin America, but the Chilean experience was far more significant insofar as it provided a viable model. The success of the Chilean experience was very much noted by other regional leaders." He added, "Southeast Asia also had some relevance as a model for Latin America, but it was viewed with some doubts because the Asian region was made up of many diverse countries with different social and cultural environments...whereas Chile presented a far more relevant example to emulate" (1994: 493–94).

In the same vein, Allan Bollard, referring to the reforms in New Zealand, argued that "the reform experience in the Southern Cone countries was not seen as relevant to New Zealand, given the problems of hyperinflation, political instability, and capital flight that existed there. Margaret Thatcher was putting into place some microeconomic reforms and spending restraints in Britain at the time, and there were certainly lessons to be learned from the British restructuring recession of the early 1980s" (1994: 98).

Thus, to put all the pieces together, it seems that governments' preferences for market reforms were informed by what they learned. Very bad experiences discredited a particular course of action and successful experiences gave credit to an alternative one. How these contrasting experiences were interpreted was crucial: The diagnostic of the cases of success (less state intervention and more outward-oriented policies) was exactly the opposite of the diagnostic of the cases of failure (too much state involvement and inward-oriented development). Apparently, lessons were drawn somewhat selectively on the basis of geographic propinquity or linguistic, historical, and cultural similarities. As a result of this learning process, switches to market-oriented policies occurred.

Note that the question of whether governments successfully *sustained* market-oriented policies as a result of learning from experience is more complex.[12] The literature on economic policy reform relates the *launch* of

---

[12] It is very common to study the launching of market reforms as a different political process than their implementation and maintenance over time. The literature on market reforms agrees that the dynamics and variables that influence the one and the other process are different (Nelson 1990a; Haggard and Kaufman 1992).

1.1. Governments, Market Reforms, and Learning 13

radical policy switches to the existence of an autonomous state. In turn, state autonomy may be related to multiple institutional features such as the existence of authoritarian regimes.[13] In democracies, autonomy can be achieved if a big electoral mandate exists, if a temporal recourse to extraordinary politics is made, or if popular discontent is not organized. An economic crisis frequently precipitates institutional changes that, by concentrating power in a few hands, facilitate swift action. Regardless of the specific source of state autonomy, it seems an empirical regularity that state autonomy is a necessary precondition for radical reforms (Nelson 1990a; Haggard and Kaufman 1992; Waterbury 1992; Bates and Krueger 1993; Haggard and Kaufman 1995; Evans 1995). However, state autonomy is uninformative about which particular course of action will be preferred.[14] Therefore, to account for economic policy choices, one needs to understand what shapes the preferences of autonomous politicians and the preferences of the technocrats they empower. Since learning may be crucial in determining agents' preferences, focusing on learning by these strategic actors at the moment of launching radical policy switches seems warranted.

For the reforms to be sustained, however, learning should transcend insulated change teams and become social (discussed subsequently). The room for special politics generally decreases with time, and the autonomy of change teams decreases with it. The most urgent aspects of economic crises, such as hyperinflation, are generally resolved after a relatively short period; honeymoons end, and political opposition may reorganize. On the other hand, if successful, reforms may create their own basis of support among specific groups, facilitating their sustainability. Thus, after reforms have been launched, the variables that influence whether reforms stall or endure increase dramatically (Haggard and Kaufman 1992, 1995;

---

[13] This, of course, does not imply that authoritarian regimes are autonomous per se.

[14] The empirical regularity is that governments that reformed did so after concentrating power in the hands of a reformist president and/or cohesive economic agencies. Yet not all governments that enjoy a stock of autonomy engaged in reforms. Autonomy is a necessary but not a sufficient condition. A state may be autonomous, but may be weak. Thus, it may not have the capacity to undertake the policies it prefers. Moreover, an autonomous state may prefer the status quo or may believe that an orthodox course of action is not superior. According to Van de Walle (2001), both factors explain why the autonomous states in Sub-Saharan Africa made inaction a permanent policy feature.

14 *The Question*

Haggard and Webb 1994; Haggard and Kaufman 1995; Weyland 2002). I also explore the question whether learning from experience under the reforms was one of the variables that influenced their sustainability. Due to the factors mentioned earlier, I anticipate that the beliefs of particular politicians and technocrats will be less consequential for the decision to sustain market reforms than for the decision to launch them.

Do the stories and illustrations presented amount to simple anecdotes or do they reveal the existence of a general pattern? To what extent is it true that learning was mostly driven by nearby experiences? Is it possible to systematically test whether policy switches across time, space, and policies were motivated by a process of learning? Answering these questions is precisely the task I undertake in this book.

1.2. Varieties of Learning

Discussions on learning have been extensive in the fields of public policy analysis and international relations. In their thorough review of available notions of learning, Bennett and Howlett conclude that "there is no shortage of theorization. Our review suggests that, if anything, the concept has been overtheorized and underapplied" (1992: 280). In the same vein, Bennett (in Stone, 1999: 52) points to "the paucity of systematic research that can convincingly make the case that cross-national policy learning has had a determining influence on policy choice." And Levy states that "the concept of learning is difficult to define, isolate, measure and apply empirically" (1994: 282). These statements are certainly an accurate description of the state of the art, which is clearly biased toward a conceptual discussion not matched by empirical analysis.

In their review article, Bennett and Howlett (1992) discuss the concepts of political learning (Heclo 1974), policy-oriented learning (Sabatier and Jenkins-Smith 1993), lesson drawing (Rose 1991, 1993), governmental learning (Etheredge 1981), and social learning (Hall 1993). The available notions of learning do not end there. May (1992) adds the notion of instrumental learning, and Levy (1994) contributes a distinction between causal and diagnostic learning.

All notions of learning entail an improved understanding of the cause-and-effect relationships of policies in light of experience. However, these definitions frequently overlap, and concepts vary regarding the subject (who learns) and the object of learning (about what). Also, different concepts entail different consequences. For instance, sometimes learning is merely procedural. It refers to changes in the policy process or in the capacity of policy advocates to advance their ideas (Etheredge's governmental learning or May's definition of political learning). At other times, learning is about policy content, ranging from particular policy instruments (Rose's lesson drawing) to the ultimate goals of policies and the terms of the policy discourse (Hall's social learning). Finally, some definitions of learning entail a change in behavior (for instance, in Heclo's and Hall's versions of the concept), whereas others define learning as a change in beliefs that may or may not induce a behavioral change (as in Levy). It is obvious that a conceptual discussion of learning is not lacking.

For their connection with the question I address here, several ideas in this literature deserve special attention: Peter Hall's concepts of *social learning* and *paradigm shifts* provide an accurate description of the kind of event I seek to explain. In turn, *rational learning* and *bounded learning* are the two competing theoretical approaches to explaining how learning may take place. I discuss these concepts in turn.

Social Learning

Using as an illustration the British shift from Keynesianism to monetarism between 1970 and 1989, Peter Hall conceptualizes social learning as a three-level change that affects the setting of the instruments of policy making (*first-order change*), the instruments themselves (*second-order change*), and the ultimate goals of policies – for instance, to give priority to inflation over unemployment. When these changes occur simultaneously, Hall describes the process as one of *third-order change*. The distinctive characteristic of this type of policy change is that it affects "the framework of ideas and standards that specifies, not only the goals of policy and the kind of instruments that can be used to attain them, but also the very nature of the problems they are meant to be addressing" (p. 278). Hall defines these frameworks as policy paradigms. First-order and second-order changes constitute instances of "normal policy making" – that

16 *The Question*

is, adjustments in policies that are compatible with continuity under a particular policy paradigm. However, third-order changes are characterized by discontinuities in policy – a change in policy paradigm – that occur relatively rarely.

Following Kuhn's work on changes in scientific paradigms, Peter Hall (1993) contends that the accumulation of anomalies and puzzles that cannot be explained in terms of a policy paradigm will gradually undermine its authority, eventually causing its abandonment. Thus, policy failure appears fundamental in triggering the learning process. Hall's account of social learning has some advantages compared with the panoply of other concepts of learning. The notions of first-order change and second-order change embrace all other notions of learning that refer to changes in processes, programs, and instruments, hence simplifying the conceptual discussion. Hall also introduces the notion of *paradigm shift*, which has relevance for my research question: The switch from statism to market policies that I study in this book is considered to be an illustration of paradigm shift.[15]

The switch from inward-oriented to outward-oriented policies and from statism to marketization that took place in much of the developing world constitutes an excellent illustration of paradigm shift that might have resulted from a process of learning. Thomas Biersteker contends that the shift in economic thinking witnessed during the 1980s and 1990s might have been the result of a process in which "developing countries may have finally been 'educated' and accepted the superiority of the liberal economic ideas they resisted for decades" (1995: 180).

---

[15] The main point in Hall's article is to demonstrate that a paradigm shift requires a broad societal debate including the media, interest groups, and political parties. Yet, the author also acknowledges the importance of shifts in the locus of authority over policy in the person of the prime minister. He states that ". . . Thatcher played a key role in institutionalizing the new policy paradigm. She packed the influential economic committees of the cabinet with its supporters, appointed an outside monetarist to be chief economic advisor at the Treasury, and in conjunction with a few advisors, virtually dictated the outlines of macroeconomic policy for several years. The locus of authority over policymaking in this period again shifted dramatically towards the prime minister" (p. 287). Thus, even if the author is making an argument against state autonomy, it seems clear that, for radical changes to be *launched,* a temporary concentration of power is required; and, if reforms are to be sustained, additional actors have to learn. Once more, the distinction between launching and sustaining reforms seems to be analytically important for defining whose learning and when it takes place are relevant.

1.2. Varieties of Learning   17

Miles Kahler (1990) pursues the same line of reasoning to explain what he describes as a shift in the supply of economic ideas toward orthodoxy. However, these authors do not succeed in making a strong argument in favor of the learning hypothesis, let alone in testing the argument empirically.

Whereas social learning provides a good description of what is to be researched – namely, changes in policy paradigms – this concept does not offer any hint about how to demonstrate that an observed paradigm shift is the consequence of a process of social learning. Note that, by definition, social learning cannot be observed in isolation from the change in paradigm that is being explained. However, in turn, a change in paradigm may be caused by a myriad of factors, social learning being just one possibility. This takes us directly to the complex issue of how to measure learning and how to test its impact on observed policy switches.

Kahler (1992: 124) poses the knotty problems involved in testing the hypothesis that a process of learning caused the shift to economic liberalism.[16] He characterizes as "demanding" "the empirical task of demonstrating that a particular behavioral change is the result of a clearly specified cognitive alteration at one level or another." He adds:

The investigation of shared beliefs is not an impossible empirical task but, once again, it has rarely been attempted in a rigorous fashion. Nor have alternative explanations for policy change been carefully compared to an explanation based on change in ideology or beliefs.

This, then, is the challenge.

Rational Learning and Bounded Learning

In public policy, two competing empirical approaches have being used to measure learning and to test its impact on policy change: *Bounded learning* and *rational learning* (Gowda and Fox 2002).[17] The two approaches

---

[16] In the article cited, Kahler's social learning is limited to elite networking. At the center of this type of learning are "transnational epistemic communities who share a common set of 'cause-and-effect beliefs' and appropriate control over policy in a particular issue area" (p. 126).

[17] The seminal work on bounded learning and individuals as *satisficers* rather than utility maximizers is Simons (1956).

18   *The Question*

assume that policy makers deciding under uncertainty engage in a purposive search for information about the possible results of policies, observing vicarious experiences. Thus, learning has a utilitarian motivation.
Also, and importantly, gathering information is costly for both types of
learning. However, processing the information is costly only for bounded
learners (Grossman and Stiglitz 1976). While rational learning assumes
that policy makers process information efficiently and in the same way,
the bounded learning approach argues that policy makers' ability to process overabundant information is limited and costly. In other words,
policy makers resort to cognitive short cuts and cognitive heuristics,
acquiring biases when processing the available experience.[18]

In a rational learning framework, policy makers are assumed to have
some prior beliefs about the expected outcomes of alternative policies
(Meseguer 2005). These beliefs entail a certain degree of uncertainty
about the consequences of policies. To reduce that uncertainty, policy
makers can look at the available experience with alternative policies in
the past and elsewhere. With that information, policy makers update
their initial beliefs – that is, they learn about the consequences of policies. It is important to note that, if the available information is abundant
and consistent (that is, it is not noisy), rational learning predicts that
what is observed will eventually override what was initially believed.
In other words, observed experience will eventually be the only factor
shaping governments' beliefs about the results of policies. Moreover,
rational learning entails that two different policy makers with different
initial beliefs confronted with the same information will eventually converge in their posterior beliefs (beliefs after learning) as more and more
information about the results of policies is gathered. This is a powerful
prediction.

In contrast, in a bounded learning framework, policy makers do not
have full analytical capabilities. Policy makers do not look at all available
information, they do not process the available information in the same

---

[18] Jervis argues that "people pay more attention to what has happened than to why it has
happened." Thus, learning is superficial, overgeneralized, and based on *post hoc ergo
propter hoc* reasoning (Jervis 1976). March and Levitt argue that learning is frequently
superstitious, suggesting that "beliefs about effectiveness of particular actions (...)
dominate any understanding or evaluation of performance" (in May 1992: 336). See
also Kyburg (1988), Hacking (1988), March and Olsen (1989).

1.2. Varieties of Learning

way, and they acquire a series of cognitive biases when analyzing the flow of information (Kahneman and Tversky 1988; Popkin 1991; Lupia and McCubbins 1998; Gowda and Fox 2002).[19] Although such an approach has been used to explain policy convergence, what one would actually expect is the opposite – that is, policy makers arriving at very different conclusions about the consequences of policies, and hence choosing divergent policies.

In a series of interesting studies, Kurt Weyland (2004, 2005, 2007) explained the diffusion of *policy innovations* using a bounded learning approach.[20] His illustration is the diffusion of the radical Chilean model of pension privatization and the moderate spread of health reforms in Latin America in the 1990s. According to the author, the diffusion of policy innovations is characterized by (1) an S-shape in time, that is, a pioneer country takes the lead and many other countries jump rapidly on the bandwagon until this trend eventually tapers off; (2) geographical clustering; and (3) commonality amid diversity; that is, the same policy framework is adopted in varied national settings (2007: chapters 1 and 2). Weyland contends that these features of the diffusion of innovations are better explained in terms of particular cognitive heuristics that policy makers use to process the information. First, the diffusion of policy innovations evolves in an S-shape because policy makers overemphasize initial success. Based on a minimal track record, policy makers jumped to the conclusion that the Chilean pension model had been a success with

---

[19] Clarifying the sense in which rational learning and bounded learning coincide or contradict each other in policy making is important. Opinion is divided. Researchers talk about limited utility maximization as opposed to standard utility maximization. Critics of the bounded approach hold that demonstrating that ordinary citizens are not utility maximizers and that they incur biases in processing information does not entail irrationality. Critics also argue that, at the most, research on bounded rationality shows that human beings are not perfectly rational, not that they are systematically irrational. From this perspective, cognitive heuristics typical of bounded learning would be *approximations* to utility-maximizing strategies. Consequently, the heuristics are still useful for efficient decision making (Elkins and Simmons 2005). Other authors radically disagree with this view, and contend that the bounced approach is something completely different, bearing no relation to the rational approach (see the contributions in Gowda and Fox 2002).

[20] Research on policy diffusion is far from new, but in recent years it has experienced a revival, especially among international political economists. The classic book on this topic is Rogers', first published in 1962.

much promise elsewhere. This is due to the *representativeness heuristic*. Second, the diffusion of innovations shows a geographic pattern because policy diffusion seems to require a close and successful example. This is the *availability heuristic*. And third, the same policy innovation is adopted in countries with very different functional needs due to the *heuristic of anchoring*. This heuristic limits the adaptation of the policy innovation to the particular context, producing the fundamental feature of diffusion – namely, commonality in diversity.

For Weyland, this mode of proceeding makes it evident that policy makers are far from being rational: Rather than carefully evaluating the results of the Chilean pension privatization after enough evidence was available, politicians rapidly drew (wrong) conclusions. Rather than scanning all available worldwide evidence about pension privatization, policy makers turned to the experience that was close and relevant to them. Rather than adopting the pension privatization model that could have fit best the characteristics of their national economies, politicians copied the Chilean model in toto, making adjustments at the margin. Thus, the author concludes, learning from the Chilean experience proceeded in a clearly nonrational fashion.

While Weyland's work makes an important contribution, it is not a convincing rebuttal of rational learning, nor is it a persuasive defense of bounded learning beyond the policy domain that the author studies (pension and health privatization) and his geographic focus (Latin America). Would this psychological approach be useful to explain the diffusion of policy innovations globally and not regionally? Why do some policy innovations transcend the regional setting and diffuse worldwide? Moreover, is the bounded approach useful in explaining the diffusion of policies that are *not* policy innovations? Consider, for instance, some of the policies that were advocated by the Washington Consensus, such as financial openness and trade liberalization. Changes in those policies toward more liberal stances do not constitute policy innovations and yet they were part of the change in paradigm addressed in this book. What does the cognitive approach contribute to explaining changes in these (non-innovative) policies? Finally, why do successful policy innovations sometimes fail to spread even in the regions where they emerge?

1.2. Varieties of Learning

Also, there are a couple of contradictions in the author's defense of bounded learning. For instance, Weyland contends that the reason why the pace of the adoption of the policy innovations eventually tapers off is that the initial upsurge in enthusiasm is followed by a sober evaluation "as more information becomes available" (2005: 286). What I read here is that policy makers may be temporally bounded, but eventually they carefully evaluate the results of policies much as rational learners would.[21] In the same vein, the author minimizes the relevance of the subsequent adaptations that several countries incorporated in their reforms in response to other policy experiences (interestingly, the adaptations where inspired by Latvia and Sweden) and to solve the shortcomings of the Chilean model as more came to be known about its performance.[22] Again, what I read here are not irrelevant adjustments but important deviations that demonstrate that, after a while, policy makers look at other experiences beyond their geographic area of "availability," and closely scrutinize the results of policies. In sum, policy makers may be bounded learners in the short run, but eventually "whether we know the term or not, we are all Bayesians – or almost all of us" (Stiglitz 1998: 40).[23]

[21] Also, there is a simpler explanation for the tapering off in the S-shape curve: It may be due to the simple fact that as the innovation is adopted, there are fewer and fewer countries left to adopt it.

[22] For instance, Brazil, rather than privatizing its public pay-as-you-go pension system, opted for making changes to strengthen its financial viability. It was agreed that full privatization could be very harmful in an already very unequal country. Thus, Brazilian policymakers looked at the notional defined-contribution reforms that had been implemented outside Latin America, notably in western and Eastern Europe.

[23] Elsewhere (Meseguer 2006), I argued that rational learning and bounded learning are not necessarily incompatible. A rational learner takes into account not only how much information exists but also how consistent that information is. The weight a rational learner will give to observed experience vis-à-vis what was initially believed about the performance of policies is negatively related to the noise that the observed results convey. It is sensible to think that the variability of results (the noise) increases as the geographic area of application of a policy expands. For example, the results of trade liberalization in Latin America may vary a lot; but it makes sense to hypothesize that the variability of those results is less than when the African, the East Asian, South Asian, and the European experiences with trade liberalization are considered together. Thus, policymakers may look at the experience in the region not because it is available (bounded learning) but because it is less noisy (rational learning). Moreover, if it is demonstrated that "available experience" *is* indeed "less noisy experience," then there is no substantive difference between bounded learning and rational learning. I tentatively explored this possibility using as an illustration the decision to liberalize the trade regime. The experience of a successful country is less noisy than the experience

22   *The Question*

Overall, bounded learning may be a good tool to explain the regional diffusion of policy *innovations*, but it has not been demonstrated that this approach can explain the *global* convergence of policies that are not strictly *new*. Policy stances are eventually adjusted in the light of the evidence. Thus, bounded learning may be an adequate characterization of *short-term* behavior. Rational learning seems superior when it comes to explaining behavior in the *long* run (see Gilardi, Flüglister, and Luyet 2008). Moreover, policy makers frequently transcended the regional setting in their search for models. For instance, Mexican policy makers looked at the Philippine experience to reform the stock exchange market (Minushkin 2001). Finance Minister Pedro Aspe quoted the experience of Italy and the Dominican Republic as an inspiration to promote a development strategy based on small firms (Aspe 1993: 86). His Deputy Minister, Guillermo Ortiz (1994), cited the experience of France and Portugal as an inspiration to privatize the banking sector. In his assessment of the overall Mexican development strategy, Centeno (1994: 194, 196) compares the Mexican elite with the elite of Meiji Japan, "searching the globe for models in order to strengthen their own state." The author asserts that "[t]he model was Taiwan or South Korea, not Friedman Chile." Bounded learning has obvious problems in explaining why Mexican policy makers paid attention to such distant experiences.[24] In sum, rational learning offers a theoretical and empirical approach to learning, the capacity of which to explain policy switches is well worth exploring.

1.3. Policy Convergence, Learning, and Alternative Hypotheses

So far, I have provided narrative accounts of scholars and policy makers that support the argument that a process of learning was behind the

> of a whole region. And the experience of a successful region is less noisy than the experience of the whole world. With all the statistical caveats borne in mind, it turned out that rational learning from the experience of Chile and of East Asia with trade liberalization explained the decision to open up the trade regimes in Latin America. Two miraculous – less noisy – performances could explain what average experience (in Latin America and the world) could not. Thus, a rational learning model confirmed a prediction of the bounded learning approach.
>
> [24] Stating that attention was paid to these distant experiences because they were somehow made available to decision makers raises immediate tautological concerns.

1.3. Policy Convergence, Learning, and Alternative Hypotheses   23

Table 1.1. *Mechanisms of policy convergence*

Bottom-up (1)	Top-down (2)	Horizontal diffusion (3)
Independent but the same response	Coercion	Learning (Rational and Bounded) Imitation Competition

paradigm shift that took place in the 1980s and 1990s. I also argued that the main obstacle to testing learning across time and space is the lack of an empirical measure of learning. I discussed two competing approaches to the issue of conceptualizing learning – namely, rational learning and bounded learning – and concluded that rational learning is substantively and methodologically superior for the purpose of this cross-national study. However, a strong case in favor of the hypothesis that learning caused the change in policy paradigm must take other, competing, explanations into account.

There has recently been an enormous interest in identifying and testing the possible mechanisms causing the convergence on liberal policies (Simmons and Elkins 2004; Levi-Faur and Jordana 2005; Knill 2005; Weyland 2005; Brooks 2005; Meseguer and Gilardi 2005; Holzinger and Knill 2005; Elkins and Simmons 2005; Simmons, Dobbin, and Garrett 2006; Braun and Gilardi 2006; Lee and Strang 2006; Swank 2006; Shipan and Volden 2008). These mechanisms may be classified as bottom-up, top-down, and horizontal mechanisms of policy convergence. Learning from experience falls into the horizontal category. There is a crucial distinction between convergence and diffusion. Diffusion entails the adoption of policies in an *interdependent* and *voluntary* way. However, policy choices may converge as a result of nonvoluntary decisions if, for instance, policies are imposed on countries. Thus, diffusion is only one reason why policies may converge (Meseguer and Gilardi 2005; Knill 2005).[25] See Table 1.1 for a summary of diffusion mechanisms.

---

[25] As Elkins and Simmons (2005) state, classifications of alternative diffusion mechanisms have recently become a cottage industry, with more or fewer categories depending on researchers' taste for parsimony.

1. *Bottom-up convergence* originates in national economies and polities that, confronted with the same external environment, adopt the same policy *independently* of each other. A frequently cited example of this situation is individuals opening their umbrellas when it starts raining, thus reacting in the same way to the same phenomenon but without communicating with one another. For instance, imagine that, in the light of the inflationary environment of the 1980s, governments discovered that granting independence to central banks achieved the objective of keeping inflation in check. What one would observe is an increase in the number of independent central banks as an *independent* reaction to the same problem. To give another example, it could have been the case that different governments confronted with similar demographic trends discovered that the privatization of pensions was the best response to the increasing pressure on their social security systems. Of particular interest is to test whether the wave of democratization that took place in the 1980s is related to the wave of economic reforms adopted immediately afterwards. Therefore, the empirical tests of the impact of learning on policy choices have to control for possible shared domestic characteristics (inflation, demographic trends, political characteristics, and others) that may have induced policy makers to adopt the same economic policies as a result of independent discoveries or shared local circumstances.

2. *Top-down policy convergence* results from the adoption of particular policies, not voluntarily, but as a result of external imposition, as epitomized by the conditionality imposed by IFIs. Briefly, to avoid the moral hazard problems that may arise from the existence of a lender of last resort, IFIs make their loans conditional on adjustment measures the content of which is aligned with the policy prescriptions of the Washington Consensus. Thus, the convergence on liberal economic policies in the 1980s and 1990s might have been the price paid by less developed countries for access to IFIs' loans. In this case, liberal economic policies would not have been voluntarily chosen.

   However, external coercion is a problematic mechanism of policy convergence. It is not always correct to identify conditionality

1.3. Policy Convergence, Learning, and Alternative Hypotheses   25

with imposition. Some authors argue that IFIs do not "force" but "teach," spreading norms and ideas (Barnett and Finnemore 2004; Finnemore 1996). According to this view, IFIs contributed to policy makers' learning process through dialogue and persuasion. Thus, what appears as imposition may actually be a case of "technocratic alignment" or, in other words, a coincidence of interests between IFIs and local policy-making elites socialized in the same set of ideas.[26] As Kahler puts it, "[t]he IFIs and other external agencies have a strong interest in shaping the process of learning by national governments in directions that will lead to greater alignment with external policy preferences" (1992: 125).

Also, it has been shown that some governments may deliberately seek IFIs' conditionality in order to legitimize the adoption of policies that those governments privately want. A closer scrutiny of the interaction between the IMF and governments shows that, in many cases, governments actually use the IMF as a scapegoat to overcome domestic opposition to their preferred policies. Calling in an "external villain" allows governments to avoid the responsibility for adopting unpopular measures. And since a rejection by the IMF sends a bad signal to creditors and investors, domestic opposition may acquiesce in the conditions (Vreeland 2003). This is not to say that IFIs played no role in the adoption and implementation of market reforms. As I discuss in Chapter 6, IFIs provided financial assistance that made economic adjustment feasible and sustainable in quite a few episodes of reform. But their role is ambivalent. At times, international aid helped to sustain corrupt governments and thus to delay reform (Van de Walle 2001; Easterly 2003). In any case, the claim that governments were yielding to IFIs' pressure when they endorsed those policies may not always be correct. All in all, detailed case studies show that governments frequently have more room to maneuver than the imposition hypothesis implies (Nelson 1990a;

---

[26] Much has been written about the role played by technocrats as epistemic communities in some of the most relevant cases of policy reform. The "Chicago Boys" in Chile is the archetypical case. The "Berkeley mafia" in Indonesia, MIT economists in Mexico, and Harvard technocrats in Poland are other examples (Centeno 1994; Valdés 1995; Domínguez 1996; Williamson 1994).

26   *The Question*

Kahler 1992; Stallings 1992; Haggard and Webb 1994; Weyland 2007).

In most quantitative studies, possible coercion by IFIs and supranational institutions is controlled for by including some variable measuring whether a particular country in a particular year is under an IMF agreement, a variable that measures the amount of aid received from IFIs such as the World Bank, or some variable measuring institutional memberships such as the EU or GATT/WTO.[27] I adopt this strategy, although, admittedly, this approach is rough: I shall be able to state whether being under an IMF agreement is significant in explaining a particular change in policy, but I shall not be able to discern whether this is because of imposition or persuasion.

3. Finally, *horizontal policy convergence* results when policy choices in one country are shown to affect the policy choices in another country. As opposed to bottom-up convergence, horizontal convergence entails *interdependent* policy making. And, unlike top-down convergence, horizontal convergence entails *voluntary* adoption.

Learning is a *horizontal* mechanism of policy convergence. Testing the role of learning is still a pending task. Despite the amount of conceptual work that has been undertaken on the topic, the most recent wave of quantitative research on policy convergence mostly fails to address the challenges of measuring learning and testing its effects in a systematic way. For instance, Simmons and Elkins' (2004) interesting study of capital and current account liberalization operationalizes learning using only the policy stance of successful countries (Simmons and Elkins 2004; see also Swank 2006; Elkins, Guzman, and Simmons 2006). Yet, both theory and narrative accounts suggest that learning from policy failures is probably more relevant than learning from success. In other words, policy choice is usually, most of the time, a choice among alternative

---

[27] Belonging to clubs such as the GATT/WTO entails a commitment to particular policy stances. For instance, membership of GATT/WTO entails a commitment to liberalize trade. More recently, membership in the European Monetary Union (EMU) has entailed tight constraints regarding budget deficits and orthodox monetary policies and an extensive process of "Europeanization" of policies.

1.3. Policy Convergence, Learning, and Alternative Hypotheses 27

policies (Weyland 2007).[28] In sum, empirical research on the impact of learning on policy choices, even in the most recent and sophisticated research on policy diffusion, is no more than marginal.

Emulation falls in the same category of *horizontal* mechanisms of diffusion. Distinguishing learning from emulation is far from simple, but I have argued elsewhere that there are at least two differences between these mechanisms (Meseguer 2005). First, unlike learning, emulation does not imply a reassessment of causal maps that link policies to outcomes. Thus, emulation does not entail an improved understanding of cause-and-effect relations (May 1992: 333). Second, I argued earlier that learning is a utilitarian search for information: A problem is in place and a solution is sought. However, governments may want to imitate the policies carried out elsewhere for a host of reasons other than problem solving. Credibility and reputation are among them. Governments may copy the policies implemented by countries acclaimed as successful in an attempt to win international favor and avoid the stigma of backwardness.[29] Whatever the reason, this type of behavior has been

---

[28] Lee and Strang's paper (2006) on public sector employment in developed countries takes this fact into account with an interesting outcome: Politicians learned from the good results of those countries in which the public sector was downsized, yet they ignored the good (bad) results of those countries in which the public sector was upsized (downsized). The authors conclude that the existence of a prevailing discourse regarding the desirable size of the public sector meant that governments paid more attention to the policy that was seen as "correct." Particular ideas biased the interpretation of the outcomes under the two policy alternatives. To the authors, this behavior is evidence that learning is not rational. Note that prevailing discourses (or, in other words, hegemonic ideas) are also crucial to understanding why particular policies "win". The debate on the role of ideas in politics and policymaking is as fascinating as it is inconclusive. On the specific issue of economic policymaking and the role of ideas, very influential works have been written by Hall (1989, 1993), Sikkink (1991), Goldstein and Keohane (1993), Hood (1994), and Blyth (2002). Convincing criticisms of this cognitive turn in economic policymaking by Jacobsen (1995), Woods (1995), Yee (1996), and Blyth (1997) have shown that the above authors did not demonstrate that economic ideas have an independent impact on policymaking but only that ideas operate through the institutions in which they are embedded and as long as particular interests support them. Thus, ideas have not been shown to have a life of their own.

[29] Emulation may also have utilitarian purposes. For instance, signals of commitment to "good policies" may be a requisite for access to scarce external financial resources. Also, policies that are carried out by a majority of other governments are easier to justify domestically, especially when those policies are unpopular (Ikenberry 1990; Maxfield 1997; Bagheri and Habibi 1998; Vreeland 2003; Mosley 2003). However, in this study I

28   *The Question*

described in "tipping" and "threshold" models in which a certain number of adopters are determinant in making others follow suit (Schelling 1978; Granovetter 1978).

From an empirical point of view, scholars have used several indicators to operationalize emulation. The number or proportion of countries in the region or in the world that have previously adopted a particular policy is taken to be a proxy for the climate of opinion in favor of that policy. The hypothesis is that the greater the density of previous adoptions, particularly in a country's region, the more likely a country is to switch to that policy. In the empirical chapters that follow, this is the indicator I use. More refined measures of emulation are those that consider that, beyond geographical proximity, shared traits such as a common religion, a common language, common legal traditions, or a shared colonial past drive imitation. In general, these operationalizations of emulation perform well in the empirical tests relating to a wide range of policy choices (Brooks 2005; Gleditsch and Ward 2006; Elkins, Guzman, and Simmons, 2006; Wotipka and Ramírez 2008).[30]

To summarize, in order to evaluate whether countries switched to market-oriented policies as a result of learning from their own past experience and the experience of other countries with alternative policies, an operational concept of learning is needed. Although learning is central to several discussions in the literature, there is a dearth of empirical studies that test its presumed role in causing policy switches and convergence. Moreover, a convincing proof of the impact of learning on the decision to engage in market reforms requires pitting this hypothesis against alternative ones. A strong case in favor of the learning hypothesis would entail showing that the change in policy paradigm toward a more liberal stance was not the result of (1) an independent response to the same critical

shall consider emulation to be legitimacy driven, and will not enter into the discussion about how rational imitating others may actually be.

[30] Competition may be another mechanism of policy convergence. It has to do with strategic responses to the policies adopted by others. For instance, if country A reduces the taxes it imposes on capital, country B, which competes against A for the same pool of international capital, will also reduce taxes in order not to lose its share of the pool. Note, however, that competition only sometimes leads to convergence. On occasions, adopting a different policy from that of a competitor may be the best strategic response. In such cases, divergence rather than convergence would occur.

economic environment, (2) an external imposition, or (3) a process of symbolic emulation. These mechanisms are unlikely to exclude each other or to operate in isolation, though. Hence, in the empirical chapters, I test whether learning explained the switch to four liberal economic policies (trade liberalization, privatization, capital account openness, and agreements with the IMF) controlling for the aforementioned alternative mechanisms of policy convergence (coercion and imitation) and for a battery of domestic and economic variables (bottom-up convergence).

1.4. Plan of the Book

I should start with a caveat. The hypothesis that market reforms were adopted after learning from their success in some locations and from the failure of state interventions in others is not a naïve endorsement of the infallibility of market reforms. The financial crises of the late 1990s and early 2000s that hit some of the star pupils of the reform movement opened a discussion about the virtues of the Washington Consensus as a blueprint for development. Among the things that "we now know better" is that for the reforms to succeed, the correct sequencing in their implementation is essential. Also, some of the reforms need institutional preconditions for them to bear fruit. Importantly, there is not a unique path to reforming the economy, and some of the alternative paths require active state involvement. Blueprints have to be carefully tailored to match local conditions. Finally, the goals of stabilization and growth must be accompanied by policies that address poverty (World Bank 2005). Thus, the reform agenda is much more cautious and complex these days.

While aware of it, I explore only marginally the learning process motivated by the most recent financial crises. This learning is still an ongoing process and the time span to empirically evaluate its impact on current policy making is still insufficient. Hence, although I comment on this issue in the concluding chapter, this study does not cover the learning and the progress of market reforms during the 2000s.

In Chapter 2, I present rational updating and discuss why it is a suitable approach to operationalize learning. Briefly, Bayesian updating allows combining particular prior beliefs about the expected outcomes of alternative policies with actual (observed) results. Using Bayes's rule, it is possible to combine these prior beliefs with observed experience and to generate posterior beliefs about the outcomes of policies. Thus, posterior beliefs are a combination of uncertain prior beliefs and available experience. I shall use those posterior beliefs to operationalize learning, that is, posterior beliefs after observing the outcomes of policies will be the independent variables of interest. To allow for possibly distinguishing information on the basis of geographic proximity and to account for the fact that even for a rational learner the acquisition of information is costly, I assume that governments rationally learned from their own past experience, the experience of the regions they belong to, and the experience of the rest of the world, excluding their own and the regional experience.[31] I distinguish between learning from normal times and learning from shocks, modeling the latter as an increase in the uncertainty of governments' beliefs following a major economic disruption. The Costa Rican decision to adopt a more liberal trade regime in the mid-1980s is used as an illustration of the updating process. This exercise shows that the model is grounded in reality and that it is capable of producing realistic predictions.

As explained earlier, the models include operationalizations of alternative hypotheses, particularly imitation and coercion. A dynamic probit model, which captures temporary dependency in the choice of policies, is used to relate learning and alternative hypotheses to choices actually made. This model allows estimating the impact of learning on the probability of *adopting* market reforms and on the probability of *sustaining* them. As I discuss in detail in Chapter 2, this simple model assumes that politicians care and learn only about the economic results – specifically growth – of the adoption of policies. But it is obvious that politicians care about other things. Most prominently, they care about whether the policies they adopt are popular. Whereas in this project I do not undertake the complicated task of modeling updating from political results, I do control for political variables in the specification of the models of policy choice. Chapter 2 concludes spelling out the testable hypotheses that flow from the model of rational learning and rational choice.

---

[31] The regional classification is Sub-Saharan Africa, Middle East and North Africa, South Asia, East Asia, South East Asia, Pacific Islands/Oceania, Latin American, Caribbean and Non-Iberian America, Eastern and Central Europe, and Industrial Countries.

1.4. Plan of the Book

Chapters 3–6 are the empirical chapters. I apply the aforementioned model of learning and decision making to explain the decision to adopt an export-oriented development strategy and to liberalize the trade regime (Chapter 3), the decision to privatize (Chapter 4), the decision to liberalize the capital account (Chapter 5), and the decision to enter into agreements with the IMF (Chapter 6). All chapters have a similar structure: First, a review of the political economy of each of the policy decisions is presented and a case for an explanation based on learning is advanced. Second, the data are described and discussed. Third, the results of applying the learning model to each of the policy choices are interpreted and evaluated in light of the main question posed in this project.

Note that in this research design, economic policies take the form of case studies. The policies I explore display interesting similarities and differences.[32] First, privatization, trade, and financial openness are first-generation economic reforms as opposed to reforms that pertain to social policies (such as education and health) and/or institutional changes (such as judicial system reform). The latter are known as second-generation reforms, and the labels first and second refer to the sequence in which these policies typically have been undertaken. First-generation reforms are considered easier to adopt and implement than second-generation reforms because there is a fair amount of technical consensus, at least about their desirability. A technical blueprint similar to the Washington Consensus that could act as a focal point for decision makers is generally lacking for second-generation reform (Naím 1999; Krueger 2000; Kuczynski and Williamson 2003). All in all, there has been far more progress and hence experience with first- than with second-generation reforms (Krueger 2000). Thus, to study the impact of learning, focusing on first-generation economic policies seems appropriate.[33]

Second, as much as the three policies share the status of first-generation reforms, they differ in important aspects. Policies concerning trade and

---

[32] Brooks and Kurtz (2007) make an interesting case for exploring the particular determinants of different market reforms rather than treating them as uniform.

[33] For instance, Krueger (2000: 63) posits that "while the first generation of reforms benefited from accumulated knowledge, much remains to be learned about the most appropriate way to implement this second generation of reforms."

capital movements have long histories. Tariffs, quotas, and exchange controls have been used extensively since the beginning of economics. Even though what is known about the impact of these instruments on growth has changed over time, there is a wealth of accumulated experience that could inform learning. However, privatization had no precedent prior to the Chilean and British experiments starting in the mid- and late 1970s. Thus, among all the policies surveyed, only privatization has the status of a policy innovation. A politician eager and willing to learn about privatization would have to rely on the information that exists, which, by definition, is scant (otherwise it would not be an innovation). A policy maker eager and willing to learn about an established policy would have much more experience and historical materials to learn from. Thus, it is sensible to expect that experience in the world (other than own and regional experience) will be more relevant in the learning of policies that are *not* innovations.

Third, IMF agreements typically included, among others, all three policy recommendations: To eliminate barriers to trade, to liberalize finance, and to privatize. Thus, it could be hypothesized that learning from experience with IMF agreements should display similar patterns to learning from the policies they prescribed. However, it is also the case that IMF agreements raise sovereignty costs that the adoption of the very same policies on a country's own initiative would rarely pose. This should have consequences for the way in which policy makers learn from the outcomes of IMF agreements.

In Chapter 3, I study the decision to switch development strategies (from import substitution to export orientation) using two databases. The first database covers 51 developing countries from 1964 through 1990. This database is particularly interesting to test the impact of the 1982 debt crisis on policy makers' beliefs, learning, and policy choices. After the shock is modeled, the estimation reveals that countries found the outcomes under import substitution industrialization (ISI) too volatile to be reliable, which spurred the change. Therefore, the model shows that the failure of ISI was the major motivation to adopt export orientation (EO). The second database I employ covers data on trade liberalization for 87 developing countries during 1970 through 1999. This database is interesting because its time coverage allows

1.4. Plan of the Book

testing the impact of learning from trade liberalization as experience with this policy accumulated. It also allows testing the impact of the diffusion of democracy in the developing world on the diffusion of trade liberalization. Both variables (accumulated experience and especially the extension of the franchise) turned out to be relevant. Finally, the results of the estimations across models and databases show that emulating others was systematically related to a greater probability of liberalizing. Additional domestic conditions had no impact.

In Chapter 4, I enquire whether thirty-seven governments in industrialized and Latin American countries privatized as a result of learning from experience in the 1980s and 1990s. Using narrative accounts about the privatization process in both groups and statistical techniques, I examine whether the decision to streamline the public sector was the outcome of a revision of beliefs about the effectiveness of privatization or whether, alternatively, it was triggered by international pressures or mimicry. The results suggest that rational learning and especially emulation were important factors in the decision to privatize. International pressures, proxied by the presence or absence of an agreement with the IMF and by EU membership, were irrelevant. Finally, domestic political conditions appeared consequential to the decision to launch privatization but only when the analysis is carried out for each of the regional subsamples. In the countries in the Organization for Economic Co-operation and Development (OECD), center-left governments were more likely to privatize, whereas in Latin America, repressive regimes were more likely to divest.

The decision to allow the free movement of capital in and out the country is explored in Chapter 5. Applying the learning model to 129 developed and developing countries in the period 1970 through 1996, I show that learning from experience had hardly any impact on the decision to open the capital account; it was more consequential in the decision to sustain an open capital account, though. It is important to emphasize two points. First, in the aggregate, this is the policy in which the least global convergence is observed. Capital account openness was mainly concentrated in advanced countries. In contrast, developing countries exhibited great variation. Given the variation and mild convergence, it is not surprising that the model predicts a marginal role for learning, on average. Other than the structure of the data, both theory and practice relating capital account liberalization and economic growth are much less conclusive than theory and practice for other policy domains – say, trade liberalization (Stiglitz 1998, 2000). Thus, policy makers who desire to learn about the growth impact of capital account liberalization would have difficulties in drawing clear conclusions. Conclusions are even harder to extract in the face of recent financial crises associated with mistakes during the process of capital account opening. Whereas there is broad consensus that ill-informed opening processes caused the financial crises of the late 1990s, there is less consensus about what the best response (to remain open or to establish controls) is to minimize the impact of crises on economic growth. Overall, theory, practice, and malpractice are still objects of much debate (Srinivasan 2000).

I use the Mexican experience with financial openness and reform to illustrate how learning and other mechanisms of policy convergence influenced policy decisions. I then test an explanatory model against a large sample of developed and developing countries. Capital account liberalization appears related to the preceding and parallel process of trade openness. It is also related to the need to be competitive in an increasingly integrated environment. There are some signs that learning from experience in the world with and without capital controls was related to the decisions to open and to remain open. However, this result holds only after the Exchange Rate Mechanism (ERM) crisis of the early 1990s and the Mexican 1994/1995 financial crisis are modeled in the updating of beliefs. Finally, a country's being under an IMF agreement is always a significant (but weak) predictor of the decision to liberalize capital flows.

Chapter 6 is the last empirical case study. It explores the role that learning from the outcomes of IMF agreements played in their adoption, using data for 135 developed and developing countries in the period 1960 through 1990. The content of IMF agreements was aligned for the most part with the Washington Consensus. Therefore, one would, a priori, stipulate that the impact of learning on the decision to sign these agreements should not be very different from the impact that learning had (or did not have) on each of the policies individually. In fact, this is the case: Learning from experience in the world is a robust determinant of the

1.4. Plan of the Book

decision to sign agreements. However, other findings suggest that IMF agreements are politically more costly than the individual policies they prescribe. Indeed, the accusation of selling out to international powers (sovereignty costs) motivates countries to abandon IMF agreements even when performance under them is better than without them. Overall, it seems that being under IMF agreements is a status that governments do not seek to prolong. The results of several specifications show the decision to enter into agreements with the IMF as fundamentally driven by domestic conditions.

Finally, Chapter 7 discusses the main results of this study and the future research agenda. I argue that this book makes contributions on several fronts. First, it gives an answer to the substantive question posed by this project. Thus, the book provides evidence that *in the 1980s and 1990s governments did privatize and did change development strategies in part as a result of learning. Yet, learning from experience was marginal in the decision to open the capital account (but less marginal in the decision to sustain it).* Moreover, whereas there is weak evidence that third-party imposition was crucial in the adoption of market policies (only the decisions to change development strategies and to open the capital account were related to the presence of an IMF agreement), emulating others was an important factor in the adoption of privatization and trade liberalization. The concluding chapter summarizes important findings concerning the role of economic crises in learning and of crises *and* learning in policy choices.

This study also makes an important methodological contribution – namely, testing learning across time and space. It constitutes a first attempt to provide scholars with a tool that overcomes the operational-ization conundrum. Although my approach is far from being definitive or problem-free, it should be suggestive enough to encourage other scholars to improve it and use it.

Finally, the book deals with relevant normative issues. Does it matter at all whether or not politicians and policy makers learn? If "yes," does it matter how they learn? What can be expected about the quality of policy making if politicians learn or if they mindlessly imitate others rather than learning in a more systematic way? Can we anticipate or at least speculate about the welfare consequences of treating the information provided by the world in one way or another? Can rational learning be something other than a normative (but unrealistic) approach to policy making? Given that learning matters, what are the consequences of learning from more than two decades of reforms expected to be? In other words, what are the implications of this study for the post-Washington Consensus debate on market reforms? I address these important questions at length in the conclusions to this book.

TWO

The Model

[P]eople ought to learn from their mistakes.
Dani Rodrik (1996: 23)

Imagine the following situation. A new government headed by Alberto Monge Alvárez of the National Liberation Party (Partido de Liberación Nacional, PLN) is elected in Costa Rica in mid-1982.[1] The government considers reducing quotas and tariffs, and eliminating subsidies that encourage import substitution. The economic team, however, is concerned about the impact that liberalizing the trade regime will have on Costa Rican rates of growth. It is very likely that the team, led by the central bank governor Carlos Manuel Castillo, has some established beliefs about the consequences of liberalizing based on either economic theory or previous experience. Despite these "informed hunches," there is some uncertainty about the economic consequences of liberalizing.

One simple way to reduce the uncertainty is to compare the experience of countries that chose to liberalize their trade regime in the past with that of those that opted to continue under a protectionist development model. Which of the two models performed better? To answer this question, the dedicated economic team gathers the relevant information. Again, imagine that the evidence is overwhelming: Not only did the countries that opened up their trade regimes grow more on average, but *all* of them grew more. By contrast, the data on the countries that opted for a protectionist trade regime was "confusing": On average, they grew less

[1] Information about Costa Rica's market reforms is based on Nelson (1990b) and Clark (2001).

than those that opened up their trade regimes. However, some countries performed badly under a strategy of import substitution whereas others did remarkably well. To use a technical term, the evidence on the impact of protectionism was "noisy." Finally, imagine that this pattern was repeated year after year.

It is sensible to assume that the economic team, regardless of its initial informed hunches, finds the evidence so overwhelming that it concludes that a liberal trade regime clearly outperforms a protectionist one. Consequently, after learning from the experience of others, the government decides to change its trade policy regime. The Costa Rican economic team acts like Bayesian learners, most likely without knowing it.[2]

Is it possible to test empirically stories such as this one across time and space? How far does this sort of stylized account take us when it comes to explaining policy switches? Is it possible to conclude that the adoption of more liberal trade regimes, more open capital accounts, and smaller public sectors was the consequence of a learning process? In order to answer this question, we need an operational concept of learning. As discussed in Chapter 1, although there has been much theoretical discussion about learning and economic policy reforms, an empirical test of this relationship remains to be done. Given that "learning" is an elusive concept, this is not surprising.

In this study, I assume that politicians are rational learners. Politicians are often uncertain about the consequences of policies. Governments do not know how alternative economic policies will affect performance. They may have some prior beliefs about economic results based on historical experience, theoretical relationships, or ideology.[3] Moreover, governments can observe their own and others' past experience with policies, and update their beliefs on the basis of those observations. The combination of prior beliefs and available data using Bayes's rule provides posterior beliefs about economic results. I hypothesize that governments

---

[2] As I describe subsequently, the real story matches this imaginary tale quite well.

[3] As Freeman states (2006: 374), a precondition for learning is a moderate level of commitment to a belief (in statistical terms, holding beliefs with some variance). If policy makers are strongly committed to a belief and thus do not hold uncertainty about it, they will have no ability to learn from past experience and the experience of others. Such dogmatism, I believe, is not a good characterization of behavior in the long term.

choose policies on the basis of these posterior beliefs, which embody learning from previous experience. Period after period, new information is gathered, new posteriors are derived, and a new policy choice is made on the basis of what has been learned. The updating process proceeds sequentially.

As illustrated in the example earlier, Bayesian updating is an intuitive, simple, and appealing mechanism to operationalize learning; but it is mathematically complicated. In the presentation that follows, I focus on concepts and relegate the more technical details to the appendices. The Costa Rican experience with market reforms (1978–88) is used as an illustration to depict the behavior derived from an "ideal" process of rational learning and rational choice. This small Central American country is interesting for several reasons. First, it shows that, even in an established democracy in which political institutions play against the concentration of power, governments may acquire a temporary space for autonomous policy making, particularly if the economic situation is generally perceived as requiring prompt action. However, again, if this space opens, it becomes crucial to explore the evolution of beliefs and preferences of those enjoying the autonomous space. Also, Costa Rica is a good case to pinpoint alternative explanations of policy choices. Domestic characteristics such as the small size of the country, and geopolitical ones such as its strategic importance to the United States during the 1980s, should certainly be taken into account in order to frame an accurate explanation of economic policy choices.

My approach to testing learning involves two steps. The first is to come up with some measure of learning. The second step is to relate that measure of learning to the choices actually observed and to evaluate whether learning had any impact on those policy choices. For the first step, I use Bayesian updating: I generate point estimates of posterior beliefs (posterior probability distributions that combine prior beliefs with observed experience) about average growth results and about the dispersion of the results under alternative policies. I proceed in this way for each of the four policy issues surveyed in the book (trade liberalization, privatization, capital liberalization, and IMF agreements). Together with a set of control variables, the differences in posterior beliefs are used as independent variables in a model that regards policy choices

40   *The Model*

as dependent over time. This makes it possible to test, whether learning explains the decisions to launch and to sustain different economic policies.[4]

Subsequently, I present the essentials of Bayesian learning. Using Costa Rican choices and switches of development strategies as an illustration, I discuss some features of Bayesian updating. Where possible, I rely on intuitions, providing examples all along the presentation. After that, the decision problem is spelled out together with the complete model relating policy learning and policy choice. Finally, I conclude by presenting the set of hypotheses to be tested in each of the empirical chapters.

2.1. Essentials[5]

On Priors

Suppose that governments want to learn about the expected rate of growth that would follow the application of two alternative policies, A and B. Politicians may, of course, want to learn about other policy outcomes: For instance, the rate of unemployment, inflation, or the public deficit. The model easily can be extended to those variables.[6] Governments are uncertain about the outcomes that will result from the adoption of each policy, but they have some prior beliefs about the outcomes. The distinctive feature of the Bayesian approach is the operationalization of prior beliefs in a probability distribution. Prior beliefs are especially relevant when decisions are made about "unique" events – that is, about events the repetition of which, under the same circumstances, is unfeasible. This is the case with most political phenomena.

---

[4] Therefore, I use a Bayesian approach to generate only posterior point estimates. The use of the dynamic probit model to evaluate the impact of learning is an instance of classical, not Bayesian, inference (or Bayesian inference with uninformative priors).

[5] This section is based on Leamer (1991), West and Harrison (1997), Lee (1997), Gill (2002) and Gelman, Carlin, Stern, and Rubin (2004). On Bayesian decision theory, see De Groot (1970), Winkler (1972), Raiffa (1972), Coyle (1972), Berger (1985), Gärdenfors and Sahlin (1988), Pericchi (n.d.), and Gill and Walker (2005). Interesting applications to political science and sociology include Berk, Campbell, Klap, and Western (1992), Western and Jackman (1994), Gerber and Green (1998), and Western (1998).

[6] It would be very interesting to model learning about the political results of policies that are obviously crucial to politicians' utility functions. However, that challenge is not tackled here.

2.1. Essentials

There are two conditions in which we can be confident that the impact of prior beliefs will be minimal: If information is abundant and the data are consistent, the latter will override prior beliefs in the formation of posterior beliefs. This result entails that different policy makers with different prior beliefs will converge in their posterior beliefs because the data will overwhelm the prior beliefs, whatever they are. For instance, suppose that the Costa Rican and Peruvian finance ministers are exposed to the same information about the results of reducing tariffs and import quotas. It does not matter whether the Costa Rican policy makers were more or less certain than their Peruvian peers about the anticipated results of opening up to trade. If they are rational learners confronted with the same data, their posterior beliefs will converge. Also, provided these policy makers choose policies on the basis of what they have learned, they will converge not only in their posterior beliefs about the results of lowering barriers to trade but also, and importantly, in their policy choices. Thus, Bayesian updating anticipates the policy convergence that this study seeks to explain.

Prior beliefs can be uninformative – flat, diffuse, reference priors – or informative. With uniform priors, classical inference and Bayesian inference give the same results because the posteriors are driven by the data – the prior beliefs convey no information. One may want to choose diffuse priors if the aim is to "let the data speak for themselves." This is relevant in settings in which gathering new information is costly. Above all, because, in this case, only the data influence the posteriors, choosing uninformative priors is a convenient way to avoid the criticism of subjectivity.[7]

In this project, I use empirical data to propose governments' prior beliefs. I take as priors the average rate of growth and the variability of growth rates in the world under a particular policy the year before a

---

[7] Conjugate priors entail selecting prior distributions such that the posterior distribution belongs to the same class of prior distributions. They are convenient because they guarantee the analytical calculation of the posterior distributions of the parameters of interest. Conjugacy also guarantees that the posterior distributions are well behaved. Natural conjugate priors arise by taking the class of prior distributions to be the set of all densities having the same functional form as the likelihood (Gill 2002; Gelman, Carlin, Stern, and Rubin 2004). Finding solutions for the posteriors has recently become much less of a problem. The development of Markov Chain Monte Carlo techniques allows us to deal with model specifications that, being realistic and interesting, were until recently mathematically intractable.

42 *The Model*

country enters the database. For instance, the prior belief about growth under export promotion for Costa Rica is taken to be the average rate of growth and the variability of results under export promotion in the world the year before Costa Rica enters the database.[8] Note that, although this choice of priors is intended on my part to be nonintrusive, these priors are informative.

The Setting

I assume that governments can express their initial uncertainty about the expected economic growth following the implementation of alternative policies, $j = \{A, B\}$, by means of a probability distribution. Growth, X, is assumed to be a random variable, normally distributed, with an unknown mean, M, and an unknown variance, V. Governments learn about these two unknown parameters by observing the results of other countries under alternative policies. These two parameters are random variables, too.

In the prior specification for this kind of setup, the conditional distribution of the mean is normally distributed.[9] The marginal distribution of the variance is *scaled Inverse-χ^2*. In this prior *Normal/scaled Inv-χ^2*, the distributions of the mean and the variance are interdependent.[10] Thus, for policies $j = \{A, B\}$

$$X_j \sim N(M_j, V_j) \tag{1}$$
$$M_j | V_j \sim N\left(\mu_j, \sigma_j^2 / \tau_j\right)$$
$$V_j \sim Scaled\ Inv - \chi^2\left(\upsilon_j, \sigma_j^2\right)$$

The four parameters are the location (μ) and the scale (σ^2/τ) of the mean, M, the degrees of freedom (υ), and the scale (σ^2) of the variance, V. τ_j is the factor that relates the prior variance of the mean to the sampling variance.

At time t, governments observe the performance of alternative policies A and B in other countries. Suppose that n_A countries followed policy A

---

[8] The entry year for Costa Rica varies with the policy illustrations.
[9] Marginally, the mean has a t-Student distribution.
[10] This is a strong assumption but it does not seem to be unrealistic. The dependency means that if σ^2 (which is the sampling variance of growth) is large, then a prior distribution with high variance is induced on μ.

2.1. Essentials

and that n_B countries followed policy B. Hence, the following information about performance of policies A and B becomes available at time t.

$$X_t^j = x_{t1}^A, x_{t2}^A, \ldots, x_{tnA}^A, x_{t1}^B, x_{t2}^B, \ldots, x_{tnB}^B; \quad j = \{A, B\} \qquad (2)$$

These new data are assumed to be drawn from normal distributions. Also, it is assumed that these observations are independent and identically distributed (i.i.d.). The sample mean, $\overline{x}_j$, and the sample sum of squares, S_j, are sufficient statistics to summarize the information in the sample of countries under each of the policies A and B.

New information in combination with prior beliefs produces posterior beliefs – that is, updated beliefs embodying observed policy results under A and B. The useful feature of Bayesian updating is that it offers a mechanism of rational learning based on Bayes's theorem. The expression that follows states that beliefs about a particular parameter θ conditional on data X – posterior beliefs – is proportional to the prior beliefs about the parameter times the likelihood.

$$p(\theta_j | X_j) = \frac{p(\theta_j) \, p(X_j | \theta_j)}{p(X_j)}; \quad \theta_j = M_j, V_j; \quad i = \{A, B\} \qquad (3)$$

Bayesian updating provides updating equations for the parameters of interest – that is, mean and variance – after observing n_j outcomes of policy.

In common parlance, governments start with certain prior beliefs about average growth and the variability of growth for policies A and B. New information is gathered and governments update their beliefs about growth and its variability under the alternative policies according to equations (4)–(5), which follow. Equations (4) and (5) provide the posterior point estimates for the two parameters that I use as operationalizations of learning in the statistical analysis: The posterior for the *location* and the posterior for *the scale*.[11] These posterior beliefs become

---

[11] Reporting point estimates of the posterior distributions of the parameters is less common than reporting other summary information of the posterior distribution. What is commonly done is to run simulations of the joint posterior and then to summarize the quantities of interest by using quantiles, credible intervals (the analog of the frequentist confidence intervals), credible sets, or highest posterior density intervals (Gill 2002: 68). However, the point estimates are useful for my purpose of having an operational measure of learning included as independent variables in the dynamic probit model.

44 *The Model*

priors the following year. Based on the posterior beliefs, I assume that policy makers choose a policy. Under the assumption that samples gathered consecutively are independent, the rational updating of beliefs proceeds sequentially.[12]

With a *Normal/scaled Inv-χ²* conjugate prior and a normal likelihood as described earlier, the posterior value of the location (4) and the posterior value for the scale (5) have the following shapes.[13] For each country i, time t, and policies $j = \{A, B\}$

$$\mu_{it} = \frac{\tau_{it-1}}{\tau_{it}}\mu_{it-1} + \frac{n}{\tau_{it}}\bar{x}_{it} = \rho\mu_{it-1} + (1-\rho)\bar{x}_{it}; \ \ 0 < \rho < 1 \quad (4)$$

$$s_{it}^2 = \frac{S_{it}}{\upsilon_{it}} \quad (5)$$

n is the sample size, S_{it} is the posterior for the sum of squares, υ_{it} is the posterior for the degrees of freedom, and τ_{it} is the posterior for the factor that relates the prior variance of the mean to the sampling variance.[14]

The equations just given may look rather obscure, and an immediate reaction to them is that no real policy maker would ever undertake the heroic task of calculating posterior beliefs in order to make a decision. Yet, what the equations tell us is nothing different from the example that opened this chapter. For all its complication, equation (4) implies that posterior beliefs are a compromise between prior beliefs and the information conveyed in the observed sample of countries carrying out alternative policies. The bigger the sample size, n, the more weight the sample information has in forming posterior beliefs compared with prior beliefs.

To give a numerical example, imagine that the Costa Rican government, in view of the average rate of growth under import substitution in the world at $t - 1$, expects that the average annual rate of growth at t will be 2.24%, with a variance of 13.42 (priors).[15] Yet, the government

---

[12] A similar example can be found in Gill (2002: 72–73).

[13] Gelman, Carlin, Stern, and Rubin (2004: 79).

[14] See the Appendix to learn about the updating equations for S_{it}, υ_{it}, and τ_{it}.

[15] Prior sum of squares = 255; prior degrees of freedom = 19. As I explain in detail in the Appendix to this chapter, I use this empirical information and the method of matching moments – taking into account that the marginal distribution of the mean, M, is t-Student and that the marginal distribution of the variance, V, is *scaled Inv-χ²* – to obtain the prior values for all the parameters in equations (4) and (5). This method assigns values to the expected value and the variance of the mean, M, and to the

2.1. Essentials

observes that the *actual* average rate of growth in the world at t has been 0.13% with a variance of 42.55, in a sample of $n = 21$ countries. With $\tau = 0.9$, which, according to (1), means that the prior variance attributed to the mean is very close to the sampling variance, posterior beliefs about growth after the actual rate of growth and the variability of results at t have been observed will be 0.21% with a variance of 27.66. Note that both posteriors are a compromise between the prior belief and the observed data. Note also that the posterior belief about average growth is closer to the observed value than to the prior belief. This is because, given the values of τ and n, the weight given to the prior belief in the formation of the posterior is $\rho = 4\%$. Thus, the prior belief hardly affects the value of the posterior belief.[16]

It is realistic and substantively interesting to assume that governments learn from average growth results and from the variability of those results. Take the example of the Costa Rican economic team learning from the noisy evidence about rates of growth under a protectionist trade regime. A high variability of the outcomes following a particular policy may be interpreted as outcomes driven by underlying conditions and not by the policy in question. Hence, the variability of results can be taken as a proxy of the responsibility of a particular policy for observed outcomes. If governments are risk averse, they will be reluctant to adopt a policy that displays great variation in performance.

Also, in the empirical chapters of this book, I assume that governments update their prior beliefs on the basis of three different sources of information: Their own experience, the average experience in the region a country belongs to, and the average experience in the world, excluding own and regional experience. For example, in the model, the Costa Rican government learns from its own past experience under alternative

---

expected value and variance of the variance, V, with the marginal distributions of both parameters taken into account. By using different specifications for the priors, I show in the Appendix that priors are practically inconsequential in the formation of posterior beliefs. This is particularly notorious when the samples used in the updating process are large (regional and world samples as opposed to learning from own experience). See also Gill and Walker (2005).

[16] Note that strong assumptions have been made in setting up this model. I have assumed that (1) the rates of growth are normally distributed, (2) the rates of growth of a sample of countries under a particular policy are independent of each other, and (3) the variance of the mean and the sampling variance are dependent.

46 *The Model*

policies, the experience in its region (Latin America), and the experience in the rest of the world (excluding Latin America). Recall that gathering information is costly for rational learners, too. Thus, governments may find it optimal to learn from the experience in their regions or from their own experience only. Structuring information at these three levels allows us to test whether governments exercised some discrimination with respect to the information on the basis of geographic proximity. World experience is more abundant, and thus a rational learner should find it more informative. However, gathering it may be too costly. On the other hand, experience coming from the region allows controlling for characteristics such as shared institutional affiliations, common language, common religion, and shared colonial past. These traits are often highly correlated with the region category. To the extent that these shared traits may translate into less volatile outcomes, a rational learner might find the regional experience more informative than the world experience.[17] Moreover, when it comes to policy innovations (such as privatization) for which world experience is scant, regional experience is likely to matter if learning does take place.

Finally, note that own experience is based, at best, on a single piece of information at any one time. Thus, the sample size is minimal. This lowers $(1 - \rho)$, which is the rate of adaptation to new data. Also, note that equations (4)–(5) imply that, in a sequential updating process, posterior beliefs equal prior beliefs when there is no experience with a policy. Given that a particular country is under either one policy alternative or the other, the government in question will not have experience with which to update its beliefs based on its own experience. For instance, if Costa Rica is under an import-oriented strategy for ten years, the Costa Rican government will learn about this particular policy but it

---

[17] Elkins and Simmons (2005: 44) propose that looking at what is familiar may be, in part, a strategy of *risk reduction*. Put differently, the reason why closer experiences capture policy makers' attention is that those experiences are less noisy; but, as I explained earlier, the same preference for less noisy information is part of a rational framework and can be made part of the choice rule. Thus, the jargon may be different but some substantive ideas behind both rational and bounded learning may not differ. This is a relationship that would be worth exploring and that I only speculate about here. If it were proved to be an empirical regularity, then it would be easy to build a bridge between rational learning (which prioritizes less volatile outcomes) and bounded learning (which prioritizes nearby outcomes, in turn less noisy).

will not be able to update its beliefs about export orientation based on (nonexisting) experience. Of course, in that case the economic team can still update its beliefs by observing the experience in Latin America and the rest of the world. This fact is of concern in that the influence of prior beliefs is expected to be more persistent in the updating of *own experience* than in the updating of experience in the region and in the world, where information is greater. Thus, without such abundant information, there is little guarantee that the impact of prior beliefs will vanish. As a consequence, I expect the coefficients of own experience to be not very robust to changes in the model specifications.

The next section is designed to illustrate the characteristics of the sequential process of belief updating, where I also set out the limitations and the potential of this approach. I connect the model to a real example – namely, the choices of development strategies in Costa Rica. The aim is to clarify the nuts and bolts of rational belief updating.

2.2. On Posteriors

In order to make the model more intuitive, I use empirical data to describe how the updating process operates. I am interested in addressing two concerns. First, to what extent can the results be trusted if we take into account the fact that the prior beliefs are a modeling choice? Can we be confident that the results are not driven by the choice of prior beliefs? Second, is it possible to predict policy switches within a Bayesian updating framework? I argue and demonstrate that, providing prior beliefs are vague and information is abundant, the impact of prior beliefs vanishes rapidly in the updating process. Also, provided policy choices are modeled as a choice between policy alternatives, policy switches can be predicted by setting up a simple decision rule comparing posterior beliefs.

When external shocks are presumably the cause that spurs the learning process, modeling the shock as an increase in the uncertainty about the parameters of the model makes policy makers automatically more receptive to new information. This allows incorporating external information in the updating process. By so doing, posterior beliefs closely match the observed data.

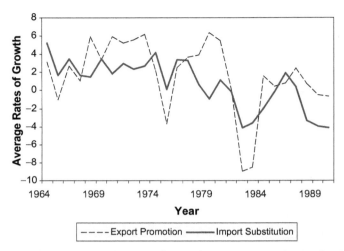

Figure 2.1. Average Regional Rates of Growth in Latin America Under Export Orientation and Import Substitution (1964–90).

Figure 2.1 shows the *observed* average rates of growth under export orientation and under import substitution in Latin America during 1964 through 1990. These figures do not include rates of growth for Costa Rica, the country whose policy choices I explore.

A priori, it is sensible to expect governments to choose the policy that performs better. Had Costa Rican governments used this criterion of policy choice, they would have embarked on export orientation in 1968, again between 1970 and 1973, and again in the periods 1977–81, 1984–85, and 1987–90. These are the spells in which, in Latin America, average rates of growth under export orientation were greater than the average rates of growth under import substitution. Thus, Costa Rica would have changed its development strategy nine times. According to World Bank data (1987), Costa Rica changed it only twice: It switched to a moderate import-substitution strategy in 1974 and embraced a moderately export-oriented strategy in 1986. According to the dichotomous Sachs and Warner (1995) measure of trade liberalization, Costa Rica was a closed economy until 1986.[18] A brief historical background will help to frame the Costa Rican government's choice of development strategies.

[18] Information about these measures of trade liberalization is provided in Chapter 3.

2.2. On Posteriors 49

Costa Rica is a small middle-income country, highly trade dependent, and traditionally within the geopolitical orbit of the United States. The latter is Costa Rica's major trading partner, major source of investment, and major provider of concessionary assistance. Coffee, bananas, and beef have traditionally been the most important country exports and, in fact, make up the majority of them.

Under the PLN administrations of José Figueres (1970–74) and Daniel Oduber (1974–78), the country embraced a strategy of state-led growth in a mixed economy. Manufacturing was highly protected and very dependent on imported inputs, which, by the late 1970s, was translating into a growing trade deficit. The 1970s also witnessed the creation of the state holding company *Corporación para el Desarrollo de Costa Rica* (CODESA) and the expansion of the state sector with many firms operating at a loss and adding to a growing budget deficit. External borrowing covered the fiscal and trade deficits, increasing sixfold between 1970 and 1978. The illusion of continuing high coffee prices postponed the need for reforms. Yet, the global drop in coffee prices in 1978–79, soaring oil prices, and the disruption of the important Central American markets mired in conflict hit Costa Rica early (Nelson 1990b).

The first timid and unsuccessful attempts at reforming the economy took place under the government of Rodrigo Carazo, who was elected in 1978. However, his weak political position, which included a divided cabinet and a small majority in the Assembly, allowed him to undertake only minor reforms. With failed attempts to raise taxes, the public deficit amounted to twelve percent of gross domestic product (GDP). By mid-1980, the country's reserves covered only a week's imports. Despite the fact that Carazo considered devaluation as politically suicidal, at the end of the year, the local currency, the *colón*, was floating. In autumn 1981, Carazo announced restrictive measures, such as drastic import controls and a debt moratorium. By the elections of February 1982, the economic situation was so bad that most Costa Ricans saw their standards of living and the country's social achievements facing severe risk.

The elections provided a clear winner – Alberto Monge, with a clear majority – who moved quickly to regain control of the economy. A unified economic team led by central bank governor Carlos Manuel Castillo and the window of opportunity opened by the economic crisis allowed a

50   *The Model*

temporary concentration of power. In turn, state autonomy translated
into a swift stabilization program supported by an IMF standby agreement. The stabilization program included rescheduling of the external
public debt early in 1983. That same year, the program bore fruit: The
public deficit and the inflation rate were slashed, the currency was stabilized, real wages rose, and economic growth resumed.

However, there was a dark side to the impressive success of the stabilization program. With improving economic conditions, calls to persevere
on the reform path faced the opposition of vested interests and the public. Protracted reform attempts characterized the rest of Monge's mandate (1982–86) and that of his successor, Oscar Arias. Gradual reforms
included the partial privatization of the state holding company CODESA,
a renegotiation of the tariff structure shared with Costa Rica's partners
in the Central American Common Market, import-tariff liberalization
starting in 1986 under the auspices of the World Bank, slow progress in
reducing subsidies for agricultural credit, and steps to reform the financial
sector under the umbrella of the United States Agency for International
Development (USAID).[19] All in all, during the 1990s, the Costa Rican
reform process proceeded gradually (Nelson 1990b; Clark 2001).

As shown in this historical account, radical policy changes are rare,
and policy persistence is more the rule than the exception. Therefore, the
comparison of observed rates of growth under alternative policies seems
not to be a good characterization of the actual policy choice process. The
latter better fits a pattern of change, continuity, and change rather than
one of frequent switches. Does the comparison of posterior beliefs about
growth generated by a rational updating process provide a more realistic
portrait of choices than the comparison of observed growth rates?

Figures 2.2 and 2.3 are based on the same data as Figure 2.1. Figure 2.2 shows the *observed* rates of growth under import substitution
in Latin America and the *posterior beliefs* about average rates of growth
under the same development strategy, with the actual path of growth
outcomes being used as the basis for the updating. As it is possible to see,
at the beginning of the updating process, the posterior series matches

---

[19] The executive branch had the power to decree an end to basic grain subsidies and to
reduce import tariffs (Clark 2001: 63).

2.2. On Posteriors

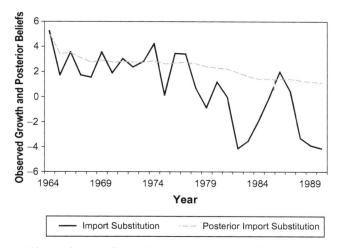

Figure 2.2. Observed Rates of Growth and Posterior Beliefs (Import Substitution in Latin America). The posterior series represents posterior average results calculated as in equation (4). For instance, for 1964, some prior belief about growth under import substitution is combined with actual average results in the region under that development strategy. The rate of adaptation to new data determines how much weight the observation will receive relative to the prior.

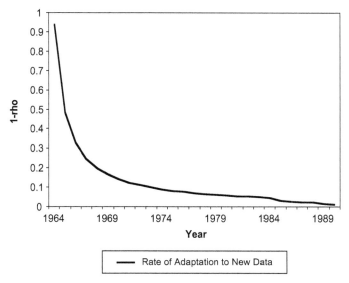

Figure 2.3. Costa Rica: Rate of Adaptation to Regional Information, Import Substitution.

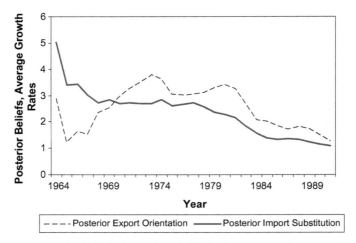

Figure 2.4. Posterior Beliefs About Growth Under Import Substitution and Export Orientation Based on Regional Experience. Both posterior series have been calculated using the observed average rates of growth in the region under both development strategies – that is, the average rates of growth as shown in Figure 2.1.

the observed path of growth quite closely. Later, posterior beliefs become enduring. This results in a posterior series that is much smoother than the original.

A look at the shape of the rate of adaptation to new data, $(1 - \rho)$ in equation (4), helps to explain why the posterior series is so smooth.

If initial priors are vague, the rate of adaptation to new data converges very fast. Such a property entails learning to take place swiftly at the beginning. Later in the updating process, new information has much less impact on the formation of posterior beliefs. This feature poses a legitimate question: Does such a low receptivity to new information make Bayesian updating less useful to predict policy changes? As long as the policy choice is modeled as a comparative exercise, the answer is 'no.'

For example, Figure 2.4 shows the *posterior beliefs* about average growth for export promotion and import substitution in Latin America.

Under the assumption that Costa Rican governments compare those posterior beliefs and choose the policy for which the posterior is greater, export orientation would have been chosen in 1970 and sustained thereafter. Thus, despite the persistence that Bayesian updating implies, it can predict policy changes. Note also that the dynamics involved in Bayesian

2.2. On Posteriors

learning resemble better the kind of behavior one observes in reality: One of continuity, change, and continuity again.

Comparison of Figures 2.1 and 2.4 throws light on the conditions under which Bayesian updating and rational decision making would predict a policy switch. Since the choice of policy is a comparative exercise, the performance of the two policies matters. It takes the results of both policies (1) to change in the opposite direction for a switch to occur. Later, when the receptivity to new information is weaker, changes in the results of the two policies will have to be (2) not only in the opposite direction, but also (3) big in magnitude and sustained over time for a switch to take place. Otherwise, peaks and troughs will be considered "anecdotal." This feature explains why Bayesian updating does not predict a change in 1982 and 1983, despite the dramatic downturn in average rates of growth under export promotion. Not only was this slowdown brief, but growth rates of the countries under import substitution were also slowing at the same time, albeit less dramatically.

The shape of the rate of adaptation to new data may be altered with an intervention (West and Harrison 1997). An intervention allows the incorporation of external information that carries with it a high level of uncertainty – for instance, an external shock. After all, one feels uneasy with the fact that Bayesian updating as presented so far does not account for the dramatic drop in rates of growth that followed the Latin American debt crisis that broke in 1982. In her study about Costa Rican market reforms, Mary Clark (2001: 43) asserts that "[L]ike many of their foreign counterparts, prominent economists saw the crisis as a proof that the regional import substitution industrialization scheme has exhausted itself." Recall also that the argument that relates learning to market reforms revolves crucially around the idea that an economic crisis is likely to spur a revision of beliefs by showing how mistaken the previous economic model was (Tommasi and Velasco 1995). By changing the priors to account for the uncertainty that accompanies a shock, the rate of adaptation to new data reaches a new peak. Modeling the uncertainty attached to a shock – attributing a greater uncertainty to the parameters of the model – makes the decision maker automatically more attentive to new data. From a substantive point of view, this is reasonable. Policy making occurs mostly under a pattern of continuity

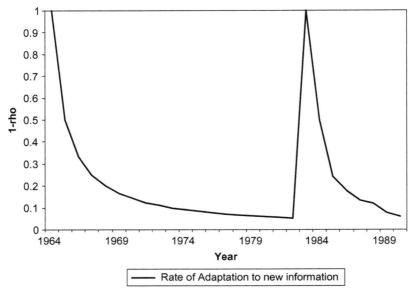

Figure 2.5. Costa Rica: Rate of Adaptation to Regional Information After Modeling an Intervention to Account for the 1982 Debt Shock, Import Substitution.

in which mild ups and downs do not bring into question the validity of the economic model. Changes are usually gradual, reflecting continuous slow modifications in environmental conditions. However, a shock that affects the performance of the economy increases dramatically the uncertainty about the "correct" model. Reasonably, this increased uncertainty makes policy makers more receptive to the information that actual outcomes could reveal about the validity of one or the other development strategy.

Figure 2.5 shows the effect on the adaptive coefficient of modeling an intervention in the year 1983, that is, of altering the updating process by introducing new prior beliefs about growth and its variability, conveying great uncertainty.[20] The uncertainty has the effect of increasing dramatically the weight given to observed data in the formation of new posterior beliefs. As it is possible to see, due to the introduction of this intervention, a new peak of "attention" is given to the 1983 average growth

[20] For simplicity, I use the same prior beliefs as in t_0.

2.2. On Posteriors

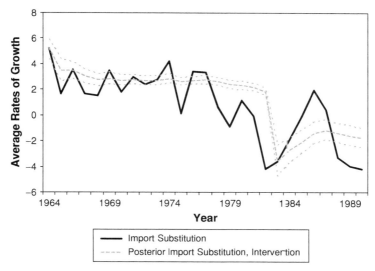

Figure 2.6. Observed Rates of Growth and Posterior Beliefs (Import Substitution in Latin America, Intervention). The intervention in 1983 – increase in prior uncertainty for that year – approaches governments' posterior beliefs versus the actual observation. The figure also shows +/− one standard deviation around the level of the mean, illustrating that the uncertainty of posterior beliefs diminishes as more experience is gained. The shock, however, increases the uncertainty about the value of the parameter.

rates and the years immediately following in the formation of posterior beliefs.[21]

Figure 2.6 shows the *observed average* rate of growth under import substitution and the posterior beliefs about growth also under import substitution. However, I modeled the intervention to account for the external shock – the debt crisis – in 1983. If we compare this figure with its "sister" Figure 2.2, it is possible to appreciate how the intervention dramatically increases the receptivity to new information. The increase in uncertainty associated with the economic shock makes politicians receptive to observed data, and by so doing, the posterior series matches the observed series after a period of gradual change without major shifts in the beliefs about the validity of the economic model.

---

[21] It is reasonable to assume that the effect of this shock on growth was felt with a lag. I therefore model the intervention in the year 1983.

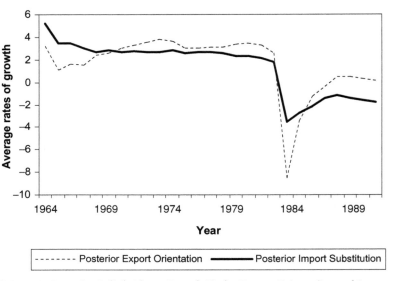

Figure 2.7. Posterior Beliefs About Growth Under Export Orientation and Import Substitution After Having Modeled the Uncertainty Surrounding the 1982 Shock, Based on Experience with Alternative Development Strategies in Latin America.

Finally, Figure 2.7 compares the posterior beliefs about growth under import substitution and under export orientation when an intervention is modeled in 1983 in the updating of the two series. It is interesting to compare this figure with its "sister" Figure 2.4, in which no intervention was modeled. In that case, the 1982 shock and the subsequent recession had practically no effect on the formation of posterior beliefs about growth under the two alternative strategies. Yet, after conditioning on the data *and* the economic shock, the actual rates of growth under both policy alternatives do affect the formation of the posteriors, which match closely the observed rates of growth. Also, and importantly, the posterior series accounts for the faster recovery of those countries in the region that adopted an export-oriented development strategy. Thus, having learned from experience in the region *and* the shock, governments in Costa Rica would have switched to an export-oriented strategy in 1970, reverted to a protectionist stance to muddle through the debt crisis, and liberalized by the mid-1980s. Interestingly, this is the actual pattern of development strategy choices followed by a good number

2.2. On Posteriors

of countries in Latin America during the period of this illustration. As Edwards's (1995) account shows, countries such as Brazil, Uruguay, and Argentina eased their import-substitution strategies in the 1970s, raised their trade barriers to secure the generation of the surpluses needed to repay their external debts during the shock, and eased the barriers to trade starting in the mid-1980s. Whereas it is true that Costa Rica did not follow its Latin American counterparts in relaxing its moderate import-substitution strategy before the 1980s, it also is true that the model of sequential updating based on regional experience predicts a switch to export orientation in Costa Rica in the mid-1980s, exactly when it occurred.[22]

It is important to note a limitation of interventions. Shocks will have an impact on the formation of posterior beliefs as long as they have consequences for growth rates. Imagine a political shock that does not produce a global recession but nonetheless has strong implications for which model of how the economy works is correct. The collapse of Communist rule in the late 1980s and early 1990s fits this description. It was a political watershed that clearly affected politicians' views about the viability of the command economy, discrediting that policy option. However, the economic consequences of that event in terms of global rates of growth were not as sweeping as the political consequences. Thus, using an intervention to model that political shock is likely to have no clear consequences in terms of posterior beliefs. Yet, it is clear that the fall of the Berlin Wall did affect politicians' beliefs about feasible economic strategies.

Also, I am following the vast literature on economic policy reform in depicting the 1982 debt shock as a crisis of beliefs about policy ideas. Contrary to previous crises triggered by external shocks – such as the oil

---

[22] Recall that the main purpose of this exercise is to illustrate the operation of Bayesian updating. Thus, learning from the experience of other Latin American countries is only part of the story. As a Costa Rican scholar recognized, "... the transformations that are being advocated in Costa Rica derived not only from an orthodox conceptual framework that promotes free trade at the global level and indebted countries meeting their financial commitments. They also derive from the example of what some authors describe as the success of the East Asian dragons" (Villalluso 1990: 99, my translation). The author also discusses in depth why the East Asian model could not be replicated in Costa Rica in toto.

58   *The Model*

crises – the 1982 collapse was related to bad policy, not to bad luck. It was excessive debt, in turn caused by the onerous financial requirements of import substitution, that brought about the debacle (Iglesias 1992; Krueger 1993; Edwards 1995). Arguably, politicians have little to learn from shocks caused by exogenous factors – such as the rise or fall in the price of some strategic commodity – about the validity of their beliefs, yet in principle they have a lot to learn from crises generated by bad economic management. It therefore makes sense to portray as crises of belief only the shocks of the latter type. It is an empirical question whether learning from such shocks rather than routine learning had any impact on the decision to launch and sustain market reforms. I employ the same strategy to evaluate the impact of the financial crises of the early and mid-1990s.

Finally, it is fundamental to emphasize that this operationalization of learning does not inevitably impose policy changes. Policy makers may be rational learners and yet they may *not* choose policies rationally, for a host of reasons (discussed subsequently). Moreover, policy makers may be rational learners, and yet the evidence may be so confusing that, even if one is a rational learner and chooses policies rationally, a change of policy is not justified on the basis of experience alone. Thus, rational choices do not automatically follow rational learning.

2.3. Policy Choices

Governments are interested in adopting policies that enhance growth. The motives for this interest may vary. Governments may be benevolent. Alternatively, they may be interested in holding on to office and believe that a good record of achievement increases their chances of re-election. Autocrats may also promote economic growth as a way to legitimize their regimes and make them endure. Regardless of motivation, I portray governments as actors that "invest" in a policy. Like any risk-averse investor, governments prefer the policy that yields the best outcome with the least volatility.

A decision problem can be specified in which, every period, governments maximize the expected utility from alternative policies. I assume that politicians' expected utility is a function of their *posterior beliefs*

2.3. Policy Choices

about average results and about the variability of results (posteriors calculated as explained earlier). Again, the variability of results matters because, if governments observe a high average rate of growth with very little noise, then the average will convey a great amount of information about the responsibility of the policy for the observed outcome.

Suppose that government i derives utility from a high rate of growth. For policies, $j = \{A, B\}$, the expected utility has the following shape:

$$EU_{it}^{j}(\mu, s) = \beta_1 \mu_{it}^{j} + \beta_2 s_{it}^{j} + \varepsilon_{it}^{j}; \; j = \{A, B\} \tag{6}$$

where μ_{it} is the *posterior belief* about average growth results, s_{it} is the *posterior belief* about the variability of growth results, and ε_{it} is a stochastic component.[23] Thus, expected utility is a function of the posterior average and the posterior standard deviation, which vary from government to government and over time.

I assume that expected utility increases in posterior beliefs about the average rate of growth. If decision makers are risk averse, expected utility decreases in posterior beliefs about the volatility (standard deviation) of observed results. Governments are indifferent between a policy that yields less average growth and less variability of results and a policy that yields greater growth but is noisier. Also, under the assumption that governments' utility increases with average growth and decreases with noise, governments prefer policies that yield greater growth for a particular level of noise, and they prefer a less volatile policy for the same growth outcome.[24] For the sake of clarity and for the time being, I assume that policy choices over time are independent. I drop this assumption subsequently.

Thus, government i faces a choice at t between policy A and policy B. The decision maker i will choose policy A if and only if the

---

[23] It is assumed to be normally distributed and independent over time and among governments.

[24] There is extensive debate about the conditions that are necessary for a mean-standard deviation preference function to yield the same ranking of preferences as the expected utility criterion. These conditions are a quadratic utility function and normally distributed alternatives. However, recent research contends that the only requirement is that the alternatives should have distributions that differ in their location and scale. The shape of the utility function in (6) allows a more intuitive interpretation of results than a quadratic utility function. Moreover, models were estimated using the latter specification with minor qualitative changes in the results. On this topic, see for example, Meyer (1987) and Frankfurter and Phillips (1995).

60   *The Model*

expected utility from option A is greater that the expected utility from option B.

$$EU_{it}^A \geq EU_{it}^B \tag{7}$$

This implies:

$$\beta_1\mu_{it}^A + \beta_2 s_{it}^A + \varepsilon_{it}^A \geq \beta_1\mu_{it}^B + \beta_2 s_{it}^B + \varepsilon_{it}^B \tag{8}$$

Rearranging terms,

$$\beta_1\left(\mu_{it}^A - \mu_{it}^B\right) + \beta_2\left(s_{it}^A - s_{it}^B\right) \geq -\left(\varepsilon_{it}^A - \varepsilon_{it}^B\right) \tag{9}$$

To simplify, let $\mu_{it}^A - \mu_{it}^B = \mu_{it}$; $s_{it}^A - s_{it}^B = s_{it}$, $\varepsilon_{it}^A - \varepsilon_{it}^B = \varepsilon_{it}$.

Note that μ_{it} is the *difference in posterior beliefs* about average growth whereas s_{it} is the *difference in posterior beliefs* about the variability of results under one and the other policy.

Hence, the probability that policy maker i chooses policy A at t is:

$$P(A_{it}) = P\left(EU_{it}^A \geq EU_{it}^B\right) = P(\varepsilon_{it} \geq (\beta_1 + \beta_2 s_{it}))$$
$$= 1 - F\left[-(\beta_1\mu_{it} + \beta_2 s_{it})\right] = F(\beta_1\mu_{it} + \beta_2 s_{it}) \tag{10}$$

This setup allows us to estimate β_1 and β_2. My main task in the next chapters is to obtain empirical information about those parameters for each of the four policy choices under scrutiny, thus to explore whether rational learning is significant and, if so, by how much and in what direction.

I expect that the greater the difference in posterior beliefs about average results following policy A with respect to policy B, the greater the probability of a *switch* to policy A will be. Thus, a positive sign is expected for β_1. I also expect that, the greater the posterior beliefs about the variability of results following policy A compared with policy B, the less likely a change to policy A will be. Hence, β_2 is expected to be negative. Ultimately, the sign of this coefficient will depend on governments' attitudes toward risk.

The comparison of a politician choosing between policies and an investor choosing among risky assets is intuitive. However, assuming that a politician will show an unequivocal preference for a policy that performs consistently better is a working hypothesis. It could be the case that governments are guided by a miraculous performance instead of

2.3. Policy Choices

average performance. If that is the case, a high variability of results could be positively related to the probability of a switch, since high variability entails the existence of very bad but also very good performers in the sample. For instance, in the example of the Costa Rican economic team that opened this chapter, I assumed that the average rate of growth under import substitution was lower than that under export orientation. I also assumed that the rates of growth under import substitution showed greater variability: Some countries grew remarkably but others did badly. The Costa Rican economic team could be deterred by this high variability of results, wondering what might be expected from a policy that exhibited so very different results. Alternatively, the Costa Rican change team might be seduced by the experience of the country or countries in that cluster that did very well, and decide to pursue the same strategy. Whereas the first reaction accords with risk-averse behavior, the second reveals a risk-loving attitude. Finally, even if a policy performs comparatively worse, it may not be abandoned if it is ideologically preferred, if the policy is imposed on politicians, if an alternative course of action is not envisaged, or if there is some exogenous or ideational justification for poor results.[25]

Also, I expect the relationships spelled out earlier to hold in the decision *to sustain* a particular policy. However, note that the Costa Rican example is also illuminating in pointing to the complexity of factors that affect policy *sustainability*. The Costa Rican case resembles many other instances of market reforms in that sustaining them has proved much more difficult than launching them (Nelson 1990a; Grindle and Thomas 1991; Haggard and Kaufman 1992, 1995; Nelson 1994; Williamson 1994; Haggard and Webb 1994; Haggard and Kaufman 1995; Krueger 2000; Weyland 2002). The panoply of interests that opposed the reforms and other institutional veto players will resume their activities after a period of extraordinary politics. Thus, the shared beliefs of a cohesive economic team are less likely to be consequential during "normal times." Interestingly, the statistical model employed in this study distinguishes

---

[25] One example is that of a Polish policy maker who judged the success of the reforms in the light of the unemployment they yielded (Przeworski 1991). It is also common to consider that economic reforms bear fruit along a J-curve. This implies that things have to get worse before economic performance eventually improves. See, for instance, Piñera (in Williamson 1994) and Aspe (1993). Thus, a policy that gives bad results may not be revised if those bad results are expected and explained by theory.

62 *The Model*

both phases (launching and sustainability) and, thus, I shall be able to provide information about the impact of learning from experience in both stages. For the reasons already mentioned, I expect learning to be more relevant during the stage of launching the reforms than during the stage of sustaining them.

So far, I have focused on how to obtain a measure of learning from experience and on how this measure of learning may inform policy choices. I assumed that policy choices over time were independent. However, policies tend to be highly inertial, and policy switches are exceptional. Thus, the most accurate way to depict the policy choice process over time is to drop the assumption that policy choices are independent by specifying the problem as one of learning and dynamic choice. The last step in this modeling process is to relate learning from experience to the observed path of policy choices. Using a dynamic version of probit, I estimate the probability of transitions between policies as well as the probability of remaining under the same policy.[26] Therefore, the empirical test consists of, first, producing posterior beliefs for average results and the variability of results under alternative strategies using Bayesian updating; second, comparing those posterior beliefs; and third, relating the difference in posterior beliefs to *observed* policy choices by using a dynamic model. In this model of transitions, current policy choices of country i, y_{it}, are modeled as a function of a country's prior history of policies, y_{it-1} (first-order Markov chain).[27] The transition matrix for this type of model with a binary outcome is:

$$\begin{bmatrix} p_{AA} & p_{AB} \\ p_{BA} & p_{BB} \end{bmatrix}$$

where p_{AB} indicates the probability of a policy switch, or the probability that $y_{it} = A$ given that $y_{it-1} = B$. Alternatively, p_{AA} indicates the probability that country i will continue under the same policy – that is, the probability that $y_{it} = A$ given that $y_{it-1} = A$.

[26] Recent applications of this statistical model in political science include Vreeland (2003), Boix (2003), and Gledistch and Ward (2006).

[27] Note that the dynamic probit model is an event history/survival model. In fact, it is equivalent to a discrete-time exponential hazard model in which all that matters for a transition to take place is the previous period.

2.3. Policy Choices   63

Given some set of predictors Z_{it-1}, these conditional transition probabilities can be estimated by

$$\Pr(y_{it} = 1 | y_{it-1}) = F[Z_{it-1}\beta + y_{it-1}Z_{it-1}\alpha] \qquad (11)$$

where F is a probit link. β indicates the effect of the independent variables on the probability of adopting a particular policy, A, at time t given that this adoption did not occur at $t - 1$. The probability of remaining under the same policy, A, at $t - 1$ and t is given by the vector of parameters $\gamma = \alpha + \beta$. Hence γ gives the probability of sustaining a particular policy.[28]

As independent variables, I include the learning variables – that is, the *difference in posterior beliefs* about average results under alternative policies and the *difference in posterior beliefs* about the variability of results, also under alternative policies, and this for own, regional, and world experience. Thus,

$$Z_{it-1} = \mu_{it-1}^{O}, s_{it-1}^{O}, \mu_{it-1}^{R}, s_{it-1}^{R}, \mu_{it-1}^{W}, s_{it-1}^{W}$$

with μ_{it-1} and s_{it-1} defined as previously. O stands for own experience, R for experience in the region, and W for world experience.

To account for alternative explanations of policy diffusion, two other control variables were added to the baseline models of learning. These variables are (1) the number of other countries (NUMBER) in the world under a particular policy in a particular year and (2) a dummy variable coded 1 for countries and years under an IMF agreement (IMF). The first control variable is a proxy for symbolic emulation. As explained in Chapter 1, governments may believe that a policy embraced by many other countries has to be good. Moreover, governments may see high reputation costs in not jumping on a particular policy bandwagon or want to avoid the stigma of backwardness for not adopting a generally well-regarded policy. The second control variable accounts for the

---

[28] In practical terms, these transitional probabilities can be obtained by estimating two separate probits. Transitions to a new policy can be calculated by focusing on the observations where the lagged dependent variable, y_{it-1}, equals 0. Estimations of the probability of remaining under the same policy status can be calculated using the observations where the lagged dependent variable equals 1. Proceeding in this way simplifies enormously the calculation of standard errors, z scores, and the post-estimation interpretation of results. For the post-estimation interpretation, I used Clarify (King, Tomz, and Wittenberg 2000) and Spost (Long and Freese 2006).

external imposition of policies. For instance, in Costa Rica, coercion and persuasion by international actors were important during the stabilization period and especially after 1983. The Costa Rican case shows that external finance and conditionality played a major role in shaping the timing and the content of the adjustment. IFIs and USAID were very active in proposing, helping to design, and sometimes openly pressing for specific macroeconomic policies and structural reforms, such as the liberalization of import tariffs and reform of the financial sector (Nelson 1990b; Clark 2001).

My expectation is that the number of other countries that have already adopted a particular policy will exert a positive impact on the decision to adopt and to remain under each of the policies. Finally, switches are expected to be positively related to the existence of an agreement with the IMF.

One obvious objection to the model presented so far is that it is politically simplistic. When governments decide whether to adopt a particular policy, they obviously care about things other than the economic results of policies. Most prominently, governments care about the expected political results of policies. Politicians consider whether a particular policy will damage the interests of a relevant constituency, and they care about their ideological preferences and about whether there is any chance that their preferred policy will be enacted given the set of domestic political institutions. In other words, the political results of policies should be as much part of governments' utility as are economic results.

Unfortunately, modeling learning from political results within the framework just presented seems far from simple: Which piece of information would politicians look at to judge the *political* success of a particular policy? If that indicator existed, could the same logic of rational updating be applied? This question is interesting and very likely worth exploring in a different project. However, for the time being, modeling learning only from economic results offers a very good pilot experiment of the potential of this approach. I do not ignore politics, though. In this project I employ the simpler strategy of including as controls in the different model specifications those political and socioeconomic domestic variables that the international political economy literature regards as

2.3. Policy Choices

relevant for each of the policies under scrutiny. For instance, the economic reform literature considers electoral honeymoons as a likely time for launching radical reforms. To return to the Costa Rican illustration, the 1982 stabilization program was embraced after a new government and a new, homogeneous economic team was installed. Moreover, the Costa Rican political system diffuses power among the different branches of government, and the principle of no presidential re-election encourages the formation of rival factions within the governing party prior to elections. Both features pose an obstacle to prompt action that, for instance, precluded a quick reaction to the deteriorating economic situation under the Carazo government (1978–82). However, the combination of a deep economic crisis and the arrival of a new PLN government with a majority in the legislature opened a temporary space for highly autonomous action. With the improvement in economic conditions, both the centralization of authority and the cohesion of the economic team disappeared, which stalled the reform process.

One domestic control included in all empirical chapters is the type of political regime (democratic or authoritarian). An established belief, yet one hardly backed up by existing evidence, is that democracies have a disadvantage with respect to their authoritarian counterparts when it comes to launching market reforms. Distributive pressures and the fear of losing elections would play against the introduction of austerity measures, whereas authoritarian regimes can more easily circumvent distributive pressures and popular opposition to reforms. This conclusion was mostly drawn from the experience of military and rightist dictatorial regimes, particularly in East Asia and Latin America. However, as the Costa Rican example illustrates, even old democracies can enjoy periods of high political autonomy to adopt important economic reforms. Besides, as the chapter on privatization discusses, reforms can be and usually are designed to generate their own supporters. Finally, democracies can also engineer compensations with which to appease losers' opposition to reforms. Given that many new and old democratic countries have been able to launch at least first-generation economic reforms, the hypothesis that democracies are at a disadvantage has less leverage today (Haggard and Kaufman 1992; Bresser, Maravall, and Przeworski

66   *The Model*

Table 2.1. *Independent variables and expected effects on policy decisions*

Dependent Variables

Switch to and Sustainability of Trade Liberalization, Privatization, Capital Account
    Openness, IMF Agreements

Independent variables	Expected sign
Learning from Average Experience, Own	+
Learning from Volatility of Experience, Own	−
Learning from Average Experience, Region	+
Learning from Volatility of Experience, Region	−
Learning from Average Experience, World	+
Learning from Volatility of Experience, World	−
Coercion	+
Emulation	+
Other Domestic Controls	Depends on Control

Note: A negative sign for the variables "Learning from the Volatility of Results" is expected under
the assumption of risk aversion.

1993; Haggard and Web 1994; see the contributions in Williamson 1994).
However, it is an interesting exercise to assess its performance in a cross-
country, cross-time, and cross-policy study such as this one.

Hence, the variables in the control models are:

$$Z_{i,t-1} = \mu_{i,t-1}^{O}, s_{i,t-1}^{O}, \mu_{i,t-1}^{R}, s_{i,t-1}^{R}, \mu_{i,t-1}^{W}, s_{i,t-1}^{W}, \; EMULATION,$$
$$COERCION, DEMOCRACY, OTHER \; DOMESTIC \; POLITICAL$$
$$AND \, ECONOMIC \; CONTROLS.$$

Table 2.1 summarizes the expected effects of the explanatory variables
on the probability of adopting and the probability of sustaining several
market reforms. Note that, as explained earlier: (1) The negative sign
for the volatility of results is expected on the assumption that decision
makers are risk averse; (2) since world experience is more abundant, a
rational learner should find it more relevant. This, however, depends
on the costs of gathering information and on whether the policy in
question is an innovation with or without historical precedents from
which to learn. Also, (3) the impact of learning is expected to be more
influential and stronger in magnitude in the decision to adopt, rather

than in the decision to sustain, market policies. Finally, according to the literature on market reform, I expect deep crises to affect policy decisions via an increase in the uncertainty about cause-and-effect relationships contained in policy ideas. Thus, (4) I expect learning from shocks to be more consequential than routine learning for policy switches.

2.4. Discussion

In this chapter, I have tackled the issue of how to measure learning and how to evaluate its impact on economic policy choices. In order to answer the central question posed by this book – namely, whether the spread of market-oriented policies had to do with a process of learning from the experience of others – an operational measure of learning is needed. Whereas the discussion on learning and the spread of public policies has been prolific, testing learning across time, space, and policies is a harder task. This paralysis has to do with difficulties in coming up with an empirical measure of learning.

In this study I assume that politicians are rational learners who seek to reduce the uncertainty about the consequences of their policy choices by inspecting the experience of others. No matter what their initial beliefs about the results of policies are, if confronted with a good deal of information, all policy makers will converge in their beliefs about the outcomes of policies, and will also, I hypothesize, converge in their policy choices.

Although rational learning as expressed in its mathematical form may lead us to think that policy makers will never apply that rule (unless blessed with heroic statistical power), the fact is that the substantive meaning of that rule is pretty simple: Observe all available information and, in evaluating average information, consider also the consistency of what you see. This can be done even by a statistical antihero. Moreover, at least in the realm of economic policy making, in quite a few developing countries, technocrats with extensive training in economics increasingly took over political positions (Domínguez 1996). Decision making was left in the hands of experts with above-average training in data gathering and analysis (Centeno 1994; Valdés 1995). This is not to say that these policy makers are free from cognitive limitations or immune from making

68 The Model

mistakes (see Tetlock 2005); however, they have been trained to minimize them. I think it realistic to portray expert policymakers as less bounded than the average citizen.[29]

Bayesian updating is a very intuitive idea. I use it to produce the independent variables of a model that is, in turn, estimated "classically." I produce posterior beliefs about average growth and its volatility under different policy choices. Those posteriors are compared and the differences in posterior beliefs about growth and its variance after learning from own, regional, and world experience are then used as explanatory variables of the observed policy choices. Other possible mechanisms of policy convergence and domestic economic and sociopolitical controls are used to obtain a better sense of the true responsibility of learning for observed policy switches.

Chapters 3–6 apply this model of learning to four policy choices: The decisions to privatize, liberalize trade, sign agreements with the IMF, and open the capital account. For each policy, the difference in posterior beliefs about growth and its variability – (1) under a liberal and a protectionist trade regime, (2) privatizing and not privatizing, (3) with an open and a closed capital account, and (4) with and without an IMF agreement – will be used to explain the decision to switch to and to sustain those policies over time. Interestingly, the model performs differently depending on policy domain: Whereas trade liberalization emerges as the policy mostly driven by international factors, entering into IMF contracts appears as overwhelmingly grounded in domestic conditions. Learning has the strongest impact on the decisions to privatize, to adopt export orientation, and to sustain an open capital account. In practically all policy illustrations, it is learning from shocks, rather than routine learning, that explained policy switches. A robust result across policies is that learning from experience in the world, rather than learning from the other sources of experience, did matter in the decision to liberalize the trade regime, to privatize, to sustain an open capital account, and to enter into agreements with the IMF.

---

[29] Studies of bounded and rational decision making have shown that people with training in probability and statistics are less prone to certain kinds of error (Swoyer 2002).

APPENDIX

Conjugate Families for Samples from a Normal Distribution. Sampling from a Normal Distribution with Unknown Mean and Unknown Precision.

This section is based on De Groot (1970), Lee (1997), Zellner (1997), Gill (2002) and Gelman, Carlin, Stern, and Rubin (2004).

Suppose growth, X, is a random variable that follows a normal distribution with an unknown value of the mean, μ, and an unknown value of the variance σ^2. Suppose that their prior joint conjugate distribution is as follows: The conditional distribution of μ given σ^2 is a normal distribution. The marginal distribution of σ^2 is *scaled Inverse-χ^2*. With this specification, the marginal distribution of μ follows a t-Student distribution.

Thus,

$$\mu|\sigma^2 \sim N\left(\mu_0, \sigma_0^2\right)$$
$$\sigma^2 \sim Inv - \chi^2\left(\nu_0, \sigma_0^2\right)$$

or

$$(\mu|\sigma^2, \sigma^2) \sim N \sim Inv - \chi^2(\mu_0, \sigma^2/\tau_0; \nu_0, \sigma^2)$$

The parameters are the location and scale of μ and the degrees of freedom and scale of σ^2 respectively. Note that this specification implies that μ and σ^2 are dependent in their prior specification. If σ^2 is large, a high-variance prior distribution is induced for μ. Prior beliefs about μ are calibrated by the scale of measurement of X and are equivalent to τ_0 prior measurements on this scale (Gelman, Carlin, Stern, and Rubin, 2004).

Suppose now that a sample, χ_n, of n i.i.d. observations on growth, also normally distributed, is gathered.

1. *The joint posterior distribution, $p(\mu, \sigma^2|x_n)$.*

   The posterior parameters for the location and scale of the mean and the degrees of freedom and scale of the variance are as follows:

$$\mu_{it} = \frac{\tau_{it-1}}{\tau_{it}}\mu_{it-1} + \frac{n}{\tau_{it}}\overline{x}_{it} = \rho\mu_{it-1} + (1-\rho)\overline{x}_{i\cdot}; 0 < \rho < 1 \quad (A1)$$

$$s_{it}^2 = \frac{S_{it}}{v_{it}} \tag{A2}$$

$$\tau_{it} = \tau_{it-1} + n \tag{A3}$$

$$v_{it} = v_{it-1} + n \tag{A4}$$

$$S_{it} = S_{it-1} + S_{it} + \frac{\tau_{it-1} n (\bar{x}_{it} - \mu_{it-1})^2}{\tau_{it}} \tag{A5}$$

where v_0 are the prior degrees of freedom, S_0 is the prior sum of squares, and S_t is the sample sum of squares.

2. The marginal posterior distribution of σ^2, $p(\mu, \sigma^2 | x_n)$

$$\sigma^2 | x_n \sim Inv - \chi^2 (v_n, \sigma_n^2) \tag{A6}$$

with v_n and σ_n^2 as in (A4) and (A2).

3. *The conditional posterior distribution of μ, $p(\mu | \sigma^2, x_n)$*

$$\mu | \sigma^2, x_n \sim N(\mu_n, \sigma^2 / \tau_n) \tag{A7}$$

with μ_n, τ_n as in (A1) and (A3). One way to proceed to sample from the joint posterior distribution is to draw σ^2 from its marginal posterior distribution as in (A6) and then draw μ from its normal posterior distribution using the simulated value σ^2.

4. The marginal posterior distribution of μ, $p(\mu / x_n)$

$$\mu | x \sim t_{vn}(\mu_n, \sigma_n^2 / \tau_n)$$

with v_n, μ_0, σ_n^2, and τ_n as in (A4), (A1), (A2), and (A3) previously.

5. Specifying the prior parameters.

Since σ^2 follows an $Inv - \chi^2$, the following formulas apply.

$$E(\sigma^2) = \frac{S_0}{(v_0 - 2)} \tag{A8}$$

$$Var(\sigma^2) = \frac{2 S_0^2}{(v_0 - 2)^2 (v_0 - 4)} \tag{A9}$$

Thus, after values for the mean of the variance and the variance of the variance have been specified, prior values for S and v can be

Appendix 71

obtained solving those equations. Also, since μ marginally follows a t-Student distribution:

$$E(\mu) = \mu_0 \tag{A10}$$

$$Var(\mu) = \frac{S_0}{\upsilon_0 \tau_0} \tag{A11}$$

from which τ_0 can be obtained after the variance of the mean has been specified and after S_0 and υ_0 have been obtained.

Example: Obtaining the Prior Parameters

Suppose that growth under a certain policy in year t has been observed to be 1.87 with variance 14. I use this information to come up with a prior distribution of the mean, the variance, and prior beliefs for all parameters. The mean and variance of the mean distribution equal 1.87 and 14 respectively. The mean and variance of the variance distribution equal 14 and twice this value, 28. Hence,

$$E(\mu) = 1.87; Var(\mu) = 14.$$

$$E(\sigma^2) = 14; Var(\mu) = 28.$$

With this information and by using equations (A8), (A9), (A10), and (A11), the following priors are obtained:

$$\mu_0 = 1.87; \upsilon_0 = 18, S_0 = 224 \text{ and } \tau_0 = 0.88.$$

The same priors but with $Var(\mu) = 28$ – that is, with double the uncertainty adjudicated to the prior of the mean – would yield $\tau_0 = 0.44$, which is half the value found earlier.

With these prior parameters, the updating process is set in motion.

Example: Different Priors, Very Similar Posteriors

The figures that follow are the summary statistics of the posterior beliefs about average growth and variability of results for own, regional, and world experience under and not under a liberal trade regime (see Chapter 3 for information about the database). The first set of posteriors has been obtained by using as priors the observed sample information the

72   *The Model*

year before a country enters the database, exactly as explained earlier. In
the second set of posteriors, the expected values of both the mean and
the variance have been taken to be the observed values, but the variance
(the uncertainty) attached to the parameters was very large.[30]

As expected, the differences in posteriors are more sizable when it
comes to learning from the own experience. The differences in posterior
beliefs, on average, are minor thanks to big sample sizes for updating
based on regional and world experiences.

Difference in posteriors, relatively uncertain priors

Variable	Mean	s.d.	Minimum	Maximum
Average Growth, Own	.68	2.76	−7.80	20.09
Volatility, Own	−.13	1.55	−9.20	2.58
Average Growth, Region	1.07	1.41	−4.52	9.87
Volatility, Region	−1.36	1.70	−4.96	1.74
Average Growth, World	2.51	1.10	−1.08	5.86
Volatility, World	−1.60	0.97	−3.30	0.38

Difference in posteriors, very uncertain priors

Variable	Mean	s.d.	Minimum	Maximum
Average Growth, Own	.70	3.36	−13.72	29.42
Volatility, Own	− .95	2.41	−13.26	4.53
Average Growth, Region	1.10	1.56	−6.71	12.28
Volatility, Region	−1.73	1.98	−6.85	2.63
Average Growth, World	2.54	1.12	−1.46	5.84
Volatility, World	−1.87	1.00	−4.01	0.09

---

[30] Note that Gill (2002: 120) calls for caution when using conjugate priors as ignorance
priors because, actually, conjugate priors convey a large amount of information.

THREE

Learning and Development Strategies

[M]any developing countries learned the hard way by following IS policies too long and seeing the fortunate few pursuing the EP strategy [export promotion] do much better. Perhaps learning by others doing and one's undoing is the most common form of education.

Jagdish Bhagwati (1985: 41)

In this chapter, I explore the question of whether governments adopted an EO development strategy as a result of learning.

During the 1980s, a growing consensus emerged about the failure of ISI to promote growth. Poor economic performance in countries pursuing ISI contrasted with outstanding growth figures in the East Asian newly industrialized countries (NICs). In turn, the good performance of the East Asian NICs was associated with the adoption of a radically different strategy based on export promotion. Failure of ISI coupled with the success of EO triggered a process of learning in theory and practice. As a result, trade policy stances converged. This story is obviously sketchy. Yet, it is an accurate summary of a well-established argument: Governments adopted EO because they learned from experience (Haggard 1990; Iglesias 1992; Edwards 1995, chapter 3; Krueger 1997). I test this argument here.

The debate about development strategies had profound normative implications. Initially, the triumph of EO over ISI was interpreted as a triumph of markets over the state. Policy recommendations of less state involvement in development became the rule. However, a closer look at country stories and other empirical research showed that the reality was far more complicated. State withdrawal and EO are far from equivalent.

74 *Learning and Development Strategies*

Replicating policies does not guarantee success. In fact, results under the same strategy showed a considerable variation across regions (World Bank 2005; Simmons, Dobbin, and Garrett, 2006).

This chapter proceeds as follows. I briefly introduce the different development strategies and advance several alternative explanations found in the literature. I then describe the data on development strategies and growth for fifty-one developing countries from 1960 through 1990. I also use data on trade liberalization for eighty-seven developing countries in the period 1970 through 1999.[1] Following this, I present the results of several learning models. The baseline model of learning reveals that governments were systematically risk averse in their decisions to switch to EO, which is consistent with the high variability of growth outcomes observed under alternative strategies, and especially under ISI. Yet, beginning in the mid-1980s, switches toward more liberal trade regimes did happen. I show that modeling the uncertainty associated with the 1982 debt crisis is relevant to understand those switches in the late 1980s. I also show that emulating others was related to the decision to open up the trade regime. Other control variables such as the size of the country and membership in the General Agreement on Tariffs and Trade/World Trade Organization (GATT/WTO) are not significant in explaining moves toward less restrictive trade regimes.

Finally, I concentrate on trade liberalization using a database covering 1970 through 1999. Given the time period surveyed, this database is particularly suitable to test the influence of the diffusion of democracy (Brinks and Coppedge 2006; Gledistch and Ward 2006) on the diffusion of trade liberalization (Milner and Kubota 2005; Guisinger 2005). The results suggest that it is not possible to reject the hypothesis that the diffusion of trade liberalization was related to the diffusion of democracy. In fact, diffusion of democracy appears as the most influential variable. Overall, international factors fare better than domestic ones when it comes to explaining the global trend toward more liberal trade regimes.

---

[1] Note that I use data on both trade regimes and development strategies. As I will show, the trade regime is part of the development strategy but does not fully describe it. On the other hand, I think it accurate to state that the trade regime is the central feature of the alternative development strategy. To complement the results and check their robustness, I use data on trade liberalization based on the Sachs–Warner index of trade liberalization up to 1999.

3.1. Development Strategies: A Description and Alternative Explanations[2]

Development strategies are a central issue in development and international economics. The topic has generated an impressive amount of research and debate. However, many of the issues at stake are still controversial. Since the literature on the topic is monumental, I briefly present the main characteristics of each alternative strategy.[3] I then focus on a few aspects on which consensus is still absent. Finally, I review the extant explanations to address the choice of different development strategies. Only recently have scholars considered the possibility that the liberalization of trade might have been related to the policy stance adopted by others via competition or social emulation (Guisinger 2005). However, learning from the experience of others has not been explored as one of the interdependent mechanisms causing countries to liberalize.

Development strategies are packages of policies that aim to allocate resources among domestic industries and social groups. They also shape countries' relations with the global economy. An EO development strategy consists of trade and industrial policies that do not discriminate between purchases of domestic goods and foreign goods. By contrast, an ISI strategy favors production for the domestic over the export market. Exporting is discouraged by the increasing cost of domestic inputs relative to the prices received by exporters. This may happen due to domestic inflation or an appreciation of the exchange rate following the imposition of import barriers. I summarize the main characteristics and instruments of each strategy in Table 3.1.

ISI has been identified with the strategy pursued by Latin American NICs during the 1950s and 1960s. It was inspired by the Economic Commission for Latin America and the Caribbean (ECLAC). Two arguments were used to defend this strategy. First, infant industries needed to be protected, at least temporarily. Second, Latin American countries could not generate foreign exchange out of their specialization in the export

---

[2] Unless otherwise stated, this section is based on Haggard (1990) and the contributions in Gereffi and Wyman (1991).

[3] See, for instance, Balassa (1980), Krueger (1983, 1984, 1985, 1990), Bhagwati (1985), Balassa (1989) and Meier (1990).

76 *Learning and Development Strategies*

Table 3.1. *Features and policy instruments of development strategies*

Export promotion	Import substitution
* Ready access to imports of intermediate and capital goods. Provision of similar production incentives for domestic and for export markets.	* Strict and time-consuming licensing procedures for imports of manufactured goods.
* Export incentives provided uniformly and automatically.	* Protection is not uniform or automatic.
* Realistic exchange rates.	* Overvalued exchange rates.
* Normally avoidance of quantitative restrictions and use of low or zero tariffs. Exporters have access to the international market at international prices for their inputs.	* Imports are prohibited; there are quantitative restrictions or high tariffs that make imports uneconomic. Exporters do not have a free choice between domestic and imported inputs.
* Temporary protection of infant industries.	* Permanent protection of infant industries.
* Positive real interest rates.	* Low or even negative real interest rates.
* Realistic pricing of public utilities.	* Underpriced public utilities.

Note: Based on Balassa (1980), Krueger (1983; 1985) and Krueger and Jones (1990).

of primary commodities subject to declining terms of trade. Following this path, countries such as Brazil and Mexico achieved high rates of growth prior to 1960s. After that, chronic balance-of-payment crises, increasing public deficits, rampant inflation, and rent-seeking practices led to the belief that ISI had outlived its initial purposes (Krueger 1983, 1984, 1997; Edwards 1995). This perception was accentuated by the experience of the East Asian Tigers. Singapore, Hong Kong, South Korea, and Taiwan grew at impressive rates while Latin America stagnated. The success of the former was attributed to the adoption of a strategy of export promotion, in turn inspired by the Japanese experience. In policy circles, that success was interpreted as clear evidence of the virtues of the market and the daunting failures of the state. Growth under EO was fast, even during periods of crisis. Moreover, under the EO strategy, growth and equity seemed not to be incompatible. As a result of these contrasting experiences or, better, the interpretation of them, EO became the accepted orthodoxy in international policy circles.

Whereas it is undeniable that the East Asian countries performed remarkably well, the extent to which this performance can be attributed to an export-led policy alone has been highly contested. A closer look at countries' experiences reveals that the story of the East Asian miracle

3.1. Development Strategies

was simplified in several respects. For instance, the ex post reading of the Asian success as being primarily the result of the withdrawal of the state is profoundly misleading. This interpretation overlooks the fact that there are different types of states in terms of size, capacity, and autonomy, as well as different forms of state intervention. Indeed, according to a good number of studies, it is impossible to understand the success of East Asian countries without taking into account the active role played by the state. For instance, the experience of South Korea with selective intervention and infant industry promotion showed that reducing the bias of the regime may require active state involvement, not the opposite. Under the centralized public authority of Park Chung Hee (1961–79), and with the support of a good-quality bureaucracy, the state took steps to facilitate the provision of capital, labor, and technology. The provision of capital was boosted thanks to a good system of tax collection and, at times, by using public banks to direct credit to specific sectors and industries. In turn, continuing support for firms was contingent upon performance. With the use of repression, labor was cheap, disciplined, and readily available. Research and development were actively supported. These measures were carried out in a context of macroeconomic orthodoxy. Overall, the state was highly interventionist (Wade 1990; Westphal 1990; Evans 1995; Rodrik 1996, 2003; Kohli 2004).

Thus, it is true that the Latin American experience showed that state failures could be disastrous; but the East Asian experience does not establish that markets alone are enough to succeed.[4] Paradoxically, it seems that the state is, at the same time, the problem and the solution.[5] However, policy recommendations of neutral development regimes came along with broader recommendations for state dismantling.[6]

---

[4] An interesting debate on the roles of the private and public sectors in economic development can be found in the *Proceedings of the World Bank Annual Conference on Development Economics*, 1990.

[5] This is Kahler's (1990) "orthodox paradox."

[6] Another two simplifications are that the East Asian countries were following a strategy and that ISI was exclusively pursued in Latin America and EO in East Asia. On the first point, stories show that improvisation and ad hoc responses to problems as they arose were the rule. It seems that the idea of development strategies makes more sense "the second time around." On the second point, cross-regional and within-region research shows that both strategies were pursued in the two regions and that the same strategy had local variations. Development strategies are better described as a succession of phases in which elements of EO were borrowed by ISI and vice versa.

Concerning the explanations of the choice of development strategies, stylized accounts distinguish three levels of analysis: (i) the *international system*, (ii) *social, political, and institutional features* of the domestic polity, and, finally, (iii) *values, ideas, culture, or beliefs*. Another relevant distinction is that between static and dynamic factors. Among the former, size and resource endowments are the most relevant. Latin America had plentiful natural resources and big internal markets, which made ISI a particularly feasible strategy. East Asia had small markets, scarce natural resources, and cheap and educated labor. Hence, the choices of ISI and EO respectively. The story gets complicated with the consideration of dynamic factors, which include the social and political features mentioned subsequently.

At the *international level*, shocks and economic crises are frequently cited as the most important drivers of change. For instance, Latin America's choice of deepening ISI at an earlier point was related to the combination of crisis and big markets. In addition, the East Asian choice of primary EO has been attributed to economic crisis, small markets, and the availability of U.S. foreign aid. Colonial legacies and military alliances are other factors that explain different policy choices. Japan provided a viable model of development for East Asian countries (Wade 1992).

At the *domestic* level, much has been written about the influence of *sectoral interests* in the choice of development strategies: Agriculture, labor, and capital. Whether those sectoral interests influence policy or whether policy creates them is not at all clear. It seems clear, though, that the choice of development strategies created coalitions that strongly opposed policy change. For example, in Latin American NICs, the longevity of ISI was influenced by urban political constituencies in which the industrial, highly skilled working class was central (Collier and Collier 1991). EO success in East Asia was crucially related to close alliances between the state and capitalist groups (Kohli 2004).

However, the influence of sectoral interests cannot be addressed in isolation from *institutional factors*. Ultimately, the leverage of sectoral interests is a function of how vulnerable the state is to societal pressures. NIC states varied in their degree of insulation, centralization of decision-making processes, and the policy instruments policy makers controlled. East Asian countries benefited from autonomous decision-making

3.1. Development Strategies

processes and cohesive bureaucracies (Wade 1990; Evans 1995; Kohli 2004). In particular, and concerning political institutions, the relationship between development strategies and regime type has generated much debate (Nelson 1990a; Przeworski 1991; Haggard and Kaufman 1992, 1995; Haggard and Webb 1994; Williamson 1994; Kohli 2004). The radical reform processes that followed the military coups in Korea (1961), Brazil (1964), Indonesia (1966), Chile (1973), Ghana (1981), and Turkey (1980) led some analysts to conclude that dictatorships, with their repressive apparatus, were better equipped to circumvent opposition to unpopular reforms.[7] However, this is not a characteristic shared by all dictatorships regardless of their type and of their institutions (Kohli 2004; Gandhi 2004).

In recent contributions, Milner and Kubota (2005) and Guisinger (2005) contend and demonstrate that, in developing countries, democratization is positively related to the decision to liberalize the trade regime. The rationale is that in developing countries, where labor is abundant relative to capital, labor benefits from greater openness.[8] The wave of democratization that preceded and was concurrent with increased trade liberalization implied a change in the size of the group that participates in the selection of political leaders, the so-called "selectorate."[9] In other words, democratization entailed a change in the identity of the median voter, who is an unskilled worker, enfranchised as a result of democratization. Trade liberalization would then appear as the rational response of politicians facing a bigger selectorate with workers as the decisive voters. Thus, the diffusion of trade liberalization would appear as the side effect of the diffusion of democracy (Gledistch and Ward 2006). I find support for this hypothesis in the dataset that covers 1970 through year 1999.

The summary just given makes clear that the choice (and outcomes) of development strategies were the consequence of a very specific combination of multiple factors. However, although these variables can explain divergent policy choices prior to the 1980s, they are less effective in

---

[7] Against this view, other authors argue that the state does not need to be insulated but, rather, requires embedded autonomy (Evans 1995).

[8] The prediction is derived from the Heckscher–Ohlin and Stolper–Samuelson theorems.

[9] This is the terminology used in Bueno de Mesquita, Smith, Siverson, and Morrow (2003).

explaining why, in the 1980s and 1990s, trade liberalization was adopted in many countries.[10]

In an innovative work, Guisinger (2005, chapter 4) shows that modeling trade liberalization as the response of countries to the decisions of regional, economic, and income peers considerably increases the predictive capacity of explanatory models. Thus, developing countries responded to the policies of countries that were similar to them (their peers) in some respect. Models in which the decision to liberalize trade takes into account the policy stance of countries that belong to the same trade network fare much better than models in which only domestic economic and political variables are included. These findings help explain why trade liberalization has not been a race to the bottom. What one observes is countries clustering in areas of higher and lower trade tariffs depending on the level of tariffs of their network of trading partners.[11] Thus, trade liberalization appears as an interdependent policy choice rather than the outcome of an independent response to particular domestic conditions.

Learning from the policy outcomes in the past and of others is another interdependent mechanism the impact of which has not been explored thus far. In his thorough study of market reforms in Latin America, Sebastián Edwards (1995) points out that there were two successes and one failure crucial in the Latin American road to discovering EO. The two successes were the strong economic performances of East Asia and Chile. Beginning in the mid- and late 1980s, ECLAC sponsored a series of influential studies contrasting the Latin America and East Asian development strategies. As described in Chapter 1, the strong recovery of the Chilean economy after 1985 persuaded Latin American politicians that an EO strategy could also work in the tropics. The influential policy failures were the initial structuralist responses to the 1982 debt crisis in

---

[10] Interestingly, Kohli's (2004) detailed study on divergent development strategies extends to the point at which most countries embraced reforms to make their development strategies more export oriented.

[11] Note that this clustering resembles the geographic concentration of policies referred to by Weyland (2005) in his study of the diffusion of social policy innovations. However, what is interesting in the study by Guisinger (2005) is that clusters of policies can be motivated by multiple factors and not exclusively by geographic availability. In particular, policies are likely to diffuse around networks of competitors.

3.2. Learning and Development Strategies: The Data 81

Argentina under President Raúl Alfonsín (Austral Plan, 1985), in Brazil under President José Sarney (Cruzado Plan, 1986), and in Peru under President Alan García (1985–90). According to Pedro Aspe (1993: 27), Mexican Minister of Finance under Carlos Salinas de Gortari (1988–94), the discussion of the 1987 *Pacto de Solidaridad* was influenced by the failure of the Austral and the Cruzado Plans in Argentina and Brazil respectively. Aspe stated that "the government had followed closely the evolution of those South American economies [Argentine and Brazilian] trying to learn from their mistakes to make sure that Mexico did not suffer the same fate"[12] (see also de la Madrid 2004: 619, 699). Concerning Latin America, Enrique Iglesias (1992: 52) asserted that "a considerable degree of consensus has been achieved (. . .) concerning the origins of and solutions to the crisis [Latin America] experienced in the 1980s, a consensus that emerged from the lessons the Latin American countries learned at so high a cost." Corbo (2000: 65) states that "[i]n the area of structural reform there is a base of knowledge on both the theory and the practice of policy reform. It was this accumulated knowledge and experiences with the previous policy that led most governments in Latin America to ease trade restrictions by lifting nontariff barriers and reducing the mean and variance of import tariffs."

Thus, past experience and the experience of others supposedly triggered a learning process that could explain the convergence toward more open trade regimes. The next sections explore the relative importance of this explanation compared with competing ones such as the role of IFIs, revisions of beliefs in the light of the 1982 debt crisis, and the diffusion of democracy.

3.2. Learning and Development Strategies: The Data

During the late 1980s and early 1990s, a good number of developing countries took steps to liberalize their trade regimes.[13] Clearly, policy

---

[12] Translated by the author.
[13] The literature on the specific topic of trade liberalization is immense. Although there is no agreed definition of trade liberalization, it can be described as a set of measures aimed at neutralizing incentives for exports and imports through the removal of quotas, a reduction in the level and dispersion of tariffs, compensatory devaluation,

82   *Learning and Development Strategies*

converged toward lower levels of trade protection, although there was a considerable degree of regional variation (Guisinger 2005; World Bank 2005; Simmons, Dobbin, and Garrett 2006). In this section, I test whether this convergence resulted from learning, controlling for other possible diffusion mechanisms and for some domestic variables.

The first obstacle one encounters in explaining policy choices concerning development strategies is the need to come up with an acceptable measure of them. The difficulties are both conceptual and practical. They are conceptual given there is no agreement on the criteria to use in characterizing EO and ISI. Eventually, most authors use some proxy based either on aggregate indexes[14] or on disaggregated indicators of openness.[15]

At a practical level, the type of data required to characterize trade regimes – average tariffs and their dispersion, quantitative restrictions, export subsidies, tax credits, degree of exchange rate overvaluation – are rarely available in a systematic and comparable way. Thus, I relied on several ready-made lists that classify countries' development and commercial strategies. The *World Bank Development Report* (1987) provides a list of forty-one developing countries and covers the period 1963–85. This period is subdivided between the years before and after the first oil crisis (1973). Countries are classified according to their pursuit of strongly outward-oriented, moderately outward-oriented, moderately inward-oriented, and strongly inward-oriented strategies. The definitions of these categories are provided in the Appendix to this chapter. The *Report in Issues and Developments in International Trade Policy* (Kelly and McGuirk 1992) provides a second list of trade liberalization in the 1980s. In this list, thirty-six developing countries are classified as having Tight Control, Significant Control, Relatively Open, and Open trade

---

and removal or reduction of export taxes. As with development strategies, the literature is pervaded with lessons about the content and sequencing of reforms. Comprehensive studies include Nash, Edwards, and Vinod (1991), Michaely, Papageorgiou, and Choksi (1991), Rodrik (1992), Nash and Takacs (1998), and Rodríguez and Rodrik (1999).

[14] A frequently used one is the Effective Rate of Protection (ERP). This is a measure of the bias of the trade regime based on the ratio of the Effective Exchange Rate of Importables (EERm) to the Effective Exchange Rate of Exportables (EERx).

[15] Level and dispersion of tariffs, the extent of quantitative restrictions on imports and exports, the degree of exchange rate overvaluation, and the existence of export subsidies, rebates, and compensation schemes.

3.2. Learning and Development Strategies: The Data   83

regimes. As a complementary source of information, I used the 1994a World Bank Discussion Paper *Trade Policy Reform in Developing Countries since 1985*.

Because the analysis requires a dichotomous indicator of policy, I clustered in one the strong and moderate categories of the first list and the control and open categories of the second list. For instance, according to my data, Madagascar implemented a moderate inward-oriented policy between 1963 and 1973. Between 1974 and 1986, it engaged in a strongly inward-oriented strategy. In my coding, Madagascar appears as having engaged in an import-substitution strategy throughout the period 1963–86.[16] Admittedly, it could be argued that these lists measure different things. A liberal trade policy is part of a particular development strategy, but does not fully characterize it. However, I consider it accurate to put trade policy at the center of ISI and EO. Besides, when it came to allocating to one or the other alternative, the two lists were highly consistent.[17]

The *Development Strategies Database* comprises fifty-one developing countries, grouped in four regions – Africa, Latin America, East Asia, and South Asia. The list of countries included in the analysis is shown in the Appendix. The period under scrutiny extends from 1964 to 1990. Thus, it covers only the first wave of trade liberalization beginning by the mid-1980s. In this database, there are a total of 1,341 country-year observations, of which 957 were under an ISI strategy and 384 were under an EO strategy.

This database is particularly useful to study the impact of modeling learning from the 1982 debt crisis on the subsequent decision to open up the trade regime. If the crisis was relevant, its effect on politicians' beliefs must have been felt within a short time span. However, the period covered by this database makes it difficult to fully assess the role played by learning

---

[16] It is obvious that by collapsing the two categories, some nuisance is lost and some measurement error is caused. For instance, Brazil, which experimented with EO in the 1960s and 1970s, appears as a Moderately Outward Oriented country in the World Bank Report. Therefore, Brazil is classified as an open country throughout the period of study. However, other coding and country accounts place trade liberalization in Brazil much later. Particularly, the *Trade Liberalization Database* (1970–1999) places the beginning of trade liberalization in Brazil in the year 1991. Indeed, the correlation coefficient for the countries and years for which data exist for the two indicators is around 0.5. Using the two databases should help to assess the robustness of the results.
[17] The only exception is Tunisia.

84   *Learning and Development Strategies*

from the results of others with EO given the limited experience with liberalization prior to the 1990s. Since most transitions to democratic rule occurred after the mid-1980s, the *Development Strategies Database* is also of limited value in studying how democratization affected the diffusion of trade liberalization. For these reasons, I also use another database covering the period 1970–99 (Milner and Kubota 2005). This database on trade liberalization uses the Sachs–Warner (1995) index of trade liberalization and the update of the index by Horn and Wacziarg (2003). According to Sachs and Warner's definition, an economy is closed if (1) average tariff rates are forty percent or more, (2) nontrade barriers cover more than forty percent of trade, (3) the black market exchange rate depreciated by twenty or more relative to the official exchange rate during the 1970s or 1980s, (4) the economy could be described as socialist, or (5) there was a state monopoly on exports. The Sachs–Warner database has information for eighty-seven developing countries (listed in the Appendix), which I grouped in six regions – Latin America, Caribbean and non-Iberian Latin America, North Africa/Middle East, Sub-Saharan Africa, South Asia, and South East Asia. The database has 2,418 country-year observations, of which 743 correspond to countries and years with an open trade regime.

During this period, policy stances converged. Even if not all developing countries carried the reforms so far as to change their development strategy, many of them succeeded in reducing the bias of their trade regimes. Figure 3.1 shows the proportion of countries with an open trade regime. The figure is quite explicit. Toward the beginning of the 1980s, fewer than twenty percent of the countries had a liberal trade regime. This figure exceeded seventy percent at the end of the 1990s.

To make compelling the argument for learning based on past performance and the performance of others, it is necessary to have a sense of the relative growth outcomes of both development strategies. Another controversial issue is whether EO is conducive to faster growth. The problems are not only methodological but also theoretical. The links between trade and productivity are ambiguous. Arguments based on savings and innovation are not compelling enough to show that export promotion is necessarily better per se than import substitution.

3.2. Learning and Development Strategies: The Data

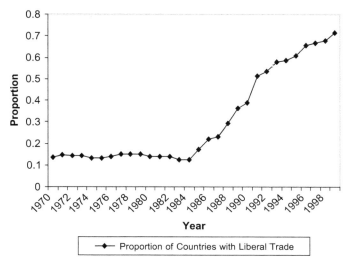

Figure 3.1. Proportion of countries with an Open Trade Regime, 1970–1999, 87 LDCs, based on Sachs–Warner (1995) and Horn and Wacziarg (2003).

According to some voices, "there is by and large a consensus among economists – based on a wealth of studies – that trade liberalization brings significant economic gains..." (Stiglitz 1998: 35). However, results are more mixed in developing countries. For instance, some Latin American countries – notably Brazil, Colombia, Argentina, and Mexico – experimented with EO during the 1970s with little success (Edwards 1995).[18] The paths of countries that liberalized their trade during the 1990s varied a lot, with less-than-impressive results in quite a few regions (World Bank 2005). Thus, if theoretical claims are not clear (Rodríguez and Rodrik 1999) and empirical evidence in developing countries is positive (Wacziarg and Welch 2003) but weak (Frankel and Romer 1999), it

---

[18] Reforms were undertaken in the 1960s and 1970s in Brazil under Minister Roberto Campos, in Uruguay under Minister Alejandro Villegas, and in Argentina under Ministers Krieger Blasena and Martínez de la Hoz. However, the reforms were not successful in resolving the overvaluation of the exchange rate. Contrary to East Asia, where overvaluation was against the interests of a large rural constituency, in Latin America, the overvaluation of the exchange rate was beneficial to powerful owners of industry and urban constituencies, who frequently were unionized (Edwards 1995).

86 *Learning and Development Strategies*

Table 3.2. *Growth rates per region and decade, development strategies*

Region	Export promotion		Import substitution	
	Growth (% change)	N	Growth (% change)	N
Africa				
1964–1973	2.67	20	1.76	178
1974–1985	1.14	23	0.53	229
1986–1990	0.60	41	−0.18	52
South Asia				
1964–1973	–	–	−0.29	43
1974–1985	–	–	3.43	60
1986–1990	0.59	4	2.65	17
Latin America				
1964–1973	3.77	40	2.69	140
1974–1985	0.44	41	0.16	175
1986–1990	0.60	59	−1.33	31
East Asia				
1964–1973	6.62	59	2.19	10
1974–1985	4.64	62	3.53	22
1986–1990	6.10	35		–
Total (N = 1341)		384		957

Growth figures taken from ACLP (1997). Growth is the annual rate of growth of real GDP per capita, 1985 international prices, chain index.

may well be the case that the East Asian success was idiosyncratic and contingent on a very particular combination of policy instruments.[19]

Table 3.2 is based on data from the *Development Strategies Database* (1964–1990). It shows descriptive information on rates of growth, which were, in general, higher under EO than under ISI. However, the good performance under EO seems to have been an exclusively East Asian phenomenon. In this region, rates of growth were remarkable also under ISI. Even in the crisis period of 1974–85, they were outstanding. However, a comparison of averages with other regions suggests that this fact may have been rather idiosyncratic, too. A look at performance during 1986 and 1990 reveals that EO succeeded in East Asia only.

[19] Performance under alternative trade regimes has also been the object of voluminous research. Summaries can be found in Edwards (1989) and Harrison and Revenga (1995). On Latin America and Africa, see Nogues and Gulati (1994) and Shafaeddin (1994) respectively. See also World Bank (2005).

3.2. Learning and Development Strategies: The Data

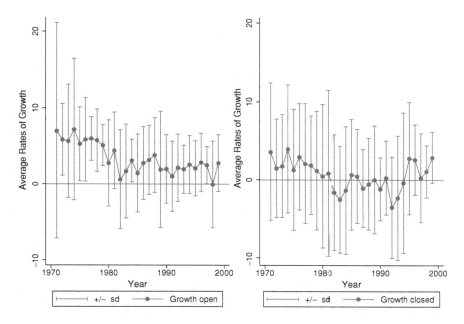

Figure 3.2. Average Rates of Growth and Volatility of Results (+/− one s.d.), Trade Protection and Trade Openness, 1970–1999.

Note that this is the period in which quite a few developing countries switched their trade regimes, apparently without the expected effects on growth.

Figure 3.2 is based on the *Trade Liberalization Database* (1970–1999). The figure unambiguously shows that the average rates of growth of countries with an open trade regime outperformed their counterparts with a close trade regime. Of course, this information is merely descriptive as there may be many other factors and policies responsible for the better performance of the open countries. Also, the figures are uninformative about the direction of the relationship between growth and trade openness. The figure also shows that the 1982 debt crisis hit countries under both trade policies but that the countries with a closed trade regime were already experiencing declining rates of growth after 1976. Also, countries under a closed trade regime experienced a new trough around 1992.

88   *Learning and Development Strategies*

Finally, the learning process as depicted in this study entails observing not only average rates of growth but also the variance of results under each strategy. High variability of results under the same strategy pervades the *Development Strategies Database* (1964–1990). For instance, in 1986, rates of growth under EO ranged from 8.29 percent in Taiwan and 9.6 percent in Korea to minus 4.56 percent in Bolivia. In Latin America, figures such as the latter coexisted with the better performance of Chile (3.02 percent) or Uruguay (8.74 percent). However, the variability of growth results under ISI was even greater (s.d. 4.63 under EO and s.d. 5.18 under ISI, year 1986). This same result holds for the *Trade Liberalization Database* (1970–1999). Figure 3.2 and Table A3.9 (in the Appendix) show that, after trade liberalization took off in 1985, average growth rates were greater for countries with an *open* trade regime in twelve out of fifteen years (up to 1999). In eleven of fifteen years, the volatility of outcomes was greater in the cluster of countries with a *closed* trade policy. These data are important, for if governments are rational, as this study portrays them to be, they will take into account not only the observed average results but whether results vary much under alternative trade policies (open and closed). If that is the case, average performance conveys little information about the true impact of trade policies on growth results.

I enquire next whether learning from the outcomes of alternative development and trade policies influenced the decision to switch to more open trade regimes. A robust test of this hypothesis requires controlling for other plausible explanations of trade liberalization. In particular, learning motivated by economic crises has been taken to be an important driver of the decision to liberalize. As explained in Chapter 2, an economic crisis may open the door for reform through two mechanisms. One is by dismantling entrenched interests in the perpetuation of a policy the crisis is showing to be a clear failure. The deeper the crisis, the more certain it is that everyone will lose from political inaction. The other mechanism is the revision of beliefs about alternative policies in the light of their relative performance. An economic crisis, we are frequently told, is decisive in making politicians reconsider their views about what policies are feasible (Rodrik 1994). I test this mechanism next and I further enquire whether the wave of trade liberalization had to do with the pressure exerted by IFIs or with emulating others. Finally, using the

3.3. Learning and Development Strategies: The Results

Trade Liberalization Database (1970–1999), I test for another unresolved contention in the political economy of trade liberalization: The effect of the extension of the franchise on trade policy reform in developing countries.

3.3. Learning and Development Strategies: The Results

I follow the procedure spelled out in Chapter 2 for testing the impact of learning on the choice of development strategies. Governments start with some prior beliefs (Appendix) about the expected growth outcomes following each policy status (EO and ISI). Each year, new information about outcomes becomes available. Prior beliefs are combined with new information to generate posterior beliefs. The updating process proceeds sequentially. Decisions on policy are stipulated to be based on those posterior beliefs.

I first calculate the posterior beliefs about the outcomes of alternative policies and compare them. The empirical test consists of relating the difference in posterior beliefs under one and the other strategy to the observed path of policy choices. I structure the policy outcomes at the level of the country, the region, and the world. Also, as explained earlier, relevant information concerns both average results and the variability of results under alternative policies.

I report the estimates of the impact of learning on the probability of a *transition* from ISI to EO. I do not report the estimates of the sustainability of this reform. This is because there were only six transitions from EO to ISI, which makes the estimators of continuity unreliable.[20]

Under the assumption of rationality, I expect that, the higher the average rate of growth under EO compared with ISI, the more likely is a transition to EO. Under the assumption that governments are risk averse, I expect that, the greater the variability of results under EO, the less likely is a switch to this strategy. Equally, the greater the variability of results under ISI compared with EO, the more likely is a switch to EO. Note that, by construction, this means that greater values of the variable LEARNING

---

[20] Also, since experience with EO is very limited in South Asia – four years in Sri Lanka – I have not included this region in the final models: With such scant regional information, there is no guarantee that the influence of prior beliefs will vanish.

90   *Learning and Development Strategies*

FROM THE VARIABILITY OF RESULTS at all levels of geography are expected to be negatively related to the likelihood of a switch.

I first use the *Development Strategies Database* (1964–1990) to test the relative impact of learning from others as opposed to learning from the 1982 debt crisis. I then use the *Trade Liberalization Database* (1970–1999) to test for the robustness of results when the period of analysis is longer and, therefore, the experience with alternative policies is greater. This database is also more suitable to test the impact of democratization on trade liberalization. The test of learning is subject to the presence of other controls regarding other mechanisms of policy convergence (EMULATION and COERCION) and a battery of domestic controls.

Learning from Others versus Learning from Shocks

Model (1) in Table 3.3 shows the results of the baseline learning model. In this model, only the learning variables from own, region, and world experience were included.[21] I expected that learning from the average experience with EO versus ISI would positively affect the probability of a switch. I also expected that learning from the variability of results with EO versus ISI would negatively affect that probability. As can be seen, the signs are as anticipated across the three levels of geography; but only the beliefs about own experience and the volatility of own results seem to have affected the decision to switch to a more liberal stance.

Model (2) adds to the baseline learning model the two alternative explanations. On the one hand, switches could have been the consequence of herding on the behavior of others (EMULATION). As explained before, the rationale is that a policy that has been previously adopted by many others may be seen as "the correct way to go." On the other hand, the adoption of liberal trade policies could have been motivated by the coercive or persuasive influence of a third party. In particular,

---

[21] As mentioned, the learning variables tend to be highly correlated. However, I decided not to exclude the variables from the models unless collinearity is shown to affect either the significance or the signs of the coefficients. For the models shown in Table 3.3, multicollinearity is not affecting the robustness of the results.

3.3. *Learning and Development Strategies: The Results* 91

Table 3.3. *Probability of adoption of an EO strategy, development strategies database (1964–1990)*

Dependent variable: Adoption of export orientation	Baseline model (1)	Alternative diffusion mechanisms (2)	1982 Crisis and other controls (3)
CONSTANT	-2.91^{***}	-4.62^{***}	-6.15^{***}
	(-4.12)	(-4.99)	(-3.32)
OWN EXPERIENCE			
AVERAGE RESULTS	0.05^{*}	0.03	0.06^{*}
	(1.84)	(0.92)	(1.65)
VARIABILITY OF RESULTS	-0.09^{**}	-0.06	-0.04
	(-2.41)	(-1.46)	(-0.80)
REGIONAL EXPERIENCE			
AVERAGE RESULTS	0.11	0.26^{*}	0.18
	(1.03)	(1.91)	(1.14)
VARIABILITY OF RESULTS	-0.05	-0.04	-0.16
	(-0.45)	(-0.29)	(-1.45)
WORLD EXPERIENCE			
AVERAGE RESULTS	0.04	0.17	0.15
	(0.41)	(1.20)	(0.90)
VARIABILITY OF RESULTS	-0.29	-0.28	-0.50^{**}
	(-1.33)	(-1.02)	(-2.49)
EMULATION		0.72^{***}	0.72^{***}
		(4.79)	(4.15)
IMF		0.50^{**}	0.49^{**}
		(2.47)	(2.23)
GATT			0.21
			(0.88)
REGIME			0.21
			(0.73)
SIZE			0.04
			(0.52)
ELECTIONS			0.07
			(0.30)
Log Likelihood	-123.63	-110.05	-104.14
LR Chi-Squared	1210.54	1237.71	859.42
P-Value for F	0.000	0.000	0.000
Observations	1171	1171	872

$^{*}p < .10$; $^{**}p < .05$; $^{***}p < .01$; z-scores in parentheses; all variables are lagged one year.
Model 3 predicts around 97% percent of the 0s and 1s correctly. The Pseudo R^2 for this model is 0.80.

I explore the impact of the IMF, which advocated trade liberalization among the conditions for accessing its loans.

As the results show, both mechanisms are significant and with the expected signs. The probability of adopting an EO development strategy was greater when a country was under an IMF agreement and when many other countries had adopted an EO strategy. The results concerning learning from own experience are no longer robust in the presence of the other mechanisms of policy convergence.[22] Overall, these two models attribute a very small and very weak role to learning as a motive for changing development strategy.

Model (3) explores another possibility. It might be that the switch to more liberal trade regimes had to do not with learning from the experience of others under "normal" times, but with learning from a shock: The 1982 debt crisis. It is reasonable to assume, and is frequently alleged, that this shock did convey important information to politicians about the viability and sustainability of ISI. Also, it is reasonable to assume that the shock increased politicians' uncertainty about the "correct" model of the world, in turn making them more attentive to the actual performance of alternative models. As I explained in Chapter 2, in a Bayesian updating framework, it is possible to model external shocks by increasing the uncertainty assigned to prior beliefs in the particular year of the shock.[23] This makes politicians automatically more receptive to the new data on performance under both strategies.

Model (3) also includes the alternative hypotheses and a few other control variables. As mentioned before, the wave of democratization preceded and accompanied the wave of trade liberalization. Thus, it could be the case that trade liberalization was the outcome of democratically elected politicians responding to the preferences of a widened and different selectorate. The variable REGIME captures this possible effect. In this specification, REGIME is a dichotomous variable that takes the value 1 for dictatorships and 0 for democracies (Przeworski, Alvarez, Cheibub, and

---

[22] When the learning variables are introduced in the sequence two by two (OWN, REGION, and WORLD) with the other diffusion mechanisms, none of the learning coefficients is significant.

[23] In this case, I modeled the intervention in the year 1983 with the idea that the shock affects growth after a lag.

3.3. Learning and Development Strategies: The Results 93

Limongi 2000). It is also argued that smaller countries have less latitude in deciding their trade policies (Katzenstein 1985; Rodrik 1997). The variable SIZE (the natural log of the population, World Development Indicators) is included to control for this effect. GATT membership, with its proactive defense of trade liberalization, may have also influenced governments' decisions to liberalize. Finally, following the literature on market reforms, it is argued that new governments are more likely to launch radical policy changes. The rationale is that new governments find it easier to overcome the status quo bias that characterizes policy making, and can benefit from electoral honeymoons (Nelson 1990a; see contributions in Williamson 1994; Weyland 2002). The variable ELECTION is included to capture the fact that it is easier to implement reforms after, rather than before, an election (Vreeland 2003). Descriptive statistics of all the variables employed are shown in the Appendix.

According to the results, the estimations suggest that learning from this shock was somewhat relevant to the move toward free trade. The signs of the learning variables (positive for averages and negative for variances) are robust and consistent with my expectations across all model specifications. Learning from average own experience is again significant in explaining the adoption of EO. Note that risk aversion is now significant, given the high variance of results under ISI as compared with EO at the level of the world.[24] This means that, after modeling the 1982 debt crisis, politicians appeared to have learned from the high uncertainty of outcomes under ISI. This, in turn, motivated the abandonment of this strategy. EMULATION and IMF agreements are robust to the inclusion of the intervention, and to the inclusion of other control variables.

However, the controls are not significant. REGIME has a positive sign – that is, dictatorships were more likely to adopt EO. This result is in line with the view that repressive regimes are better able to reform. SIZE has the opposite expected sign (big countries are more likely to liberalize). Yet, the coefficients of both REGIME and SIZE do not reach statistical significance.[25] ELECTION and GATT membership have the

---

[24] The result concerning the volatility of results in the region is also close to reaching statistical significance ($p = 0.14$).

[25] The POLITY IV indicator of democracy was also used. It was not statistically significant.

94   *Learning and Development Strategies*

expected sign (trade liberalization is more likely to be launched after an election and GATT members are more likely to open) but, again, these variables are not statistically significant. It is worth mentioning that the irrelevance of democratization may be due to the time span covered by this database. In the next section, I test this possibility using the extended database.

Thus, according to this specification, the "rush to free trade"[26] resulted from a combination of learning from the consequences of the 1982 debt shock, herding on others' behavior, and the coercion of the IMF. Note that only two of the six learning variables were significant, and that one of the variables (LEARNING FROM AVERAGE EXPERIENCE, OWN) was only marginally so. However, the most important lesson taught by the debt crisis and experience in the world was that the ISI development strategy could not be relied on consistently to deliver high growth rates.

Figure 3.3 shows the predicted probability of adopting EO against the values of learning from the variability of results in the world and the 95% confidence interval (based on model (3), Table 3.3). This variable, which is the subtraction of two positive quantities, means that values to the left of zero represent observations in which politicians' posterior beliefs about the volatility of outcomes under ISI outstripped their posterior beliefs about volatility under EO. In other words, if, after observing the outcomes in the world, governments think that what may occur under ISI (in terms of growth) is more uncertain than what may occur under an EO strategy, then governments will be more likely to choose to open. Values of the variable to the right of zero mean that the expected variance of results under EO is greater than the expected variance of results under ISI. Note that the model predicts a very low probability of a policy switch in that situation.

All in all, based on the *Development Strategies Database* (1964–1990), the learning models show that learning from the observed outcomes under alternative models had two different effects. The important volatility of growth outcomes under alternative policies, and particularly under ISI, spurred risk-averse behavior: Governments were more likely to switch to EO the greater the variance of results (hence the more unreliable

---

[26] This expression was coined by Rodrik (1994).

3.3. Learning and Development Strategies: The Results

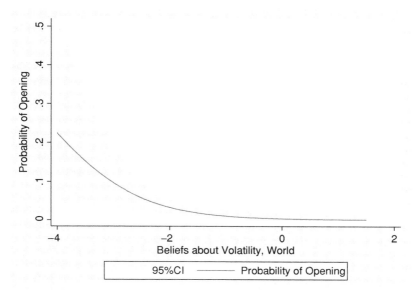

Figure 3.3. Predicted Probability of Adopting EO, as a Function of the Difference in the Volatility of Results in the World. Values of the variable less than zero mean that the volatility of ISI was greater than the volatility of EO. The opposite is true for values greater than zero. Thus, the greater the volatility of ISI in comparison with EO, the more likely is a switch to EO.

the experience) under ISI. Other than learning, EMULATION and the presence of an IMF agreement drove policy change. Contrary to domestic variables, which were irrelevant to explaining the adoption of EO, the different mechanisms of policy convergence did predict the change in trade policy stances in Less Developed Countries (LDCs).[27]

Learning from Crisis and the Diffusion of Democracy

Given that experience with trade liberalization accumulated during the late 1980s and the 1990s, looking at a longer time span appears more

---

[27] This result accords with Guisinger (2005), who finds few significant results for domestic economic and political variables in her explanatory model of tariff choices in developing countries. In particular, models of the level and changes of tariffs focusing on domestic variables explain two percent and twenty-two percent respectively of the variance in tariff levels in developing countries (Chapter 3).

96   *Learning and Development Strategies*

suitable to test the role of learning. Moreover, a fair test of the role of democratization may also require an extended period of analysis: In 1975 and in the database, only sixteen countries were coded as democracies. The figure rises to twenty-six in 1990 and to forty-one in 1995. Thus, the number of democracies more than doubled between 1975 and 1995.

Table 3.4 shows the results of running four models with roughly the same specifications as the one just described but using the *Trade Liberalization Database* (1970–1999). Model (1) is the baseline model of learning. Two results are significant at conventional statistical levels with the expected sign. First, LEARNING FROM AVERAGE EXPERIENCE, OWN is positively related to the probability of liberalizing the trade regime. Second, and again, VARIABILITY OF RESULTS, WORLD under an open and a protected trade regime is negatively related to the probability of opening. The other two significant results have the opposite expected signs but are not robust to the inclusion of further controls.[28]

Model (2) adds the alternative convergence mechanisms to the baseline model of learning. Interestingly, the stronger statistical results of the baseline model remain so after the inclusion of the two controls: Learning from average experience, own and variability of results, world have the same expected sign and are significant at 95% and 99% levels of confidence, respectively. EMULATION is also statistically significant, which means that the individual probabilities of liberalizing trade were positively related to the previous decisions of other countries. Finally, I find no evidence that being under an IMF agreement induced countries to liberalize trade, although the coefficient is correctly signed.

Models (3) and (4) include more domestic and international controls. Also, the learning variables were modeled to take into account the 1982 debt crisis. Thus, these models test the role of learning from the economic shock, controlling for a battery of other factors, as opposed to learning from the experience of others under "normal" times. In this model, the variables measuring EMULATION and VARIABILITY

---

[28] Average experience in the world and variance of results in the region are moderately correlated (0.55). When these variables are in and out the model, there are no changes in the signs of the coefficients but the weaker coefficients stop being significant depending on alternative specifications.

3.3. Learning and Development Strategies: The Results   97

Table 3.4. *Probability of trade liberalization, trade liberalization database (1970–1999)*

Dependent variable: Trade liberalization	Baseline model (1)	Controls model (2)	1982 Debt crisis and other controls (3)	1982 Debt crisis and other controls (4)
CONSTANT	−2.02***	−3.20***	−1.08	−1.61
	(−4.91)	(−3.77)	(−1.06)	(−1.55)
OWN EXPERIENCE				
AVERAGE RESULTS	**0.04****	**0.06****	**0.05****	**0.05****
	(2.03)	(2.23)	(2.33)	(2.44)
VARIABILITY OF RESULTS	**0.05***	0.02	0.07	0.04
	(1.64)	(0.66)	(1.07)	(0.58)
REGIONAL EXPERIENCE				
AVERAGE RESULTS	**−0.07***	−0.04	−0.02	−0.001
	(−1.81)	(−0.74)	(−0.06)	(−0.04)
VARIABILITY OF RESULTS	0.007	0.002	−0.01	0.002
	(0.16)	(0.05)	(−0.34)	(0.04)
WORLD EXPERIENCE				
AVERAGE RESULTS	−0.02	0.21	−0.01	0.10
	(−0.17)	(1.06)	(−0.13)	(0.67)
VARIABILITY OF RESULTS	**−0.32***	**−0.26***	**−0.21***	
	(−5.14)	(−3.64)	(−2.50)	
EMULATION		**0.19***		**0.27****
		(1.92)		(3.45)
COERCION		0.08	0.13	0.12
		(0.65)	(0.89)	(0.85)
GATT/WTO			−0.04	−0.18
			(−0.29)	(−1.09)
REGIME			**−0.52***	**−0.58***
			(−3.00)	(−3.40)
SIZE			−0.04	−0.05
			(−0.76)	(−1.09)
TIME IN OFFICE			0.002	0.001
			(0.28)	(0.12)
FDI			−0.04	−0.04
			(−1.27)	(−1.38)
Log Likelihood	−225.70	−220.04	−197.37	−194.39
LR Chi-Squared	2448.11	2442.40	1935.58	1941.39
p-value for F	0.000	0.000	0.000	0.000
Observations	2331	2323	1815	1815

$^*p < .10; ^{**}p < .05; ^{***}p < .01$; z-scores in parentheses; all variables lagged one year.
The Pseudo R^2 for specifications (3) and (4) is 0.83 with 97% correctly predicted 0s and 1s.

98   *Learning and Development Strategies*

OF RESULTS, WORLD were correlated (0.66 correlation coefficient), causing the latter to lose statistical significance in the presence of the former. Thus, I estimated two models that included one and the other variable separately.[29] The controls I include are roughly similar in substance to the ones included in Table 3.3. REGIME captures whether a country in a particular year is a democracy or a dictatorship according to Gandhi's (2004) classification. GATT/WTO is a dummy variable for countries and years of GATT/WTO membership (Milner and Kubota 2005). SIZE measures the size of the country as represented by the natural log of its population (World Development Indicators). TIME IN OFFICE counts the number of years the chief executive has been in office (Beck, Keefer, and Clark 2000). The expectation is that veteran executives are more reluctant to adopt drastic policy changes than are newcomers to power. Finally, FDI refers to foreign direct investment flows as a percentage of GDP (World Development Indicators). The anticipated sign is positive, with greater competition for FDI flows promoting trade liberalization. Descriptive statistics of all the variables are shown in the Appendix.

As can be seen, modeling the 1982 debt crisis does not add much to the significance of the learning variables. The learning result – significant in the previous specifications (from own experience and from the volatility of outcomes in the world) – is robust to the inclusion of all the controls. In this time span, learning from the 1982 shock diluted in confrontation with the accumulated evidence about trade liberalization. Two other results are robust and interesting. First, the global liberalization trend did affect the probability that countries jumped on the trade liberalization bandwagon: The coefficient on EMULATION is positive and statistically significant. Secondly, the regime variable, which, in the (1964–1990) database, did not have explanatory power, is now statistically significant: Democracies were more likely to liberalize trade than were dictatorships. Moreover, when the impact of these variables on the probability of liberalizing is simulated, REGIME appears as the strongest factor behind the liberalization of trade.

Figure 3.4 shows the predicted probability of trade liberalization and the 95% confidence intervals as a function of posterior beliefs about own

[29] EMULATION was significant at all times, but the VARIABILITY of results in the world was significant only in the absence of the emulation variable. Some of the other

3.3. Learning and Development Strategies: The Results

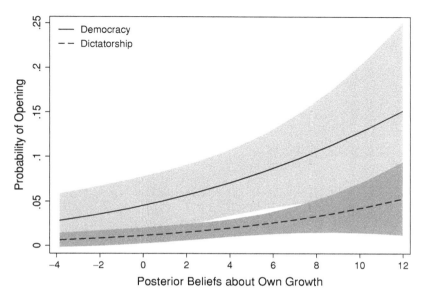

Figure 3.4. Predicted Probability of Liberalizing Trade and 95% Confidence Intervals, as a function of the difference in Posterior Beliefs about Own Growth Results, by Regime Type. All other variables were set at their mean values.

growth, by regime type (based on model (4), Table 3.4). Recall that values to the right of zero entail that governments believe that growth under trade openness will be greater than growth under trade protectionism. Consistently, the figure reveals that countries in which the difference in posterior beliefs based on own experience is the greatest (higher values of the variable) are more likely to liberalize. Democracies are always more likely to ease restrictions to trade. However, the 95% confidence intervals overlap for most of the distribution of the variable POSTERIOR BELIEFS ABOUT OWN GROWTH. For very low values of this variable (that is, when governments believe that growth under protectionism will exceed growth under openness) and for very high values (that is, when governments believe that growth under openness will clearly surpass growth under protectionism) the two regime types are indistinguishable (the 95% confidence intervals overlap). Note, however, that democracies are significantly more likely to liberalize for positive and middle-range values of this variable. This suggests that democracies switch to openness

coefficients of the learning variables changed signs, but they were never statistically significant.

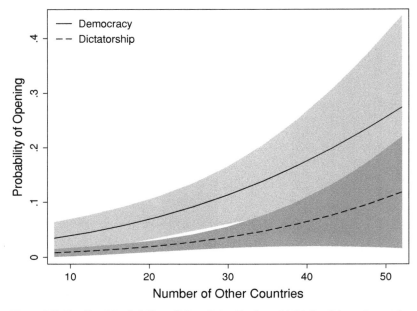

Figure 3.5. Predicted Probability of Liberalizing Trade and 95% Confidence Intervals, as a function of the Number of Other Open Countries, by Regime Type. All other variables were set at their mean values.

as long as there is positive evidence in favor of trade liberalization, even if that evidence is not overwhelming.

Figure 3.5 shows the predicted probability of opening and the 95% confidence interval (based on model (4), Table 3.4) for different values of the variable NUMBER OF OTHER COUNTRIES opening. The greater the number of other countries with a liberal trade regime, the greater the predicted probability of a switch, and this for both democracies and dictatorships. Note, however, that the probability of democracies opening is significantly different from the probability of dictatorships opening when the number of other countries ranges between 20 and 30. Again, when the number of other liberalized countries is very low or very high, both regime types are indistinguishable in their predicted probability of liberalizing. However, democracies need neither an overwhelming number of other countries liberalizing nor overwhelming evidence that trade liberalization yields better growth results than trade protectionism in order to switch. These results suggest that democracies in developing

3.3. Learning and Development Strategies: The Results   101

countries are, in general, more attentive and more ready to adopt trade liberalization than are dictatorships. As mentioned earlier, this may be related to the fact that, to the extent that trade liberalization improves the lot of the poor, who are the median voters in developing countries, democratic governments feel more compelled than dictatorships to learn about the relative performance of trade policies in their own countries and in the world.

As for the controls, again, I find practically no significant effects. GATT/WTO has the opposite sign, with member countries less likely to liberalize. This may be because countries chose to liberalize unilaterally *before* entering the GATT/WTO. Pedro Aspe, Finance Minister under Mexican President Carlos Salinas de Gortari (1988–94), stated that "the first part of the process of [trade] liberalization that includes the removal of nontariff barriers and the reduction of the level and the dispersion of tariffs generally has to be unilateral . . ." (1993: 141). The contradictory sign may also have to do with the fact that once in the system, countries take advantage of the myriad of exceptions to reductions in trade barriers (Milner and Kubota 2005). In any case, the coefficient is not statistically significant. SIZE is correctly signed: Bigger countries were less likely to liberalize, but the coefficient is not statistically significant. Contrary to theoretical expectations, older executives were not less likely to liberalize trade, but the duration of tenure of the executive is not significant after all. Finally, incoming flows of FDI did not have any impact on the decision concerning trade liberalization. Overall, the decision to liberalize the trade regime appears as an internationally driven decision. True, regime type is a domestic political feature and the mechanism laid out to explain its impact is also domestic; but to the extent that democracy has diffused (Brinks and Coppedge 2006; Gledistch and Ward 2006), it is not fully accurate to portray the impact of democratization as purely a domestic factor.

Some simulations comparing the results of the two databases may clarify persistent and varying effects over time. The figures that appear in Table 3.5 are based on model 3, Table 3.3, and on models 3 and 4, Table 3.4. In the *Development Strategies Database* (1964–1990), variation of one standard deviation around the mean of the variable LEARNING FROM THE VARIABILITY OF RESULTS, WORLD *reduces* the

102   *Learning and Development Strategies*

Table 3.5. *Change in predicted probability of opening (percentage points)*

Predictors	Development strategies database (1964–1990)	Trade liberalization database (1970–1999)
AVERAGE EXPERIENCE, OWN	0.01	0.02
	[−0.0004 0.040]	[0.006 0.045]
VARIABILITY OF RESULTS, WORLD	−0.07	−0.03
	[−0.162 −0.018]	[−0.052 −0.005]
EMULATION	0.04	0.03
	[0.018 0.068]	[0.013 0.053]
COERCION	0.03	
	[0.004 0.059]	
REGIME		−0.05
		[−0.091 −0.015]

Note: Simulations are based on models 3 and 4 of Tables 3.3 and 3.4. Changes in predicted probabilities of moving one standard deviation around the mean of the relevant predictors. For the regime and the coercion variables, the relevant change is from 0 to 1. 95% Confidence Intervals in brackets. All other variables were set at the mean values.

probability of adopting EO by around seven percentage points. This same variation in the variable EMULATION increases the probability of adopting EO by about four percentage points and, finally, moving from not having to having an agreement with the IMF increases the probability of adopting EO by roughly three percentage points. Thus, concerning the adoption of EO, learning from the volatile results of ISI in the world appears more influential in the switch to EO than EMULATION or COERCION.

In relation to *trade liberalization,* when all the variables are set at their mean value, the probability that a dictatorship liberalizes its trade regime is around four (Model 3) and five (Model 4) percentage points lower than is the case for a democracy. A one standard deviation move around the mean in the number of other countries with a liberal trade regime increases the probability of opening by roughly three percentage points (Model 4). A one standard deviation change around the mean of the variable LEARNING FROM AVERAGE RESULTS, OWN increases the probability of opening by two percentage points (Models 3 and 4). Finally, the impact of a one standard deviation in the VARIABILITY OF

RESULTS, WORLD is now smaller: A three percentage point reduction in the probability of opening.

All in all, the greatest effect on the probability of adopting EO had to do with the lessons learned from the unreliability of ISI as a strategy to promote growth. As Rodrik (1994: 82) put it, "liberalization was selected only after the alternative had been tried repeatedly and discredited." This finding accords with another frequent contention – namely, that learning from the failure of ISI, not learning from the success of EO, was the most important motivation for the adoption of liberalization (Fishlow 1990).[30] As time passed and experience with open trade regimes accumulated, own experience became slightly more relevant. Also, according to the results, the first wave of liberalization was spurred by IFIs, the power of which increased extraordinarily as a consequence of the debt crisis (Rodrik 1994). With more and more countries in dire straits and with a growing clientele, IFIs could impose tighter conditions (Vreeland 2003). Trade liberalization was one of them. However, as countries recovered from the crisis and accumulated experience with the practice and outcomes of trade liberalization, IFIs seem to have lost the leverage to impose liberalization unilaterally. The growing network of other liberalizing countries always had a positive impact on the probability that a particular country would jump on the trade liberalization bandwagon. Finally, the diffusion of democracy became an important factor in the diffusion of trade liberalization. Indeed, over time, democratization became the most relevant factor in explaining trade openness.

3.4. Discussion

The literature on economic policy reform in general and on trade liberalization in particular is full of lessons. As is common in discussions of the role of learning from the experience of others, statements are based on reasoned hunches. According to Robinson (1998: 26), "the early post-war

---

[30] I tested this hypothesis (that EO was adopted by default) by using experience under ISI only as an independent variable. The results match Fishlow's hypothesis to some extent. However, as multicollinearity is pervasive in the model, I do not report the results here. In any case, this contention makes clear the importance of modeling policy choice as a choice among alternative policies.

success of Japan seems to have been very influential in determining policy orientation in South Korea and Taiwan, just as these countries' experiences seem to have had subsequent ripple effects in Indonesia, Malaysia and Thailand." Conversely, given the great differences in historical and cultural endowments among regions, these experiences "should have had little impact in Africa and Latin America." Along the same lines, Wade (1992: 312) states that "proximity, cultural affinity, and historical familiarity all helped create an important 'neighborhood' growth effect, not just in terms of trade but also in terms of the plausibility of Japan as a model for emulation."[31]

However, other scholars tell the story of Russian visitors to Santiago seeking the advice of General Pinochet, as the architect of the Chilean miracle (Valenzuela 1997). And Krauze (2004) tells the story of African expeditions to Mexico to learn from the economic miracle under President Miguel Alemán (1946–52). Thus, it may be that geographical distance and other apparent differences did not preclude paying attention to faraway experiences.

Concerning the mechanism of learning, there are a couple of interesting results. First, modeling the 1982 crisis in the formation of posterior beliefs has little impact in making learning more significant. The effect is stronger in the *Development Strategies Database*, in which some of the learning variables are significant only *after* the crisis is modeled. The most important lesson of the debt crisis was the volatility of ISI as a growth strategy. However, in the extended database, modeling the 1982 shock did not add much to the impact of learning.[32]

---

[31] The author adds, "rulers and officials were well aware of the Japanese pre-war and post-war experience. This provided them with a tangible model of what a disciplined state could achieve both militarily and economically, which contributed to the development of a mission oriented organizational culture in key government agencies." (Wade 1992: 314–15).

[32] This result is consistent with the mixed and negative findings other scholars have reported in previous studies: Drazen and Easterly (2001) report that hyperinflation and extreme values of the black market premium are, indeed, followed by reforms, but other common indicators of crises are not. Lora (2000) finds that a falling per capita income is the best predictor of his index of reform (which includes privatization and trade, and financial, tax, and labor reforms). Yet, Milner and Kubota (2005) find no significant impact of a drop in GDP per capita, inflation, or the balance of payments on the probability of trade liberalization.

3.4. Discussion

Second, it is not possible to reject the possibility that countries adopted trade liberalization after learning from own experience that trade liberalization is conducive to greater growth than is achieved under trade protection. However, the size of this effect was very small. Also, a persistent risk-averse attitude toward the high variability of results under inward orientation and trade closure appeared in the estimations. Interestingly, whereas these effects were evident in the two databases, the positive impact of own experience was greater, and the negative impact of the volatility of results was lower, in the database that covers the period up to 1999. Thus, as experience with trade policy accumulated, learning from own performance became more relevant than learning from the relative volatility of performance in the world.

One interesting result is that learning from experience in the REGION was irrelevant to explaining the decision to liberalize the trade regime. This outcome may have to do solely with numbers: Own experience is the least noisy whereas world experience is the most abundant. Thus, any of this information beats the information coming from the region in that the regional information entails diverse experiences based on fewer observations. Another possible substantive explanation has to do with the "region" category. Regional classifications too often include very different countries and very contrasting, sometimes unique, experiences. Indeed, the impressive reduction in protection observed in some regions was the responsibility of only a few countries. This was the case with India and Bangladesh in South Asia (Guisinger 2005). In Latin American accounts of trade liberalization, Chile, not the average regional experience, appeared as the role model. For Africa, probably Botswana, Ghana, and Mauritius could have played that same role (Van de Walle 2001). If we think about the world, East Asia, rather than the combined experience of world regions, was the instigator for other countries.[33]

---

[33] Using Latin America as an illustration, I showed that the learning variables explain the adoption of EO better when the Chilean performance (rather than the average performance in the region) and the East Asian experience (rather than the average performance in the world) are used as inputs in the updating process (Meseguer 2006). Surprisingly, this result is in line with the predictions of the bounded learning approach and its emphasis on the availability of results (either due to geographic closeness or brought about by informed discussion). From a rational point of view, the cost of acquiring information can justify the results.

Relatedly, it is also interesting to confirm the marginal role that the coercive power of the IMF and the GATT/WTO played in trade liberalization. However, this does not mean that IFIs and international organizations played no function. The country stories suggest that their most important role may have been precisely to make policy experiences available to others. The Nixon-goes-to-China discovery and promotion of export orientation by ECLAC (previously a firm defender of inward-oriented development) is a telling example (Edwards 1995).

The diffusion of democracy played a nonnegligible role in the diffusion of trade liberalization. Although this result is in line with recent research, it is surprising in that, according to established views in the political economy of policy reform, democracies are ill-equipped to introduce reforms in which the losers are concentrated and the gainers are diffused. Trade policy is one example. However, democracies are systems in which politicians' perpetuation in power depends on the support of the median voter. The median voter in developing countries, who is a poor and unskilled citizen, benefits from trade openness, according to both income-earning theories (at least in the long run) and consumption-based explanations. In particular, greater access to a wide and cheap variety of goods seems to be an important determinant of the high popularity of trade liberalization in developing countries (Stokes 2001b; Baker 2003). In the (1970–1999) database, being a democracy was the strongest predictor of trade liberalization in developing countries. Also, it is apparent that countries' decision to liberalize their trade was influenced by what others did. Finally, the simulations showed that, unlike dictatorships, democracies did not need overwhelming evidence in favor of trade liberalization or an overwhelming number of other countries opening to decide to switch to trade openness.

To conclude, when it comes to explaining the wave of trade liberalization rather than its pace, depth, or content, the learning hypothesis cannot be rejected as an explanation. Its impact is moderate, though. It is this mechanism, together with demonstration effects and the pressures attached to democratization and its related popular demands, that best explain trade liberalization in the 1980s and 1990s.

APPENDIX

Table A3.6. *Prior beliefs, development strategies*

	Trade liberalization		Trade protection	
Year	Mean	Variance	Mean	Variance
1964	1.97	21	2.24	15
1965	3.83	17	2.16	24
1968	3.42	15	1.04	28
1971	8.2	26	2.21	57

Note: Based on the average rate of growth and the variability of results in the world the year before entering the database.

DEVELOPMENT STRATEGIES DATABASE, 1964–1990

World Bank Development Report (1987) Criteria for Regime Classification

- *Strongly Outward Oriented*: Trade controls are either nonexistent or very weak in the sense that any disincentives to export resulting from import barriers are more or less counterbalanced by export incentives. There is little or no use of direct control and licensing arrangements, and the exchange rate is maintained so that the effective exchange rates for importables and exportables are roughly equal.
- *Moderately Outward Oriented*: The overall incentive structure is biased toward production for domestic rather than export markets. However, the Average Effective Rate of Protection (ERP) for the home market is *relatively* low and the range of ERP is *relatively* narrow. The use of direct controls and licensing arrangements is limited and, although *some* direct incentives to exports are provided, these do not offset protection against imports. The Effective Exchange Rate (EER) is higher for imports than for exports, but only slightly.
- *Moderately Inward Oriented*: The overall incentive structure distinctly favors production for the domestic market. The ERP for home markets is *relatively* high and the range of ERP *relatively*

108   *Learning and Development Strategies*

wide. The use of direct import controls and licensing is extensive, and, although some direct incentives to export may be provided, there is a distinctive bias against exports, and the exchange rate is clearly overvalued.

- *Strongly Inward Oriented*: The overall incentive structure strongly favors production for the domestic market. The average rate of effective protection for home markets is high and the range of effective protection rates relatively wide. Direct controls and licensing disincentives in the traditional export sector are pervasive, positive incentives to nontraditional exportables are few or nonexistent, and the exchange rate is significantly overvalued.

TRADE LIBERALIZATION DATABASE, 1970–1999

Table A3.7. *Descriptive statistics, development strategies*

	Mean	s.d.	Minimum	Maximum
Beliefs Average Growth, Own	.86	3.45	−13.33	16.12
Beliefs Variability Growth, Own	−.61	2.33	−12.52	4.53
Beliefs Average Growth, Region	1.44	1.83	−6.79	12.73
Beliefs Variability Growth, Region	−1.90	2.10	−6.85	2.58
Beliefs Average Growth, World	2.93	1.11	−1.75	6.05
Beliefs Variability Growth, World	−1.72	1.27	−4.56	1.38
Regime	.69	.45	.0	1
Number of Other Countries	1.36	.66	.8	3
IMF Agreements	.43	.49	.0	1
Elections	.21	.41	.0	1
Country Size	16.69	1.43	12.72	20.25
GATT Membership	.67	.46	.0	1

Table A3.8. *Prior beliefs, trade liberalization*

	Trade liberalization		Trade protection	
Year	Mean	Variance	Mean	Variance
1970	3.83	115	3.62	61
1971	6.99	200	3.58	78
1974	7.18	86	3.94	67
1975	5.28	24	1.26	61

Note: Based on the average rate of growth and the variability of results in the world the year before entering the database.

Appendix

109

Table A3.9. *Average rates of growth and variability of results, open and closed trade regimes after 1985*

Year	Open trade regime			Closed trade regime		
	Average	s.d.	N	Average	s.d.	N
1985	1.42	5.17	15	0.65	7.12	72
1986	2.76	4.79	19	0.46	6.06	68
1987	3.17	4.56	20	−1.09	5.03	66
1988	3.82	4.91	25	−0.55	5.92	60
1989	1.90	7.69	31	0.007	6.95	54
1990	1.99	4.52	32	−1.19	4.06	50
1991	1.01	4.66	42	0.27	4.77	40
1992	2.15	4.44	44	−3.54	6.51	38
1993	1.95	3.19	47	−2.32	7.99	34
1994	2.57	3.83	48	−0.38	9.02	34
1995	2.07	3.63	50	2.77	7.22	32
1996	2.85	3.84	52	2.60	4.51	27
1997	2.49	2.45	52	0.26	5.75	26
1998	−0.06	5.75	49	1.08	3.36	23
1999	2.78	3.73	50	2.89	3.29	20

Table A3.10. *Descriptive statistics, trade liberalization*

	Mean	s.d.	Minimum	Maximum
Beliefs Average Growth, Own	3.06	3.74	−12.35	22.74
Beliefs Variability Growth, Own	2.39	1.32	−5.20	4.58
Beliefs Average Growth, Region	2.69	1.75	−10.01	13.46
Beliefs Variability Growth, Region	.96	1.70	−5.01	7.51
Beliefs Average Growth, World	3.17	.65	−3.44	6.61
Beliefs Variability Growth, World	−.01	1.19	−2.77	4.41
Number of Other Countries	2.24	1.16	.8	5.2
IMF Agreements	.49	.50	.0	1
GATT/WTO Membership	.71	.44	.0	1
Regime	.68	.46	.0	1
Time in Office	8.28	8.01	1	45
Size	16.00	1.57	12.41	20.94
Foreign Direct Investment	1.26	2.87	−27.23	56.10

Learning and Development Strategies

Table A3.11. *List of countries, development strategies and trade liberalization*

Africa	South Asia	South East Asia	North Africa Middle East	Latin America	Non-Iberian Caribbean
Angola	**Bangladesh**	China	Algeria	**Costa Rica**	Barbados
Benin	**India**	Indonesia	Egypt	**Dom. Republic**	Haiti
Bostwana	**Nepal**	**Korea**	**Morocco**	El Salvador	**Jamaica**
Burkina Faso	**Pakistan**	**Malaysia**	**Tunisia**	Guatemala	**Trinidad and Tobago**
Burundi	**Sri Lanka**	Myanmar	Iran	Honduras	Guyana
Cameroon	Taiwan*	**Philippines**	Iraq	Mexico	
Cape Verde		**Singapore**	Israel	**Nicaragua**	
Central African Republic		**Thailand**	Jordan	Panama	
Chad			Syria	**Argentina**	
Congo			Yemen	**Bolivia**	
Ethiopia			Turkey	**Brazil**	
Gabon				**Chile**	
Gambia				**Colombia**	
Ghana				**Ecuador**	
Guinea				**Paraguay**	
Guinea Bissau				**Peru**	
Côte d'Ivoire				**Uruguay**	
Kenya				**Venezuela**	
Lesotho					
Liberia					
Madagascar					
Malawi					
Mali					
Mauritania					
Mauritius					
Mozambique					
Níger					
Nigeria					
Rwanda					
Senegal					
Sierra Leone					
Somalia					
South Africa					
Sudan*					
Swaziland					
Tanzania					
Togo					
Uganda					
Zaire					
Zambia					
Zimbabwe					

Note: Countries in bold appeared in both databases.
Sudan and Taiwan are included in the Development Strategies Database only.

FOUR

Learning and Privatization

[A]lthough the Argentine and Peruvian presidents were far from being true
believers [in privatization], they turned out to be quick learners.
Luigi Manzetti (1999: 299)

In the 1980s and especially in the 1990s, privatization swept the world.
This chapter seeks to explain why. In particular, it asks whether governments in advanced and in Latin American countries engaged in privatization as a result of learning.

From the late 1970s, and especially after 1983, privatization was pio-
neered by Prime Minister Margaret Thatcher in Britain. During the 1980s,
this policy innovation was embraced hesitantly elsewhere. However, during the 1990s, privatization became an established policy in developed
and developing countries. It was also a central issue in post-Communist
societies (Stark and Brustz 1998).

Although this secular trend toward privatization exhibited important
regional variations,[1] there is no doubt that privatization has been a major
phenomenon. Moreover, it has cut across the ideological divide: Socialist
governments in Europe as well as populists in Latin America climbed
aboard the privatization bandwagon.

Explanations of this wave of divestments have been widely canvassed
but rarely tested. They range from pure efficiency considerations to more

[1] According to World Bank Data, regions rank by number of transactions in the following
order: Eastern and Central Europe (361), Latin America and the Caribbean (104), East
Asia (33), Southeast Asia (30), and the Middle East and North Africa (19). Note also
that, despite this wave, at least forty-seven developing countries did not undertake
even a single privatization in the period 1987–97 (Brune and Garrett 2000: 5). See also
Ramamurti (1999: 138).

111

complex political rationales, with both domestic and international political factors playing some role. However, Kogut and McPherson (2008) correctly claim that some countries were heavily indebted and were governed by right-wing parties – two typical domestic explanations of privatization – but were not motivated to streamline their public sectors. Accordingly, I argue that international forces better explain why so many countries adopted privatization. In fact, this is the finding of one exception to the dearth of empirical research on the causes of privatization. In their study of the determinants of privatization in developing countries, Brune and Garrett (2000) found that international diffusion explained privatization better than domestic political factors, domestic economic conditions, or a country's position in the international economy. Even when pressure to privatize from international financial institutions was controlled for, the contagion effects persisted.

As mentioned, policy diffusion is the process whereby policy choices in one country affect policy choices in other countries. Policy diffusion has certain distinctive features. First, the diffusion of *policy innovations* – in our case, of privatization – tends to cluster geographically and has quite a strong regional component. Second, the diffusion of innovations frequently exhibits an S-shaped curve: An initial innovation is followed by a rapid increase in the number of countries adopting the innovation. Finally, diffusion is essentially the spread of commonality amid diversity: Countries with very different functional needs and at very different levels of economic, social, and political development adopt similar policies (Weyland 2007).

This chapter's topic has to do with the subtle mechanisms whereby the diffusion of privatization occurred. It may be the case that the diffusion of privatization was a matter merely of imitating the policies of others and herding around fads and fashions in an attempt to avoid any stigma of backwardness. Privatization may have been imposed. Alternatively, the diffusion of privatization might have resulted from a rational revision of beliefs about the effects of privatization in the light of the experience of countries that adopted this policy. This is what I mean by learning. This chapter focuses on testing this mechanism in a sample of thirty-seven OECD and Latin American countries for the period 1980–97.

I assume that governments are rational learners. Starting with some prior beliefs about effectiveness, governments observed the outcomes in countries that privatized and in those that did not privatize. With this information, they revised their beliefs and switched to privatization as long as the expected outcomes of privatizing were expected to be superior to the outcomes of not doing so. I show that the impact of learning from experience with privatization in a country's region and in other regions was positively related to the probability of a decision being taken to adopt privatization. In particular, for Latin America, the experience with privatization in the region was a very strong determinant of other countries' decisions to privatize. This result is robust to the inclusion of domestic political and economic variables and to the inclusion of alternative mechanisms of policy convergence. Among the latter, only emulation – and not coercion – was positively related to the probability of privatizing. However, learning loses much of its explanatory power in relation to governments' decisions to continue divesting. Domestic political and economic controls were significant only in the regional samples, not in the joint one. The results show that left-wing governments were more prone to privatize in the OECD countries, whereas less democratic regimes were more likely to do so in Latin America. In both regions, emulation was a powerful and robust motivation for streamlining the public sector. Finally, only in Latin America were the fall of Communist regimes and, allegedly, the lessons associated with the collapse additional causes of privatization.

In the next section, I make a case for an explanation of privatization policies that takes into account international factors by showing that neither efficiency arguments nor domestic political factors can account for the wave-like dynamics that privatization exhibited. I then introduce the data and present the results of the learning model and its extensions. Finally, I discuss the results in the concluding section.

4.1. Explaining Privatization

I aim specifically to show that existing theories of privatization, which emphasize domestic economic and political conditions, are better at explaining divergent varieties of privatization rather than convergent policy choices. Since the main concern of this chapter is to address the question why governments engaged en masse in privatization rather than explaining the intensity and the scope of the privatization process, the current approach is insufficient.

The contingencies of the privatization process in a large number of countries have been extensively addressed (Ghosh 2000; Birsch and Haar 2000). Thus, in the next paragraphs, I focus on a few contrasting aspects of a selected group of cases later included in the empirical analysis.

Economic rationales alone cannot account for the decision to streamline the public sector. The general case for privatization, derived from principal-agent theory, overlooks the fact that public enterprises in countries such as France, Austria, Taiwan, or South Korea have performed remarkably well (Rowthorn and Chang 1994; Brune, Garrett, and Kogut 2004). Also, arguments for privatization based on efficiency considerations frequently ignore the fact that ownership alone does not guarantee a more efficient allocation of resources (Rowthorn and Chang 1994; Pitelis and Clarke 1995; Parker 1998a, 1998b; Ramamurti 1999; Hodge 2000; Stiglitz 2000). Ultimately, it is the competitive environment in which firms operate that determines the effect of this or that ownership structure. In fact, it may well be the case that privatization merely transforms a state monopoly into a private one unless the many institutions that are necessary to support the market are developed. Finally, arguments that privatization combats rent-seeking behavior usually ignore the fact that privatization has been fertile ground for the growth of corrupt practices. Assets were too frequently sold to cronies at low prices. Jan Olszewski, a former Polish prime minister, stated before the Sejm that "we've learned that the invisible hand of the market is the hand of the swindler, garnering funds from the public trust." In similar vein, a senior economic adviser to Chernomyrdin (Russian Prime Minister from 1992 to 1998) predicted that, in Russia, corruption would create a "statist private sector" and a "privatized government" (quoted in Celarier 1996: 533, 537). Corruption is not confined to former socialist economies. In India, the privatization of telecommunications was thwarted by corruption. In Mexico, the privatization of the banking system allowed drug traffickers to buy bank stocks and seek election to bank boards (Kaufmann and Siegelbaum 1996).

4.1. Explaining Privatization

Apart from efficiency, there is a more urgent, pragmatic rationale for privatization: It provides fast cash for governments that need to reduce big budget deficits, cut taxes, or finance their spending. Regardless of whether the need derived from pressure to maintain creditworthiness amid mounting debt, honor policy conditionality, or meet Maastricht criteria, privatization of public enterprises – quite often in sound financial condition – offered a relatively easy way to conform to the budget deficit constraint. Yet, the link between bad economic conditions and an increase in the willingness to privatize should not be taken for granted (World Bank 2005): Brune and Garrett (2000) found that privatization was, surprisingly, associated with good, not bad, economic conditions. Low inflation rates, low levels of short-term debt, and high per capita incomes spurred privatization. In their study, low investment levels constituted the only adverse condition that had the same effect.

As for *political rationales*, an account of the privatization process in selected Latin American and OECD countries along the lines proposed by Manzetti (1999) shows that the variation in motives within the pool of privatizers is scarcely illuminating when it comes to explaining the S-shaped curve that privatization exhibited. According to Manzetti (1999), governments' decisions to privatize result from some combination of willingness and opportunity. *Willingness* to privatize is related to both ideological and pragmatic considerations. Ideologically, the main thrust is a conscious attempt to redefine the boundaries of state action. Pragmatically, there are several factors, but the short-term objective of reducing the fiscal deficit is the most relevant.[2] In Manzetti's model, *opportunity* is related to public perceptions of privatization and nationalization. Hence, opportunity refers to the room for maneuver available to incumbents concerned with re-election.

In both Latin American and OECD countries, the balance among ideology, pragmatism, and opportunity exhibits a degree of variation that is difficult to reconcile with an otherwise uniform trend to streamline the public sector.

---

[2] Other motivations are to improve overall economic efficiency, modernize the domestic economy, strengthen capital markets, improve the business climate, rationalize state operations, and reward supporters.

The privatization stories of Margaret Thatcher in Britain (1979–90), Jacques Chirac in France (1986–88), Augusto Pinochet in Chile (1973–90), and Carlos Salinas de Gortari in Mexico (1988–94) are tales of *ideology cum opportunity*. In the well-documented British case (Vickers and Wright 1989), privatization was endorsed to create a situation in which nationalization was simply inconceivable. Privatization was envisaged as an instrument of coalition building, of transforming the common citizen into a shareholder and hence into a loyal right-wing voter. Also, in France, Gaullists launched a swift privatization programme, maintaining throughout that "privatization [was] the veritable nationalization of the economy" (Jacques Chirac, quoted in Suleiman 1990: 127). However, ideology alone cannot explain why right-wing governments in both countries enthusiastically engaged in privatization, let alone why, later, labor and socialist parties in both countries decided not to reverse that policy. Opportunity – that is, popular support for privatization – also mattered. In Britain, privatization was adopted on an appreciable scale only after the 1983 election showed that it brought notable political gains. In France, privatization was already popular a few months after the March 1986 legislative elections: According to a Gallup poll of September 1986, sixty-one percent of the public thought that privatization was a good idea and only twenty-four percent opposed it (Suleiman 1990: 123). Hence, governments were ideological, but with a clear eye on public opinion.

In Latin America, Chile (under Augusto Pinochet) and Mexico (under Carlos Salinas de Gortari) are taken to be cases in which *ideology* played a prominent role; public opinion was not so much of a constraint in view of these countries' political systems. The Chilean sequence can be described as one of re-privatization, privatization, and hyperprivatization (Sigmund 1990). In the phase of re-privatization, 259 enterprises requisitioned under Salvador Allende were returned to their owners. In the 1970s, more that 200 state-owned enterprises (SOEs) and banks were sold to private investors; but the acute economic crisis and the small size of the Chilean capital market led to a concentration of property in a few conglomerates (*los grupos*) with access to foreign capital. In 1982, a wave of bankruptcies forced the government to take over the largest private financial institutions in what some analysts described as "the Chicago road to socialism." But this proved to be a temporary reversal. Starting

4.1. Explaining Privatization

in 1985, the process of privatization gained momentum, with the clear aim of promoting "popular capitalism" (Maloney 1994).

The Mexican privatization process has also been depicted as a deliberate attempt at rolling back the state. Miguel de la Madrid's disincorporation process (1982–88) became full-fledged privatization under Carlos Salinas de Gortari. Efficiency was the official justification. Yet, relatively efficient and profitable SOEs such as Telmex or Mexicobre underwent a similar fate. Some authors interpreted the privatization drive as an attempt to restore the government–private sector partnership that had been ended by the statist policies of Luis Echeverría (1970–76) and José López Portillo (1976–82) (Schneider 1990; Ramírez 1994). Others explained the intensity of the process as an attempt to make privatization irreversible. According to James Cypher (quoted in Ramírez 1994: 41), the dismantling of the para-state sector represented "a piecemeal method of undercutting any future turn towards populism in Mexico."

However, in other European and Latin American countries, privatization was mainly a tale of *pragmatism cum opportunity*. For example, in West Germany, privatization was introduced by the coalition of the Christian Democratic Union, the Christian Social Union and the liberal Free Democratic Party (FDP). However, the program was never very ambitious, either on paper or in practice. The few transactions that were accomplished were meant to appease the demands of the FDP and its wealthy clientele. In fact, "the broad mass of the electorate did not see privatization and deregulation as self-evident political objectives." Esser (1998) concludes that privatization in Germany was purely symbolic ("we are privatizers too") and driven by fiscal considerations only in part.

In southern Europe, privatization was mostly pragmatic. The secondary role of ideology is evident in the Spanish privatizations under the Socialist Party. Felipe González (1982–96) liked to say that "the idea of nationalization was not an idea of the left" (quoted in Bermeo 1990: 145). Actually, pragmatic privatization was aided by the fact that the bulk of the SOEs had been a product of Francoist rule. Opportunity also mattered. Due to lack of support among the public, the technocratic faction of the party, and certainly its leadership, for whom the ill-fated French experiment turned out to provide a powerful lesson (Maravall 1997), nationalization played a symbolic role in the 1982 Socialist platform.

118 *Learning and Privatization*

Something similar happened in Portugal. Under the leadership of the center-right Social Democratic Party *(Partido Social Demócrata, PSD)*, Portugal amended its constitution to allow for privatization. The party platform openly canvassed denationalization. Before the July 1987 election, sixty-seven percent of the public agreed with the policy; after the elections, the figure rose to eighty percent. The election of a socialist government in the 1990s only accelerated the process (Bermeo 1990: 153; Parker 1998b).

Pragmatism cum opportunity, rather than ideology, seems to have been behind many Latin American privatization processes. In Peru, for instance, Alberto Fujimori (1990–2000) openly stated in relation to his privatization program that "there is no heterodoxy, nor orthodoxy; no liberalism, nor communism, or populism, only pragmatism" (Manzetti 1999: 246). This seems to have been the standard view of other political leaders such as Carlos Menem in Argentina (1989–99) and Fernando Collor (1990–92) or Fernando Henrique Cardoso (1995–2002) in Brazil, who engaged in privatization against a background of rampant inflation and failed neo-Keynesian experiments. Whether this change in perception took place among the public is more problematic. Privatization was popular in Argentina and to a lesser extent in Peru, but there was no public demand for privatization in Brazil.

In Argentina, privatization was seen as the centerpiece of the economic reform program and, after its inception, it enjoyed widespread popular support. To some extent, the support was the upshot of a deliberate strategy. After taking office, the government allowed the performance of SOEs in public utilities to deteriorate in order to build a consensus for divestment. This same strategy was pursued in Peru, where privatization had been notably rejected in Fujimori's campaign and was absent from his initial agenda. Despite this rejection, Alberto Fujimori endorsed privatization to please the socioeconomic elites whose political support he needed. However, he made privatization contingent on his continued popularity (Manzetti 1999).

Privatization in Brazil could not capitalize on popular dissatisfaction with SOEs, which, until the late 1970s, had performed well. Also, unlike in Peru and Argentina, privatization had no clear advocate of a party or public character to spur the debate. Hence, when Fernando Collor launched his privatization program in 1990, both the elites and the

4.1. Explaining Privatization   119

public had mixed feelings about the appropriate role of the state. Only later did the public start to conceive of privatization as a possible solution for deteriorating economic conditions. By the time Fernando Henrique Cardoso won the election in 1994, public opinion was much more supportive of his privatization plans.

Finally, in other countries, privatization was undertaken for no apparent reason, not even pragmatic or opportunistic. According to Willner (1998: 179), the motives for privatization in Denmark "do not appear to be ideological and efficiency, as such, [was] not an issue." As for the Netherlands, the issue at stake was not whether to privatize but why it should not be done if everybody else was doing it. Unnecessary from an economic point of view, the Dutch privatization program "[could] be interpreted as a curtsy to the times" (Hulsink and Schenk 1998: 255).

This account is far from exhaustive. However, it suggests that neither economic rationales (efficiency or pragmatism) nor political ones (ideology or opportunity) can explain the decision to privatize. Also, it seems that, beyond the issue of their presence or absence, these factors could interact in various ways. Exceptionally, ideology, pragmatism, and opportunity reinforced each other (Britain, especially after 1983, and Portugal under Aníbal Cavaco Silva, 1985–96). In some cases, ideology supported privatization but opportunity told against it (Germany). In other cases, ideology told against privatization but pragmatism dominated and opportunity existed or was deliberately created (Spain, Argentina, and Peru). Finally, there are cases in which none of the three factors was powerful enough to explain the decision to privatize.

Local economic, political, and historical conditions may provide a good answer to the questions of how privatization processes are carried out (Stark and Brustz 1998), what is to be privatized, and how much is to be privatized (Murillo 2002; Schamis 2002).[3] However, domestic variables do not give a good answer to the questions of "why so many

---

[3] The dual transformations (political and economic) that took place in East Central Europe made privatization a particular and intense process in that region. According to the authors' comparative study of privatization practices in East Germany, Czechoslovakia, Poland, and Hungary, the specific formula chosen (be it vouchers, universal citizen grants, or through a central institution) was intimately linked to the patterns of extrication from Communist rule (reunification, capitulation, compromise, and electoral competition) and to more or less confidence on the part of elites in the market as a transformative tool (p. 101–03).

countries and why now?" For this reason, scholars have pointed to the role that international factors may have played in the diffusion of privatization. The difficulty is to identify the particular mechanism of diffusion that operated.

I focus on learning from experience. As explained in Chapter 1, the argument that governments engaged in market reforms as the consequence of a process of learning from bad interventionist policies in the past is well established in the literature on economic reforms. One could conjecture that governments' decisions to privatize would have resulted from observing the good outcomes of existing privatizations and that those outcomes would have inspired others to follow suit. According to Ramamurti (1999: 47), a nearby "miracle" constitutes the most relevant source of lessons. Discussing why privatization was slow in Sub-Saharan Africa, the author asserted that "[p]rivatization cannot gain momentum until a cross-section of national opinion leaders is convinced that it will work in the local context. That, in turn, has to grow out of a country's local experience with privatization or with demonstrable successes in neighboring countries." He adds, "I doubt that officials in Sub-Saharan Africa will be sold on privatization just because it seems to have worked well in Argentina or Malaysia." Schamis (2002) contends that socialist coalitions in France learned from Thatcher's privatization program. French Prime Minister Edouard Balladur (1993–95) stated that "the British experience [with privatization] was, without any doubt, the best example and the one that had the greatest similarities with what we wanted to do" (quoted in Suleiman, 1990:122). In similar vein, populist parties in Argentina and Mexico acknowledged the merits of Augusto Pinochet's economic policy, whose hallmark was privatization. In relation to Latin America, Manzetti (1999: 19) asserts that emulation "based upon the positive results of previous privatization experiences in other countries" provided further incentives for privatization. He contends that in Argentina "[t]he positive results evidenced by privatization policies in a number of European countries, Mexico, and neighbouring Chile may also have had some impact on Menem's pragmatic considerations."

However, other analysts suggest that the learning process was more global, "with everyone looking over others' shoulders to see what was being done elsewhere" (World Bank 2005: 169). Discussing privatization in East Central Europe, Stark and Brustz (1998: 95) mention the Czechs' fascination with Anglo-American practices and the Poles' interest in German and Japanese experiences. Even in Thailand, the deputy minister in charge of privatization made clear that "in a way, we are starting to follow the policies of Mrs Thatcher, which seem to have been very successful in Britain" (in Ikenberry 1990: 102). Thus, proximity may not have been a binding constraint on learning.

In the next section, I test the learning hypothesis. I also test the robustness of this hypothesis against a set of domestic political and economic variables and the alternative mechanisms of emulation and coercion. In brief, it could well be the case that governments did not learn from experience but simply gave independent responses to similar economic pressures. Alternatively, it could be the case that governments privatized following fads and fashions in an attempt to look modern. It may also be the case that selling the state sector was not the result of a deliberate choice but the outcome of external pressures to do so, that is, the outcome of coercion. As I show, both learning and emulation played a relevant role in decisions to privatize, whereas outward coercion did not. Also, domestic conditions did matter, but only in the regional sub-samples.

4.2. Learning and Privatization: The Data

The test of learning is based on thirty-seven countries during 1980 through 1997. These countries were grouped as OECD or Latin America.[4] I used the World Bank Privatization Database, which contains information on approximately 8,000 privatization transactions in low- and middle-income countries during 1988–98. The Garrett, Guillén, and Kogut database (2000) *Privatization around the World* has information on more than 4,300 privatization transactions, in developing, transition, and OECD countries. Finally, I used the 1990–2000 *Privatization*

---

[4] Although the privatization trend was certainly global, important differences among regions remain. For instance, countries in Africa privatized much less than other regions. As the World Bank 2005 study reports, between 1991 and 2001, roughly 2,300 privatizations affected fewer than forty percent of Africa's state-owned enterprises. Just four countries (Ghana, Côte d'Ivoire, Nigeria, and Zambia) accounted for a third of these transactions (World Bank 2005: 165).

122   *Learning and Privatization*

Yearbooks. I completed the data with secondary literature about specific case studies.[5]

I took some decisions about where to place the beginning of the privatization process. In most cases, I placed the beginning at the inauguration of a systematic and deliberate program of slimming down the state sector. To give some examples, I disregarded the isolated privatization of British Petroleum in 1977 under a Labour government. Although Chile repriva- tized and privatized during the 1970s – to temporarily nationalize later – I placed the starting year in 1985, which coincided with the "popular capitalism" phase. By the same token, I overlooked the scattered pri- vatizations accomplished during the Mexican disincorporation process. Although some sell-offs took place in Spain from 1984 to 1986, there was no a purposive denationalization program until 1988. For statistical purposes, the dependent variable PRIVATIZATION has been coded 1 if a particular country in a particular year carried out some transaction; otherwise it has been coded 0. The list of countries included in the study is provided in the Appendix.[6]

According to my data, 308 country-year observations of the total 660 correspond to years of privatization activity. As Figure 4.1 shows, this activity was clearly concentrated in the early 1990s, reaching a peak in 1993. It was slightly reversed at the end of the period, coinciding with the Mexican (1994–95) and the East Asian (1997–98) crises.

Earlier, I argued that pragmatism alone is not a good predictor of the decision to privatize. Eventually, privatization results from a complex mixture of pragmatism and politics. Some figures may be illuminating.

For example, I coded as "bad deficit" those years in which the budget deficit was greater than minus five percent of GDP in Latin America and minus three percent in the OECD.[7] According to this criterion, there are 145 observations in which there was privatization and a "good deficit," and 158 observations in which there was no privatization and a "bad

---

[5] The World Bank database does not include OECD countries, and Garrett, Guillén, and Kogut (2000), when checked against the World Bank database, proved not to be accurate. A codebook is available on request from the author.

[6] Mexico has belonged to the OECD since 1994 but, for the purpose of regional grouping, Mexico was included in the Latin American region. Hungary and Poland were included in the OECD cluster; both countries joined the OECD in 1996.

[7] Data from World Development Indicators.

4.2. Learning and Privatization: The Data

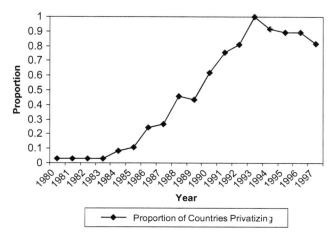

Figure 4.1. Proportion of Privatizers, 1980–97. Thirty-seven Latin American and OECD countries. *Sources:* own data, based on the World Bank Privatization Database (1998), Privatization Yearbooks (several years), and Garrett, Guillén, and Kogut (2000).

deficit." Likewise, the budget constraint is not a good predictor of privatization, nor is privatization a good predictor of a smaller budget deficit. In the 1980s, and in both regions, the budget constraint was tight in many countries. For instance, between 1980 and 1986, the average deficit was −11.03% of GDP in Belgium, −12.08% in Ireland, and −18.4% in Nicaragua. Still, very few privatizations were accomplished in those years.

Even though privatization was pervasive in the 1990s, it proved not to be a good instrument to contain the public deficit amid bad economic conditions. The French budget deficit was greater in 1993 under center-right rule and privatization than it was during socialist rule and nationalization (it was −3.51% in 1983 and −6.55% in 1995). Countries such as Britain, Spain, or Brazil experienced increases in their budget deficits despite persisting with privatization.[8] In 1980, Britain had a deficiency equal to −4.64% of GDP. It was −5.29% in 1995 and reached a peak of −6.45% in 1993.

---

[8] Admittedly, I disregard whether privatization, despite existing, involved fewer transactions. I also disregard the world economic cycle.

Also, it is striking to observe that convinced privatizers such as Chile never experienced a tight budget constraint (a deficit of −2.96% was the peak in 1984). Another suspect of fiscal indiscipline, Argentina, exhibits a better performance than some European counterparts such as Italy or Greece. The peak deficit in the period amounted to −7.9% of GDP in 1983. It was a low −0.38% the year before the privatization program was launched. Thus, it appears that the relationship between privatization and the budget is loose at best.

According to World Bank analysts, and in line with the typical pattern of the diffusion of policy innovations, governments began to privatize "emboldened by the euphoria over privatization in general and the specific successes of some countries" (World Bank 2005: 174). However, success in privatization is difficult to define yet crucial to measure in order to test whether learning from success caused the privatization wave. Success may refer to profit margins, efficiency, employment, or gains accruing to workers, owners, governments, and consumers. The World Bank's 2005 study reports an improvement in profitability and efficiency in upper-middle-income countries but not in low-income countries. Yet the study acknowledges that "because many things changed simultaneously . . . the benefits that followed privatization are not the proof that privatization was their cause" (2005: 170).[9]

Consistent with the view that the ultimate objective of the economic reforms was to spur economic development, I concentrate on the impact of privatization on growth. As for the average rate of growth, it was 3.10% ($N = 308$) for those countries and years privatizing. It was 2.09% ($N = 352$) for those countries and years that did not privatize. Thus, the aggregate picture is one of greater growth in countries and years of privatization. Figure 4.2, however, does not show a very evident superiority of privatization over nonprivatization concerning growth figures. Can we relate learning from the relative country performances with and without privatization to other countries' subsequent decisions to privatize?

---

[9] Besides, when benefits are reported, it is not clear what specific mechanism may have caused the improvement: Better oversight of owners, better management, the reduction of overstaffing, or the hardening of soft budget constraints may be good candidates. However, a selection bias in the study of privatized firms focusing on those already performing better before privatization also could explain the efficiency improvements (World Bank 2005: 170).

4.3. Learning and Privatization: The Results

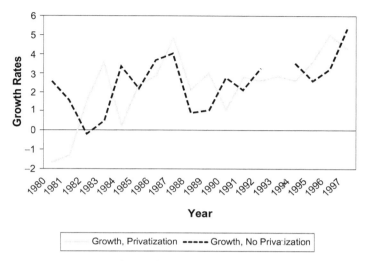

Figure 4.2. Average Rates of Growth with and without Privatization, 1980–97. All countries in the database carried out some transaction in 1993

4.3. Learning and Privatization: The Results

I model politicians' behavior as rational. Starting with some prior beliefs[10] about growth outcomes associated with the respective status of privatization and nonprivatization (Appendix), new information is produced and observed every year about the relative performance of countries under each alternative policy. Prior beliefs are updated and choices are made on the basis of posterior beliefs. As a proxy for similarity of conditions, and as explained in the previous chapters, information has been structured at the level of own, regional, and world experience.[11] If we take into account how the utility function has been defined, it is expected that, the stronger the posterior beliefs about average growth from privatizing compared with not doing so, the more likely is a switch to privatization. When results under the same policy vary greatly across

---

[10] In this illustration, the structure of the data is peculiar. Until the mid-1980s, experience with privatization is limited to Britain. Hence, not only is own experience with privatization scant, but the regional experience and world experience with privatization also are limited. Thus, the removal of the influence of priors is potentially problematic.

[11] Note that, with two regions, the world is limited to the other region, that is, the world experience for Latin America is the experience in OECD countries and vice versa.

126 *Learning and Privatization*

time and space, the perception that policy is not responsible for observed outcomes makes sense. On the assumption of risk aversion, the greater the variability of results under privatization relative to nonprivatization, the less likely a switch to that policy is expected to be. Note that this structuring of available experience at three geographical levels roughly serves as a control for shared traits such as common religion, common language, common colonial past – Catholic and Iberian – and shared affiliations and institutional memberships (EU, OECD).

In Table 4.1 (column 1) I show the estimates of the impact of learning on both the probability of switching to privatization and the probability of continuing to privatize. As can be seen, the observed path of privatization choices is positively related to the difference in posterior beliefs about average growth at own, regional, and world levels (column 1). In other words, the hypothesis that governments in OECD countries and in Latin America privatized because they learned from their own experience with privatization, experience in their regions, and experience in other regions cannot be dismissed. Their decision to privatize was also negatively influenced by the volatility of results worldwide.

Explaining the decision to continue privatizing in terms of learning is more problematic. According to the results, posterior beliefs about average growth did not influence the decision to continue privatizing. It could be the case that politicians did not look at growth rates when deciding whether to continue privatizing. They may have been interested in other economic variables, such as public deficits or performance at the firm level. It could also be the case that it was politics rather than economics that kept privatization going. Indeed, several studies suggest that the process of privatization created its own coalitions of special interests that benefited from the continuation of the selling process (Schamis 2002; Murillo 2002). In Mexico under Carlos Salinas de Gortari (1988–94), part of the proceeds of privatization were devoted to financing the poverty relief National Solidarity Program, which was channelled to the worst-off sectors of Mexican society as a "social tranquilizer" (Ramírez 2000: 59). Also, the objective of making privatization irreversible entailed curbing the opposition of the unions and management in targeted SOEs by giving them a stake in the privatization process. It further entailed giving business and the ordinary citizen lucrative investment opportunities.

Regarding Britain, Mark (1993: 38) argues that "[b]y giving tangible benefits to the participants of privatization the government created a large constituency of various political persuasions that benefited materially from privatization, and thus was opposed to any calls to end this policy (. . .)." In relation to Chile, Sigmund states that politically speaking, privatization created a new group that was likely to oppose future nationalizations (1990: 361). This strategy to garner support from the population at large may have created an extensive basis of support that made privatization highly inertial. Therefore, the support of new beneficiaries, rather than the aggregate results of privatization, was the cause of policy sustainability.

Overall, although learning was a strong predictor of the decision to privatize, and remained so in the presence of domestic controls (discussed subsequently), learning loses much of its explanatory power when it comes to predicting governments' decisions to sustain privatization.

Alternative Hypotheses

Rational learning from others' experience may be just one mechanism of policy convergence. In this subsection, I survey the possibility that governments privatized as a result of imitating others' behavior (EMULATION). Alternatively, governments may have privatized under pressure from IFIs (COERCION).

Unlike the case with learning, governments emulating others do not choose policies as a result of their improved understanding of the consequences of their choices. Emulation entails adoption of policy ideas without such understanding (Rose 1991; Bennett 1991; May 1992: 333). However, a modicum of perceived success is necessary to spur mimicry. Discussing privatization, Ikenberry (1990: 103) asserts that ". . . the watchword is copy what *seems* to work" (emphasis added). However, the crucial difference between imitation and learning has to do with the ultimate motivation to engage in one or the other process. Whereas learning is motivated by a utilitarian search for optimal solutions to objective problems, the thrust to emulate is symbolic and based on normative appeals.

128   *Learning and Privatization*

I test the hypothesis that emulation drove the choice of policies by adding to the baseline models a variable that accounts for the sheer number of other countries engaged in a particular policy in a particular year. This variable serves as a proxy for the general climate of opinion about the policy in question (Granovetter 1978). I expected this variable to have a positive effect on the probability of a switch to privatization and on the probability that the switch be sustained.

As for coercion, one widespread explanation of policy convergence is that governments privatized their public sectors under pressure from IFIs. Imposition is epitomized by IMF conditionality, which implies that policies are adopted in exchange for loans. Especially in the 1990s, privatization has usually been part and parcel of standard reform packages (Dreher 2002; Brune, Garrett, and Kogut 2004). It also has been indirectly promoted by IFIs' requirements of reducing public deficits and protecting property rights. Moreover, according to Brune, Garrett, and Kogut (2004), being under an IMF agreement and the commitment to sound economic policies that an agreement implies sends a positive signal to investors, encouraging them to buy shares and to pay a higher price for them.

If the imposition hypothesis holds, switches to privatization should be positively related to the presence of an IMF program (IMF). In hypothesizing about the impact of IMF agreements in the context of this research, I should stress that OECD countries constitute the bulk of my sample (sixty-two percent of total country-year observations). Most countries in this subsample did not need an IMF program to privatize. Of 200 country-year observations of privatization, only 17 occurred under IMF programs. In the overall sample, around twenty-eight percent of the divestments occurred under IMF surveillance. In fact, the coercion of IFIs is mentioned as a principal motivation for privatization in African countries, which were not included in the empirical analysis (World Bank 2005).

I tested the imposition hypothesis by adding a dummy variable to the baseline model. This variable accounts for the existence of an IMF agreement in a particular country in a particular year. I also included a dummy variable referring to European Union membership (EU) to take into account the fact that fourteen of the thirty-seven countries in the

4.3. Learning and Privatization: The Results

sample are EU members. EU membership might have been an active force for privatization through the imposition of tight convergence criteria to qualify for membership of the European Monetary Union. In particular, budget deficits were required not to exceed three percent of GDP.

I added to the model a few domestic political and economic controls. Many variables could not be included due to the high number of missing values and a high correlation of the controls with the learning variables. This was the case with the scale of capital accumulation, level of external indebtedness, and degree of openness. The public deficit was also considered, but, again, a good number of observations were missing. Hence, the extended model includes the ideological leaning of the government (IDEOLOGY, Left = 3, Center = 2, Right = 1, Beck, Keefer, and Clark 2000),[12] the regime type (REGIME, −10 perfect autocracy, +10 perfect democracy, Polity IV), and the level of inflation (INFLATION, World Development Indicators).[13]

Finally, I included a dummy variable for the year 1990 (YEAR 1990) to take into account the potential effect that the fall of Communist regimes, the Soviet Union, Central and Eastern Europe, and the subsequent privatization in that region might have had on governments' perceptions of privatization and its alternatives. It is generally agreed that the collapse of the East Central European economies dramatically affected views about the feasibility of socialist management of the economy, to which a large state-owned sector was central. As the World Bank (1995: 165) points out, "[T]he [privatization] trickle became a flood with the collapse of central planning in Eastern Europe and the former Soviet Union."[14]

As for the impact of controls, their effects are not a priori clear. In principle, right-wing governments, with their anti-big-state ideologies, would seem to be more inclined to privatize than left-wing ones. Yet, the earlier

---

[12] Nonapplicable = 0 recoded as missing.

[13] In the other empirical chapters, I employ a dichotomous indicator of regime, coded 1 for autocracies and 0 for democracies (Gandhi 2004). The reason why I used the scaled indicator of democracy in this illustration is that the dichotomous indicator of regime would show too little variation, particularly in OECD countries.

[14] The 2005 World Bank report also mentions that "[T]he experience of the Treuhand, created to sell the state-owned assets of East German firms after the fall of the Berlin Wall in 1989 provided early lessons [about how to carry out the transaction process and what market institutions to set up]" (World Bank 2005: 167).

130 *Learning and Privatization*

discussion showed that governments of different leanings endorsed privatization.[15] As for the impact of regime type, many countries in the Latin American region changed political regime during the 1980s. One may argue that privatization is more complicated under democracy only because democratic accountability and distributional coalitions work against a policy that is frequently unpopular. However, as mentioned earlier, privatization also creates its own supporting coalitions and may turn into a very popular policy, as the British experience and some Latin American experiences revealed (Vickers and Wright 1989; Stokes 2001; Schamis 2002; Murillo 2002). The effect of inflation on the probability of privatization also is unclear. On the one hand, governments may privatize when confronted with a macroeconomic crisis in order to signal a commitment to reform; on the other hand, hyperinflations may also constrain governments' room in which to maneuver.[16] Finally, the fall of Communist regimes is likely to have affected positively the propensity of governments to privatize to the extent that these events questioned the desirability and feasibility of big public sectors.

Columns (2), (3), and (4) in Table 4.1 show the results of the extended model with the controls and the alternative mechanisms of diffusion. To test the robustness of the results and unfold regional specificities, I ran the estimation for each category (OECD and Latin America) and for the joint sample.

Two comments on the statistical model are necessary. First, in the estimation, I did not include the learning variables about the variability of results. The reason is that these variables were not significant and yet correlated with the emulation indicator moderately in the joint sample and strongly in the regional samples. Thus, to facilitate comparison between the joint and the regional samples, I included the learning variables referring to average results only. Second, I report the estimation of the probability of launching privatization but not that of sustaining privatization. The reason is that, in the regional samples, the transitions from

---

[15] This does not mean that privatization was implemented in the same way regardless of the ideology of the governing party. According to Schamis (2002) and Murillo (2002), party ideology and preferences do affect how the selling process takes place.

[16] Brune and Garrett (2000) found that privatization is promoted by low inflation and by less democratic countries, but the latter effect was not statistically significant.

4.3. Learning and Privatization: The Results

Table 4.1. *Probability of launching and sustaining privatization (1980–1997)*

Dependent variable: privatization	(1) All countries		(2) All countries	(3) OECD	(4) LA
	Learning launching	Learning sustaining	Controls launching	Controls launching	Controls launching
CONSTANT	−1.58***	1.48**	−2.60***	−4.56***	−6.45***
	(−6.02)	(2.48)	(−5.92)	(−3.72)	(−3.06)
OWN EXPERIENCE					
AVERAGE RESULTS	0.16**	0.02	0.11	0.04	0.32*
	(2.35)	(0.44)	(1.45)	(0.34)	(1.87)
VARIABILITY OF RESULTS	0.57	−0.98*			
	(1.43)	(−1.93)			
REGIONAL EXPERIENCE					
AVERAGE RESULTS	0.35***	0.21	0.16*	−0.63	1.36**
	(2.88)	(0.70)	(1.72)	(−1.22)	(2.55)
VARIABILITY OF RESULTS	−0.05	0.84			
	(−0.18)	(0.04)			
WORLD EXPERIENCE					
AVERAGE RESULTS	0.19*	−0.20	0.21**	0.59**	−0.99
	(1.77)	(−0.95)	(2.22)	(2.10)	(−1.12)
VARIABILITY OF RESULTS	−0.82**	−0.97			
	(−2.42)	(−1.48)			
EMULATION			0.60***	0.49***	1.12***
			(5.06)	(3.39)	(3.60)
COERCION			0.22	−0.08	0.50
			(0.74)	(−0.12)	(1.15)
IDEOLOGY			0.08	0.25*	−0.37
			(0.79)	(1.74)	(−1.59)
REGIME			−0.2E-2	0.02	−0.14**
			(−0.10)	(0.60)	(−2.30)
INFLATION			0.08	1.61	−0.22
			(0.24)	(0.68)	(−0.43)
EU			0.20	0.23	
			(0.71)	(0.78)	
YEAR 1990			0.35	0.45	2.24**
			(0.95)	(0.87)	(2.43)
Log Likelihood	−177.34		−169.37	−94.02	−48.95
LR Chi-Square	508.83		399.15	285.87	165.69
P-Value for F	0.000		0.000	0.000	0.000
Observations	623		533	342	191

*$p < .10$; **$p < .05$; ***$p < .01$; z-scores in parentheses; all variables lagged one year.
The Pseudo R^2 is 0.59 (Model 1), 0.54 (Model 2), and 0.60 (Models 3 and 4). The percentage of correctly predicted 1s and 0s ranges between 87% and 89%.
OECD = Organization for Economic Co-operation and Development; LA = Latin America; EU = European Union.

the status of privatization to nonprivatization are too few to guarantee the reliability of the estimators of policy continuity.

Comparing columns (1) and (2) shows that the variables related to learning are robust to the inclusion of the controls, although learning from own experience loses significance. Surprisingly, of all the controls included in the model, only the proxy for emulation turned out to be significant. Hence, the estimation of the extended model in the joint sample shows that the decision to divest was the consequence of a diffusion process in which both learning (from others' results in the region and in the other region) and (especially) emulation were crucial.

Comparison by rows among columns (2), (3), and (4) – that is, among the joint and the regional samples – produces interesting results and confirms the suspicion that the joint estimation masked distinctive regional patterns. To start with, the most robust result of the analysis for this policy is that privatization was strongly related to the phenomenon of policy emulation. The sheer number of other countries privatizing was a powerful explanation of governments' decisions to privatize. This result applied to the joint sample as much as to each regional subsample.

The learning variables are robust in the regional samples, but apparently this learning proceeded according to distinctive patterns. Latin American countries learned from their own past experience with privatization versus nonprivatization and, more significantly, from experience in the region. Yet, the hypothesis that OECD countries privatized in response to the results of privatization in Latin America cannot be ruled out. Under the presumption that the South learned from the North, this result is somewhat counterintuitive. It can be explained, at least in part, by analyzing the rate of growth in the two regions. In the joint sample, average annual growth in countries that privatized was 3.3%, whereas countries that did not privatize grew at a rate of 2.09%. If one disaggregates the figure by region, differences are evident: Whereas in the OECD, the rates of growth were practically the same with and without privatization (2.55% and 2.67% respectively), in Latin America average growth rates in the countries that privatized were ostensibly greater than those in countries that did not privatize (4.19% and 1.23% respectively) and also better than the average rate of growth under privatization in the OECD. Obviously, responsibility for the greater dynamism in the Latin

4.3. Learning and Privatization: The Results

American region should not be attributed exclusively to privatization, but it could be that the scope of the process in Latin America, together with the improved performance of the countries in the region during the 1990s, eventually exerted some demonstration effect in the OECD countries. An alternative reading of this result is that Latin American countries privatized in an attempt to achieve OECD *levels* of income, rather than that the OECD privatized in the attempt to achieve Latin American growth *rates*.[17]

The results regarding political controls are equally interesting. They suggest that the joint analysis certainly disguised some distinctive regional features. In the OECD, the probability of privatizing was positively, although weakly, related to left-wing governments. This outcome accords with the previous narrative account, which showed that there was quite a general consensus across the ideological spectrum in the region concerning modernization via downsizing the state-owned sector (Clifton, Comín, and Díaz-Fuentes 2003: chapter 2).

In Latin America, the ideology of parties in power was not the relevant variable. Instead, it was the repressive character of the regime that mattered. In terms of launching privatization, the less democratic the regime, the more likely it was to start divesting. Chile under Augusto Pinochet, Peru under Alberto Fujimori – who, in 1992, suspended the activities of Congress – or the state of *coup de décret* under Carlos Menem in democratic Argentina are a few good examples (Weyland 2002; Schamis 2002: 138).

Note that the fall of Communist regimes influenced positively the probability of privatizing, but only in Latin America. Hence, the loss of legitimacy of the statist model brought about by the failure of the Communist countries played a relevant role in the wave of divestments in Latin America, a region that implemented highly interventionist policies for decades.

Lastly, another robust result, but in its nonsignificance, is that neither in the regional samples nor in the joint sample did the IMF or the EU influence the decision to privatize. This result accords with recent

---

[17] In other words, this result could be the consequence of using growth rates rather than income levels as the economic variables from which governments are modeled to learn. Peter Egger mentioned this possibility to me.

134 *Learning and Privatization*

Table 4.2. *Changes in predicted probability of privatizing (1980–1997)*

	(1) All countries		(2) All countries	(3) OECD	(4) LA
	Launching	Sustaining	Launching	Launching	Launching
OWN EXPERIENCE					
AVERAGE RESULTS	0.07				0.05
	(0.03)				(0.06)
VARIABILITY OF RESULTS		−0.07			
		(0.03)			
REGIONAL EXPERIENCE					
AVERAGE RESULTS	0.21		0.09		0.42
	(0.07)		(0.05)		(0.19)
VARIABILITY OF RESULTS					
WORLD EXPERIENCE					
AVERAGE RESULTS	0.11		0.12	0.13	
	(0.06)		(0.05)	(0.05)	
VARIABILITY OF RESULTS	−0.16				
	(0.07)				
EMULATION			0.17	0.13	0.12
			(0.04)	(0.05)	(0.07)
IDEOLOGY				0.06	
				(0.04)	
REGIME					−0.07
					(0.05)

Note: Standard Errors in parentheses.
Variation of one standard deviation around the mean of the predictors; all other variables are set at their means.
Note that simulations calculate 95% confidence intervals (CI). For coefficients that are significant at 90%, the 95% CI does not exclude zero.
OECD = Organization for Economic Co-operation and Development; LA = Latin America; EU = European Union.

quantitative and qualitative research on the diffusion of policies, which demonstrates that countries had more room for maneuver than the coercion hypothesis suggests (e.g. Weyland 2007). Something similar could be said about inflation levels. Although the decision to privatize is frequently associated with bad economic conditions, results show that this effect was not significant in the sample used.

Table 4.2 shows the change in the predicted probability of privatizing after changing one standard deviation around the mean of the significant predictors. These simulations provide a better understanding of the relative effect of the various diffusion mechanisms and the domestic controls on the probability of privatizing.

Some results stand out. In the joint sample and the model with controls, the impact of emulating others was considerable. A change in one standard deviation around the mean of the variable EMULATION increases the probability that a particular country will privatize by seventeen percentage points. The impact of this variable is somewhat smaller in the regional samples, but still, OECD and Latin American countries were thirteen and twelve percentage points more likely to privatize when the number of other countries privatizing moved one standard deviation around the mean. Another interesting result is the strong impact of regional experience on the decision to privatize in Latin America. A one standard deviation move in LEARNING FROM AVERAGE RESULTS, REGION concerning privatization versus nonprivatization increased the probability of privatizing by forty-two percentage points. Thus, Luigi Manzetti was right when he asserted that some Latin American leaders were indeed quick learners. I add that they turned out to be quick learners specifically from the experience with privatization in their very same region. This proves that, at least in Latin America, the diffusion of privatization was regionally clustered as a result of rational learning. Finally, note that a one standard deviation change in IDEOLOGY in OECD countries (moving, indeed, from a rightist to a leftist government in power) increases the probability of privatizing by about six percentage points. In Latin America, more democratic countries have seven percentage points less probability of privatizing.

Figure 4.3 is based on Model (2). The figure plots the predicted probabilities of privatizing along variations in the POSTERIOR BELIEFS ABOUT AVERAGE GROWTH, WORLD and the 95% confidence intervals. For this variable, a value of zero means that the posterior belief about growth with privatization equals the posterior beliefs about growth with no privatization. The greatest increase in the probability of privatizing occurs to the right of zero because positive values of the variable entail that the posterior beliefs about average growth privatizing surpassed the posterior belief about average growth not privatizing. The figure shows

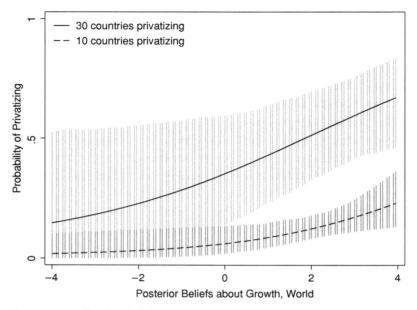

Figure 4.3. Predicted Probability and 95% Confidence Intervals of Privatizing along Posterior Beliefs about Growth Privatizing versus Nonprivatizing, World, by the Number of Other Countries Privatizing. All other variables are set at their mean values.

that the predicted probability of privatizing is, indeed, greater the more countries privatize. However, this difference is significant only for values of the posterior beliefs to the right of zero – that is, when the posterior beliefs about growth privatizing exceed the posterior beliefs about growth not privatizing. Based on Model (2), simulations show that moving from the minimum value up to zero of the predictor POSTERIOR BELIEFS ABOUT AVERAGE GROWTH, WORLD increases the probability of privatizing by 3.5 percentage points, whereas moving from zero to the maximum value of the variable, which does not show outliers, increases the probability of privatizing by about 18 percentage points. This is the reason why the predicted probability of privatizing increases as we move to the right of the X axis. However, the predicted probability of privatization varies with the number of other countries or, in other words, with the magnitude of the flood. For all the range of the variable POSTERIOR

BELIEFS ABOUT AVERAGE GROWTH, WORLD, the probability of privatizing is higher the greater the number of other countries carrying out the same policy. With all the variables at their means, the probability that a centrist country, ranked seven in the POLITY IV scale (quite democratic), under an IMF agreement, and observing eight other countries privatizing (approximately the sample mean) will privatize is around ten percent. However, when this same government observes the maximum number of other countries privatizing, the probability that it will also privatize rises to sixty percent. For this same type of country, when I allow the value of the posterior beliefs about growth in the world to vary from its mean to its maximum value, the predicted probability increases to twenty-five percent. Thus, in the joint sample, the simulations suggest a stronger impact of fads and fashions than of rational learning in the decision to privatize.

To return to the question that motivated this chapter, rational learning from the experience of others explained the decision to streamline the public sector. This result is robust to the inclusion of a set of controls. However, in the joint sample as well as in the regional subsamples, the most robust result is that herding on the policy choices of others drove the decision to privatize. Overall, it seems that policy makers processed the information as a rational learner does to some extent, but in addition, politicians' behavior matched well the expectations of a policy bandwagon effect. In fact, a government's decision to privatize was strongly and consistently predicted by what its peers did.

4.4. Discussion

The substitution of marketization for statism has been one of the most important socioeconomic changes in recent decades. Nationalization was the hallmark of statism as much as privatization was the hallmark of the marketization of economies. In this chapter, I analyzed the role that different convergence mechanisms played in the widespread adoption of this policy innovation in the belief that domestic factors cannot fully explain this trend. Within those mechanisms, I focused on learning from others.

My working hypothesis was that governments privatized in the light of the experience of those that privatized and those that had not privatized. I showed that the joint sample and the regional samples provide no grounds for rejecting this hypothesis. However, the dynamics of learning were different in the two regions. One result is very robust in its significance: When privatizing, governments herded on others' decisions. Another result is very robust in its nonsignificance: Top-down pressures or coercion did not drive governments' choices to privatize. Note, however, that the fact that blunt coercion is not reflected in the results does not rule out the possibility that IFIs influenced the process of privatization by promoting "best practices" in the field.

In Latin America, the decision to sell public enterprises was the consequence of a learning process from own experience and, particularly, from the *regional* experience. Specifically, the impact of the latter is too important to be disregarded. The regional clustering that the diffusion of privatization exhibits is a distinctive feature of the diffusion of policy *innovations*.[18] According to the results of this chapter, Latin American governments found it rational to learn from own experience and experience in the region. Learning rather than mimicry was the major motor of privatization in the region. Yet, the effect of the sheer number of others privatizing could not be discounted: Pragmatic concerns but also a certain dose of symbolism were in place. Interestingly, the joint experience of the more developed OECD counterparts did not influence the decision to privatize in Latin America. Undoubtedly, the change in the climate of opinion in favor of privatization, especially after the collapse of the former Communist economies, was a strong encouragement to divest in countries motivated by the need to show a commitment to coherent policies. Besides, privatization was more likely where the political regime was more repressive.

Somewhat surprisingly, the possibility cannot be ruled out that privatization in Latin America, and the improved efficiency results associated

[18] Regional clustering is also observed in other policy reforms that cannot be characterized as "policy innovations," but the motivation for it seems not to be bounded learning but competitive responses to the policies of others. See for instance Guisinger (2005, chapter 4, concerning trade liberalization).

4.4. Discussion

with it, exerted some influence on the adoption of privatization by OECD countries. Indeed, the average rates of growth of Latin American countries that privatized were almost double those in the OECD. And, as some authors warn (see, for example, Dolowitz and Marsh 2000), the roles of policy lenders and policy borrowers are not always as clear cut as the different country status may invite one to assume. Dolowitz and Marsh state (p. 10) that "often countries classified as borrowers act as models for other political systems." Freeman (2006: 380) argues that "standard images of cross-national 'policy borrowing', 'import' and 'export' risk obscure much of the mutualism of learning processes." In his discussion of the diffusion of pension privatization, Orenstein (2003: 172, 183) shows that semiperipheral Chile became an example for Western European pension reformers. Finally, Weyland (2007: 234–35) points out that the "shining example of third world nations may (. . .) provide an opening for reducing conservative effects of institutions and policy legacies in the first world," spurring laggards to move through reforms. Thus, it is not unreasonable to propose that latecomers in the European periphery such as Spain or Portugal had much to learn from the Latin American extensive experience with privatization. The two results showing that Latin America did not learn from OECD countries but that OECD countries did learn from Latin America back up the argument that, in this particular policy realm, learning proceeded from South to North. Also, in the OECD, symbolic emulation had some role in the decision to privatize. As pointed out in the narrative, for some European countries, privatization was primarily a "curtsy to the times." Finally, privatization in the OECD countries was favored by left-wing governments. This behavior might have been motivated by the desire of left-wing politicians to signal commitment to the rigorous policies expected in the region. Note, however, that the impact of this variable was lower than the impact of learning or of emulation.

All in all, the answer to the opening question of this chapter is, first, that governments privatized as a consequence of a diffusion process, and second, that the diffusion process, meditated by particular regional features, was related to learning from experience and strongly related to a process of emulation.

APPENDIX

Table A4.3. *Prior beliefs, privatization*

Year	Privatization mean	No privatization mean	Variance
1980	2.75	5.48	30
1981	−1.64	4.27	18
1983	1.54	4.54	21
1989	5.08	3.46	11

Note: Based on observed average and variance of results in the world the year before the entry in the database. Since only one case existed for the privatization status, priors under privatization have been attributed the same uncertainty (variance) as priors under nonprivatization.

Table A4.4. *Descriptive statistics, privatization*

	Mean	s.d.	Minimum	Maximum
Beliefs Average Growth, Own	.52	2.01	−8.33	6.31
Beliefs Average Growth, Region	.75	1.86	−3.20	4.65
Beliefs Average Growth, World	1.63	1.91	−3.85	4.34
Number of Other Countries	1.59	1.26	.0	3.6
IMF Agreements	.27	.44	.0	1
Dummy 1990	.06	.25	.0	1
Regime	7.58	4.64	−8	10
Executive Ideology	1.78	.94	1	3
Inflation	.12	.27	−.003	2.07
European Union Membership	.30	.45	.0	1

Table A4.5. *List of countries, privatization*

Region	
OECD	Latin America
Canada	Costa Rica
Japan	Honduras
South Korea	Jamaica
Austria	Mexico
Belgium	Nicaragua
Denmark	Panama
Finland	Argentina
France	Bolivia
Germany	Brazil
Greece	Chile
Hungary	Colombia
Iceland	Peru
Ireland	Uruguay
Italy	Venezuela
The Netherlands	
Norway	
Poland	
Portugal	
Spain	
Sweden	
Turkey	
United Kingdom	
New Zealand	

Sources: World Bank Privatization Database (1998); Privatization Yearbook (several years); Garrett, Guillén, and Kogut (2000).

FIVE

Learning and Capital Account Liberalization

We begin our study of the origins of financial openness with a review of what is known about consequences because we expect that government officials are likely to have first contemplated the consequences before they liberalized or not international financial markets.

Quinn and Inclán (1997: 772)

In recent decades, the internationalization of capital has been the hallmark of globalization. Starting in the late 1950s, the growth of the Euromarket boosted the opportunities for moving money across borders. The emergence of this mostly unregulated pool of capital paralleled, and is strongly related to, another important phenomenon: The increasing mobility of production and the rise of multinational corporations (MNCs) as crucial economic and political actors. With more and more opportunities to evade domestic controls, owners of capital and MNCs became empowered. Local politicians were bound to choose economic policies in accordance with capitalists' preferences to discourage capital and production from moving to more friendly environments. This is the famous "exit option" (Goodman and Pauly 1993).

The political consequences of this remarkable shift have been thoroughly discussed but continue to be controversial: In a context of the free movement of capital, can governments still pursue their preferred policies? The general answer, anticipated by Mundell and Fleming's model of open economy macroeconomics, is "no, they cannot." According to the so-called impossible trilogy, in a context in which capital is allowed to flow freely across borders, governments have to choose between two objectives: Exchange rate stability and an autonomous monetary policy.

Learning and Capital Account Liberalization   143

If they choose a fixed exchange rate, governments will have to use monetary policy to defend the exchange rate rather than to promote growth and employment. Alternatively, governments may choose an autonomous monetary policy, but, in a context of free capital flows, this implies allowing the exchange rate to float as the market dictates. Thus, capital mobility intensified the dilemma between flexibility and stability.

This is not the only political quandary that governments face in a context of free capital movements. In principle, one of the most conspicuous consequences of capital mobility is that economic policy has to court domestic and foreign capitalists in order to keep them at home and bring them in. This entails offering capitalists absolute guarantees that they will be able to move their funds and benefits in and out of the country as they wish. Moreover, mobility imposes a clear constraint on the taxes that can be levied on capital. Hence, competition to attract foreign capital would have provoked a race to the bottom in taxation with perverse consequences for the ability of governments to finance, among other things, welfare expenditures. Capital mobility imposed another dilemma on governments: The choice between the ability to compete for capital internationally and the ability to compensate domestically. However, the reality of these dilemmas continues to be the object of lively debate.[1]

If the political consequences of capital mobility are potentially so perverse, the subsequent question is why capital controls were removed in the 1990s. One possible answer is that this policy shift is the consequence of increased trade openness and greater mobility of capital and production, which are the inescapable reality in which domestic governments now *have* to operate. From this point of view, governments assume that, given the increase in the degree of openness and in the possibilities for evasion, there is no other option but to accept this new context and to adapt to it *independently* of what others do. Contrary to this passive stance, governments may have actively sought to decontrol capital movements in view of the benefits that incoming capital may bring. For instance, especially in developing countries, inflows of capital can make

---

[1] It seems that an accurate answer to this question requires recognizing the distinction between developed and developing countries (Rodrik 1997; Garrett 1998; Swank 2002; Iversen and Cusak 2000; Rudra 2002; Mosley 2003).

up for scarce local savings and crucially help to finance development. If that is the case and inflows of capital are regarded as good for economic development, governments would have lifted capital controls in order to attract those flows. *Competition* for this limited pool of resources would have been the driving force behind liberalization of the capital account. Finally, the removal of capital controls may have resulted from a shift in policy ideas embraced by influential actors. Thus, financial liberalization may have been the outcome of a shift in global views that affected policy making through persuasion, and frequently through *coercion.*

In this chapter, I enquire whether the removal of capital controls was due to a learning process. This mechanism is strongly related to the idea that the removal of capital controls has had tangible benefits for the countries that liberalized as opposed to the countries that did not. Thus, I shall be testing the hypothesis that the consequences of capital liberalization preceded the decision whether or not to liberalize, as assumed by Quinn and Inclán in the epigraph to this chapter.

As I show, learning from the experience of others was not a strong determinant of the decision to *remove* capital controls. Competition for capital and trade appears to have been a robust determinant of financial liberalization. Another persistent result is that the IMF influenced the process of capital liberalization, although the impact of this variable on the probability of opening is small. The paradox is that IMF programs may have been both the cause and the consequence of an imprudent opening. Finally, I explore the impact that the financial crises of the 1990s may have had on the process of learning about the consequences of liberalizing the capital account. Interestingly, it seems that, when learning from the financial crises is modeled, learning from own experience and the experience of the world is related to a greater probability of *sustaining* an open capital account. However, these results should be taken as preliminary since the data do not cover the late 1990s and early 2000s financial crises.

In the next section, I briefly review the political economy of capital account liberalization. Most studies, quantitative and qualitative, have focused on explaining the differences in the pace and content of liberalization in both developed and developing countries. Only a few offer explanations of the big picture – that is, why capital controls have been

5.1. The Political Economy of Capital Account Liberalization   145

eliminated or reduced regardless of the mixed theoretical case for and evidence concerning this reform. According to these studies (Simmons and Elkins 2004; Brune and Guisinger 2007; Chwieroth 2007; Quinn and Toyoda 2008), there is an apparent concentration of reforms in time and space that needs to be explained. It is in this last strand of research that diffusion appears as a plausible explanation of the liberalization of capital movements. Following the discussion, I present and discuss the data. I illustrate the different mechanisms of policy convergence, using a particular case: The Mexican experience with financial liberalization. The Mexican story is interesting in that during the period of this study, the country adopted opposite stances on the financial sector: Intervention and nationalization in the 1980s and radical liberalization in the 1990s. Moreover, the 1994–95 *peso* crisis is considered to have been "the first financial crisis of the XXI century" with allegedly relevant lessons for other reformers.[2] Finally, I comment on the results of the learning model, and I test the robustness of the learning variables under several specifications. I tentatively explore the impact that learning from financial crises may have had on the decision to lift capital controls. The connections among IMF dictates, financial crises, learning, and sustained financial liberalization seem difficult to disentangle, but are a promising avenue for future research.

5.1. The Political Economy of Capital Account Liberalization[3]

Political economists have been interested in understanding *how* domestic political factors influence the pace and scope of financial liberalization.[4] Political regimes, interest groups, party ideology, labor market institutions, and monetary institutions have been used to explain *different* ways (in terms of pace and scope) to liberalize the capital account. Do

---

[2] This label corresponds to IMF director, Michael Camdessus.

[3] Cohen (1996) and Eichengreen (1996) are two excellent historical accounts of changes in international finance and their consequences for policy making. See Simmons (1999) for a briefer account and Eichengreen (2001) for a review of studies of capital account openness, growth, and financial crises.

[4] Note that I will be exploring only one aspect of financial liberalization: Capital account openness. Other aspects of financial liberalization include the reform of domestic financial systems, and the unification of exchange rates.

146 *Learning and Capital Account Liberalization*

democracies have more open capital accounts than dictatorships? What coalitions are likely to favor or oppose financial liberalization? Given these coalitions, how does partisanship affect capital account liberalization? Do countries with fixed exchange rates have more controlled capital accounts?

Some authors argue that dictators use the control of financial resources to distribute benefits among their supporters and to finance state-led development. Democratic governments, which rely on the median voter for support, would lack the incentive to use the financial system as an instrument of patronage and thus would be more willing to liberalize. However, the preferences of the median voter with regard to capital account liberalization in democracies are far from obvious. According to the Stolper–Samuelson theorem, in advanced (capital-rich) countries, the owners of capital gain from financial liberalization, whereas in developing (labor-rich) countries, incoming capital raises wages and lowers the return to capitalists. Thus, capital account liberalization benefits labor in labor-rich countries (much as trade liberalization does). Note that the Stolper–Samuelson theorem could explain the relationship between democratization and capital account openness. Democratization, especially in less developed countries, implied the enfranchisement of labor, which, according to this theorem, has a stake in financial liberalization.[5] The studies that have tested the relevance of this hypothesis across time and space have found a positive and frequently statistically significant relationship between democracy and greater capital account liberalization (Simmons and Elkins 2004; Quinn and Toyoda 2008).

Who wins and who loses as a result of lifting capital controls? In a seminal paper, Frieden (1991b) spells out the distributional consequences of financial liberalization. The author emphasizes that there are different types of capital, not all of them equally mobile. Using the Ricardo–Viner specific factor model (as opposed to the aforementioned Stolper–Samuelson theorem), the author anticipates that, as a result of increasing capital mobility, capital moves from capital-rich (low interest rate) to capital-poor (high interest rate) countries. As a result, the owners of

---

[5] Milner and Kubota (2005) use this logic to explain the relationship between democratization and trade liberalization in LDCs.

5.1. The Political Economy of Capital Account Liberalization   147

specific factors in capital-poor countries do well whereas the owners of specific factors in capital-rich countries do badly (the former can borrow at lower interest rates now). Thus, the prediction is that, in developed countries, the owners of specific factors will mobilize against financial liberalization whereas the owners of nonspecific factors will lobby for opening. However, uncertainty is pervasive when it comes to anticipating who will win and who will lose as a result of capital account openness.[6]

As with privatization and trade liberalization, these studies provide valuable (although often inconclusive) information regarding the way in which countries liberalize their financial systems. Yet, these studies are at a loss to explain the prior question of why there was a shift toward more open finances in the 1990s. Explanatory models that rely on domestic variables are missing an important part of the story. This has been demonstrated by very recent research that has enriched the extant specifications with variables that place the major source of the drive to lift capital controls outside the domestic realm.

In line with the hypotheses that the present study considers, it could have been the case that the move toward more open finances was related to a shift in views among policy makers and IFIs. As mentioned previously,

---

[6] Quinn and Inclán (1997) go a step beyond these distributive predictions and analyze the relationship between partisanship and capital account openness. They argue that partisan preferences for capital account liberalization depend on whether skilled or unskilled labor is the relatively abundant factor. Contrary to simpler partisan predictions – such as that rightist governments would favor the generic interests of capitalists, Quinn and Inclán argue that leftist governments will *favor* capital account liberalization in countries in which skilled labor is the relatively abundant factor. Apart from the relative endowment of types of labor, the authors also take labor institutions (corporatist or otherwise) and monetary institutions into account. The picture of capital account openness they portray for *advanced countries* only is a complex and nuanced one. Chwieroth (2007) tests for the impact of societal interests on capital account openness in a sample of twenty-nine emerging economies and finds no significant effects.

Regarding exchange rate agreements and capital account liberalization, countries that choose exchange rate stability but also want to enjoy monetary policy autonomy have no option but to restrict the movement of capital. This is a logical consequence of the "impossible trilogy" described earlier. Leblang (1997), for developed countries, and Brune and Guisinger (2007), for developing countries, find that, in fact, fixed exchange rates are related to *less* capital account liberalization. This suggests that countries are reluctant to give up the possibility of using monetary policy in an autonomous way. As Eichengreen (2001) rightly points out in his review, the problems of reverse causality pervade this type of argument. Do countries fix the exchange rates because they have chosen to have a closed capital account, or does causality run in the opposite direction?

148   *Learning and Capital Account Liberalization*

IFIs influence the views of local politicians either through persuasion or through outright coercion, making the lifting of controls a prerequisite for access to their funds. The Washington Consensus did not include capital account openness among its commandments (Williamson 2000: 257). However, the IMF, which originally adopted a permissive stance regarding the use of capital controls (Chwieroth 2008), launched an active crusade in favor of capital account liberalization in the 1990s.[7] Thus, the shift to capital account openness may have resulted from this shift in views and its imposition on countries. The studies that have tested this hypothesis across time and space find little support for it, though. Moreover, some of them even find that owing money to IFIs decreases, rather than increases, the likelihood of more open capital accounts (Simmons and Elkins 2004; Quinn and Toyoda 2008). However, Brune and Guisinger (2007) and Chwieroth (2007) report that being under an IMF agreement is positively related to the degree of capital account openness.[8]

Alternatively, the decision to liberalize the capital account may have been related to horizontal connections among countries. These horizontal connections are of three types: Competitive pressures, learning, and symbolic emulation. Countries that want to have access to a limited pool of resources have to offer better, or at least similar, conditions regarding restrictions on capital mobility (Wahba and Mohieldin 1998; Simmons and Elkins 2004). Thus, if country A competes against country B for capital and country A lifts capital controls, country B will follow suit. This is what the mechanism of competitive pressures amounts to.

Countries may have engaged in financial liberalization because opening the capital account is, generally speaking, a good thing. Investors can diversify risks, investment can be allocated more efficiently, and countries

---

[7] In the original Articles of Agreement, the IMF allowed the use of capital controls that did not interfere with trade transactions. This stance was consistent with the fixed exchange rate regime adopted at Bretton Woods. With fixed exchange rates, capital controls allow monetary policy autonomy.

[8] As mentioned in Chapter 1, the coercion and the persuasion stories are difficult to disentangle in big *N* statistical studies. It may be well be that the IMF teaches rather than imposes, via the dissemination of its policy ideas among an already cohesive economics profession. Chwieroth (2007) offers an alternative test of the impact of ideas on capital account liberalization, showing that the cohesiveness of economic teams led by neo-liberal economists is positively related to the degree of capital account openness.

5.1. The Political Economy of Capital Account Liberalization 149

with insufficient local savings may borrow internationally to finance their development. Thus, capital account openness is, in general, positive for growth. Country A may have seen that country B's decision to liberalize has brought to the country much-needed resources and investment, with good growth results. Thus, country A decides to lift controls because it has learned from the experience of country B that financial liberalization is a good thing.

Finally, symbolic emulation relates to the informational cues given by countries that are similar to each other in some respect. Assume that the government of country A does not know whether to lift capital controls. Yet, this government observes that many other countries have liberalized. In this case, the actual results of financial liberalization are less important than the symbolism attached to the policy and the legitimacy that its adoption may confer. In the limit, if the government of country A observes that most countries similar or dissimilar to it have lifted capital controls, country A is likely to infer (rightly or wrongly) that financial liberalization is the right way to go.

Simmons and Elkins (2004) find evidence that competition for capital and the capital account policies of trade competitors are strong predictors of the decision to lift capital controls. Brune and Guisinger (2007) and Quinn and Toyoda (2008) find that the policies carried out by geographic peers and income peers are relevant in explaining capital account openness. Seeing the policy choices of countries in the neighborhood and of countries with similar levels of development has implications for others. Simmons and Elkins (2004) also report a surprising result: A shared religion is a trait along which capital account liberalization diffuses. This last study also finds that international coercion, proxied by different indicators, is related to capital account closure rather than openness.[9]

Finally, Simmons and Elkins (2004) and Quinn and Toyoda (2008) evaluate the impact of learning. Simmons and Elkins assume that learning is only from success: They include in the analysis the average capital account stance of the five best-performing economies on the assumption that, if learning takes place, the capital account policies of these leaders

---

[9] The most frequent indicators are being under IMF or World Bank conditionality and the amount of aid per capita received.

150 *Learning and Capital Account Liberalization*

should influence the capital account stance in other countries. For capital account openness, the authors find no evidence that this is the case. Quinn and Toyoda (2008) measure learning by including in their models an interaction term between capital account openness and the growth performance of neighboring countries. This is a more accurate indicator in that it assumes that both good performance and bad performance in neighboring countries may affect the degree of openness that others choose. Contrary to Simmons and Elkins, Quinn and Toyoda find that learning from regional peers explains the choices of others.

As I show subsequently, the evidence in favor of the learning hypothesis using a Bayesian approach (which entails learning from own, regional, and world experience, and from the results of alternative policy stances – open and closed) is weak, and not particularly robust in explaining the decision *to adopt* an open capital account. However, it is consequential in explaining the decision *to sustain* an open capital account. Capital competition, trade openness, and IMF agreements appear robust predictors of the probability of opening. However, the impact of the different diffusion variables on the probability of opening is very small.

Before discussing the results of applying the learning model to this policy choice, I describe the data in some detail. As this section makes clear, one possible explanation for the low predictive capacity of the models and the insignificance of learning is that, after all, capital account openness is a policy that is far from having being adopted worldwide. Thus, this policy constitutes an illustration of mild policy convergence in which, however, some signs of policy diffusion are evident.

5.2. Learning and Capital Account Liberalization: The Data

There are several indicators of capital account openness. Some of them are scales that measure the degree of openness (Quinn 1997; Brune and Guisinger 2007; Quinn and Toyoda 2008). Among these indicators, Quinn's (1997) is the most widely used but its geographic coverage is limited to developed countries. Alternatively, there are dichotomous indicators based on the annual IMF volumes on exchange restrictions and controls (Simmons and Elkins 2004). This indicator – which has the value of 1 if the capital account is coded as open and 0 otherwise – certainly

5.2. Learning and Capital Account Liberalization: The Data   151

misses some important information concerning the intensity of controls; but the indicator is suitable for the purpose of explaining shifts in policy (Simmons and Elkins 2004: 176–77). Also, contrary to other indexes, it is available for both developed and developing countries. Most of the experience with capital account liberalization is concentrated in developed countries and is practically nil in some developing regions. Thus, it does not make sense to make an argument about learning from the experience of others by looking at developing countries in an isolated way.[10]

In the data set, there are 3,178 country-year observations that correspond to 129 developed and developing countries grouped in nine regions for the period 1968 through 1996.[11] The list of countries included in the analysis is shown in the Appendix. As it is possible to see in Figure 5.1, the trend in the complete sample is one of mild liberalization. Whereas at the beginning of the period, twenty-nine percent of countries had an open capital account, the figure is roughly the same at the end of the period under study.[12] The years in between were mainly years of capital account closure. The increased openness observed toward the end of the period does not seem to have been motivated by an increase in openness in developing and transitional countries. Of course, talking about developing countries as a uniform group is a fiction. These aggregate figures hide important contrasts. For instance, in Sub-Saharan Africa, a meager six percent of country-year observations are observed under an open capital account, while in Latin America, the figure is thirty-six percent. The opposite is the case for the advanced countries, which are mainly responsible for the overall increase in openness observed in the

[10] Brune and Guisinger (2007) use a thirteen-point scale of capital account liberalization, and their analysis distinguishes capital inflows from outflows and different types of transactions. Their study refers to developing countries only. However, if one is to study the impact of learning from the experience of others, it seems convenient to include the advanced countries in the analysis given that the most extensive experience with capital account liberalization is located precisely in that region.

[11] The regions are Sub-Saharan Africa, South Asia, Southeast Asia, Pacific Islands/ Oceania, Latin America, Middle East/North Africa, Eastern Europe and Soviet Union, Caribbean and Non-Iberian America, and Industrial Countries.

[12] The trend was more dynamic concerning the unification of exchange rates and, above all, the liberalization of the current account. More than eighty percent of the countries had liberalized movements of the current account by the end of the period (Simmons and Elkins 2004).

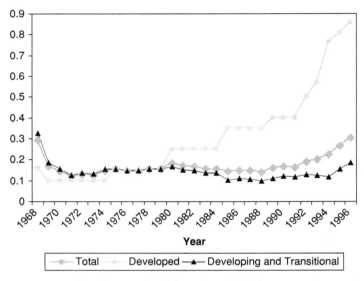

Figure 5.1. Proportion of Countries with an Open Capital Account, 1968–96. Based on 129 developed, transitional, and developing countries. Data on capital account liberalization come from the International Monetary Fund, Annual Exchange Arrangements and Restrictions.

period. In this group, a high eight-five percent of countries were open by 1996. However, the massive adoption of capital account openness is pretty unique to this region. Thus, whereas the data reveal that there has certainly been a shift toward more open capital accounts it is as important not to overstate this trend as it is not to underestimate the persistent variability among regions (see Simmons, Dobbin, and Garrett 2006).

From both theoretical and empirical points of view, there is no consensus on whether capital account openness is unambiguously good or bad for growth. The results of widely cited studies on the topic (Quinn 1997; Rodrik 1998; Obstfeld 1998; Soto 2000; Edwards 2001) are conflicting, although a majority seems to back the idea that an open capital account promotes growth, subject to a host of caveats.[13]

[13] Whereas the theory points in this direction, there are important issues of sequencing and prudential regulation that, if ignored in practice, may cause much more harm than good (Knight 1998; Wahba and Mohieldin 1998; Edwards 1999). The financial crises of the 1990s, to which I devote a subsection, have been related to mistakes in

5.2. Learning and Capital Account Liberalization: The Data   153

Given that the mechanism of learning is crucially related to the outcomes in terms of growth achieved by countries under alternative policies (open and closed), it is important to obtain a sense of what these figures are in the sample. Overall, 548 country-year observations are under an open capital account. The average annual rate of growth for those countries and years was 1.96%. This figure was 1.56% for the 2,630 country-year observations under capital account closure. These average figures point to a relatively mild difference in favor of capital account openness.

A disaggregation of the data by region reveals several facts (see Table 5.1.). First, for the period under study, the experience with capital account liberalization was minimal in South Asia, Middle East and North Africa, the Caribbean and Non-Iberian America, and Eastern Europe.[14] Second, in the developing world, Latin America is the most experienced region with capital account openness. However, the rate of growth of Latin American countries with open capital accounts barely exceeded the rate of growth of closed countries for the period of this study (1.45% versus 1.15%). In the advanced countries, where the bulk of experience with capital account openness accumulated, the average rate of growth for countries and years with an open capital account was actually less than the growth rates of closed countries (1.90% versus 2.93%). Finally, in seven of the nine regions included in the study, the volatility of growth results is higher for countries and years with a *closed* capital account. In general, the very descriptive evidence linking growth and capital account openness is limited and weak, albeit apparently less volatile than the evidence concerning growth and capital account closure.

Figures 5.2 and 5.3(a) and (b) compare the results in terms of growth under open and closed capital accounts for developed, developing, and transitional countries. The preliminary conclusion that can be extracted

---

the implementation of financial liberalization; but these mistakes do not invalidate the general case in favor of a careful and well-designed opening. A deeper discussion is provided subsequently. Edwards (2001) also warns that the positive effect of financial liberalization may accrue to countries at a certain level of economic development, but not to the least developed ones.

[14] The countries with open capital accounts are Maldives (South Asia), Iran (Middle East and North Africa), Belize, Trinidad and Tobago (Caribbean and Non-Iberian America), and Latvia (Eastern Europe).

Table 5.1. *Annual rates of growth and volatility of results by capital account stance and by region*

	Capital account openness			Capital account closure		
Region	% Average growth	Standard deviation	N	% Average growth	Standard deviation	N
Sub-Saharan Africa	1.26	7.25	61	0.55	8.17	975
South Asia	5.45	2.68	11	2.76	5.07	149
South East Asia	5.14	3.72	70	4.19	5.03	87
Pacific Islands/ Oceania	−0.79	3.74	22	1.33	6.07	80
Middle East/North Africa	−3.22	10.25	4	2.41	7.59	272
Latin America	1.45	4.78	191	1.15	5.30	331
Caribbean and Non-Iberian America	−2.35	8.64	7	1.62	7.33	272
Eastern Europe	2.41	2.82	2	0.19	8.30	61
Industrial Countries	1.90	2.40	180	2.93	3.32	403
Total			548			2630

Note: Based on 129 Developed and Developing Countries, 1968–96. IMF Annual Exchange Arrangements and Restrictions, various issues.

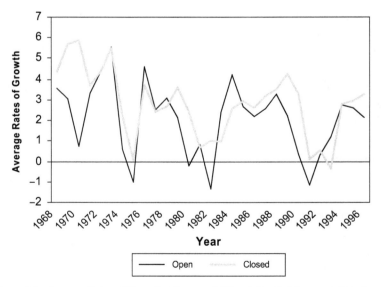

Figure 5.2. Average Rates of Growth, Open and Closed Capital Account, Developed Countries, 1968–96.

5.2. Learning and Capital Account Liberalization: The Data 155

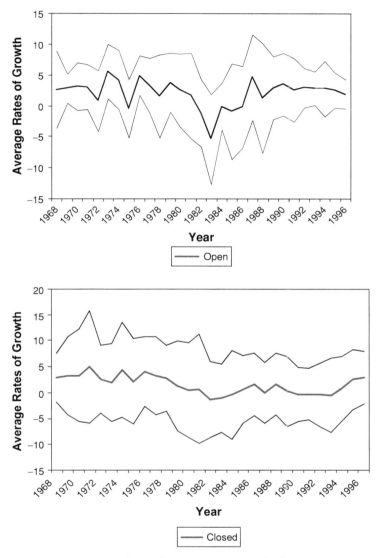

Figure 5.3. Average Rates of Growth and +/− One Standard Deviation, Open and Closed Capital Account Developing and Transitional Countries, 1968–96.

from these figures is that countries with an open capital account experienced deeper recessions in the event of an external shock than did countries with a closed capital account. However, outside the periods of economic crises, countries with an open capital account seem to do better. Also, it seems that having an open capital account is not a hindrance to resuming growth after shocks. Quite the contrary: Apparently, countries with an open capital account experience somewhat faster recoveries in post-shock periods.

In developing countries, growth rates declined and increased almost in parallel under one and the other policy status. Interestingly, in the developing and transitional economies, the countries with an open capital account experienced a dramatic recession and then a dramatic recovery after the debt crisis of the early 1980s. During the first half of the 1990s, the average rates of growth in countries with an open capital account were persistently higher than those of countries with a closed one. It should be clearly stated that these growth figures, once more, may be due to factors other than the capital account stance. Thus, their value is merely descriptive.

This graphic evidence gives preliminary support to the argument in Eichengreen and Leblang (2003). According to these authors, studies that survey the relationship between capital account openness and growth provide inconclusive results because they do not take crises into account. According to the authors, capital controls are good for muddling through financial turmoil; however, in noncrisis periods, capital controls cause the misallocation of investments and thus result in less efficient outcomes. These effects work in opposite directions. Hence, it is not surprising that the studies that measure the impact of capital controls on economic growth averaging over crisis and noncrisis periods are unable to reach clear conclusions regarding the relationship between capital account openness and growth. For sure, the view that capital controls are a good solution for deep recessions in the event of crises (Krugman 1998) is not consensual (Edwards 1999). This is a further reason to test the possible impact that financial crises may have had on the process of learning about the consequences of capital account liberalization and about the best reaction to financial shocks.

5.3. Mexico: A Narrative on Learning, Financial Liberalization, and Financial Crisis[15]

The purpose of this section is to complement the global data on capital account liberalization with a narrative about the role that different mechanisms of policy convergence played in the decision to liberalize the Mexican financial sector. In particular, I use policy makers' accounts to demonstrate that the need to compete for a limited pool of capital was a relevant factor in making decisions to liberalize in the early 1990s and to stay open after the 1995 *peso* crisis (Aspe 1993; Ortiz 1994; Maxfield 1997). I also show that the experience of other countries with certain aspects of financial sector reform – in particular, the opening of the Mexican stock exchange market and the privatization of the banking sector – was taken into account in the design of the Mexican bank disincorporation process (Ortiz 1994; Salinas de Gortari 2000). Moreover, when the financial crisis struck in the mid-1990s, the failures of others and the "lessons" of the 1992–93 ERM crisis were invoked by politicians seeking exoneration (Salinas de Gortari 2000: 1154). Unfortunately, those lessons were used as excuses rather than as a prior guide for policy making. Finally, there are few signs of outright coercion to liberalize on the part of third parties.

The *sexenio* of President José López Portillo (1976–82) ended with a dramatic political response to a dramatic economic situation: The nationalization of the banking sector and the imposition of controls on capital movements. The decision was even more controversial since it was made in opposition to the views of President-elect Miguel de la Madrid (1982–88), who would take office only three months after the nationalization. During the de la Madrid mandate, orthodox reforms such as trade liberalization and privatization of SOEs gathered steam. As in other developing countries, the adoption of market reforms responded to several factors, such as the need to reduce the public deficits (as required in several IMF agreements), abate inflation, and repay the external debt. As de la Madrid acknowledged, the failure of other Latin American countries

---

[15] Unless otherwise stated, all translations are mine.

158   *Learning and Capital Account Liberalization*

with heterodox experiments, particularly Brazil, "deterred any strident impulse" (de la Madrid 2004: 727). Therefore, openness was perceived as the only viable alternative.

However, it was not until the *sexenio* of President Carlos Salinas de Gortari (1988–94), the perfect example of a Harvard-trained technopol, that major steps were taken on all fronts of the market reform agenda, including financial reform. The reform entailed removing a framework based on reserve requirements, selective credit controls, and interest rate ceilings. It also entailed other measures such as opening the stock exchange to foreign investment, the privatization of the banking sector, and the granting of independence to the central bank. According to Santín (2001: 228) the goal of the reform was to create a financial system "where decisions on savings and investment could be made efficiently and in a growth-oriented way."

Concerning the opening of the Mexican Stock Exchange (Bolsa), both Salinas and Aspe believed that attracting foreign portfolio and direct investment was crucial to spurring growth in a country with very low savings rates. The 1989 Act to Promote Domestic Investment and Regulate Foreign Investment permitted foreigners to invest in Mexican public companies through a newly created share class. Given the strong nationalistic sentiment that characterizes Mexican economic policy, a dual system of shares, one for Mexicans and another for foreign investors, was put in place. According to Minushkin (2001: 185), this design was partly inspired by the Philippine experience. The process of financial openness was given a new impetus when, in the late 1980s, the government lifted all restrictions on foreign investment in Mexican Treasury Bills (Cetes). *Bolseros* pressed for this change while the central bank strongly opposed it. This was because the initial design of Cetes deliberately excluded foreign investors after learning from the problems that other Southern Cone countries, particularly Chile, experienced in the early 1980s (Minushkin 2001: 186). The 1989 law, along with the opening of Cetes to foreign investment in 1990, accomplished the complete removal of all barriers to the exit of foreign portfolio investment and nearly all barriers to entry in about two years (Minushkin 2001).

In 1990, the decision was taken to privatize the banking sector as part of a wider process of financial liberalization. The international context of

5.3. Mexico

increased openness and competition for capital was frequently cited as a major motivation for reform. According to Guillermo Ortiz (1994: 8, 36, 39), Deputy Minister of Finance and Director of the Banking Disincorporation Committee, the privatization of the banking sector responded to "the growing integration of financial markets and the international economy." Ortiz (p. 100) added that "the increasing efficiency of our financial system makes possible that Mexico integrates into the world economy in a more competitive, efficient and egalitarian way." The same author stated that among several reasons to liberalize the Mexican financial system was "the openness of the economy to external competition" (p. 170). In the same vein, Finance Minister Pedro Aspe (1993: 81) contended that the banking privatization sought to make Mexican banks better able to compete in an integrated economic environment. Thus, financial openness was seen as the right response to a changing and more competitive international context.

It is also interesting to observe that Mexican policy makers were attentive to lessons from past experience and the experience of others. In particular, concerning the privatization of the banking sector, Guillermo Ortiz (1994: 90) tells the story of several civil servants traveling to North America and Europe "to gather part of the experience" of different countries in the provision of banking services. The Deputy Minister recalls that "some members of the [disincorporation] Committee made a trip to Paris and Lisbon, with the aim of gathering the most relevant aspects of the French and Portuguese experiences with banking privatization..." (p. 229; see also Salinas de Gortari 2000: 437).[16] To keep the banking system in the hands of Mexicans, foreign banks were barred from owning more than thirty percent of any bank.

---

[16] In fact, the privatization of the banks was assisted by external evaluators "to take advantage of their international experience in this field" (p. 228, 232). Also, the participation of international advisors with international experience in selling financial institutions was a response to the "awareness that the involvement of foreign experts would be an extra factor to inspire the confidence that the process required" (Ortiz 1994: 232). Discussing the domestic decision to grant independence to the central bank, the author points at the cases "of New Zealand, Chile, and Colombia to which the legislative proposals currently under debate in France and Spain should be added. Thereby, the granting of independence to the Mexican Central Bank has to be seen in the context of a global trend, also responding to the conditions and the experience of our country" (1994: 124).

160   *Learning and Capital Account Liberalization*

The last year of the Salinas administration (1994) was marked by deep political and economic turmoil. US interest rates rose, making investment in Mexican debt less attractive. The indigenous *Zapatista* uprising in the state of Chiapas in January, the murder of the Partido Revolucionario Institucional (PRI) electoral candidate, Luis Donaldo Colosio, in March, and the assassination of the PRI Secretary-General José Francisco Ruiz Massieu, who was also President Carlos Salinas' brother-in-law, provoked increasing uncertainty about the sustainability of the currency. Whereas Mexican growth rates, public deficit, ratio of public debt to GDP, and inflation rates all showed good numbers, domestic savings were extremely low. Also, a large current account deficit had been developing (almost eight percent of GDP in 1994) due to massive capital inflows that kept the *peso* overvalued. Indeed, following the 1989 law, foreign investment in the stock exchange increased from $2.9 billion in 1991 to $10.7 billion in 1994. This trend made the Mexican economy extremely dependent on capital inflows (Kessler 1999; Santín 2001). Another concern was the weakness of the banking system. It was feared that a rise in interest rates could cause the banking sector to go bankrupt given the large number of bad loans after a credit boom followed the privatization of the banks.

To avoid capital flight and an increase in interest rates, the government swapped *peso*-denominated public debt (Cetes) for short-term dollar-denominated debt (Tesobonos) in what, de facto, constituted an expansionary monetary policy. This type of adjustment was achieved at the cost of depleting the international reserves. Some analysts argued that the tight exchange rate arrangement that served the purpose of stabilizing the economy in the late 1980s should have been relaxed and the *peso* devalued earlier in 1994 (Sachs, Tornell, and Velasco 1995).[17] But upcoming elections and the government's eagerness to court credibility by sticking to a rigid exchange rate commitment postponed the devaluation. Capital fled the country and the international reserves dwindled. Just after President Ernesto Zedillo (1994–2000) took power in December, the situation worsened when news leaked out of an imminent devaluation. The *peso* was finally devalued on December 20, but by then the international reserves were exhausted. Thus, investors' confidence in the

---

[17] In the context of the Solidarity Pact (1987), inflation fell from an annual rate of 159 percent in 1987 to less than twelve percent in 1992 (Santín 2001).

5.3. Mexico

ability of the Mexican government to meet its short-term debt obligations vanished, precipitating the crisis and a painful recession. In 1995, the Mexican economy contracted by seven percent.

In his exonerating account, President Salinas pointed out that Mexico's financial problems resembled the financial difficulties suffered earlier by several European countries. In 1992–93, the currencies of several European countries (Spain, Portugal, and Ireland) experienced devaluations or were forced to leave the ERM as a result of speculative runs on them (Finland, the United Kingdom, Italy, and Sweden). These difficulties were associated with the combined effects of pegged exchange rates and tight credit (Salinas 2000: 1154–55).[18] However, in his policy decisions and his subsequent accounts, Salinas ignored what analysts consider to have been the main lessons of the ERM crisis: (1) Countries should adopt more flexible exchange rate arrangements if full capital mobility is allowed and (2) devaluation has to occur before, not after, reserves are depleted (Sachs, Tornell, and Velasco 1995).

The Mexican response to the crisis was unambiguously liberal. In the face of increasing difficulties in the banking sector, the incoming administration unilaterally opened it to foreign investment and allowed foreign firms to fully own domestic banks (Santín 2001), ahead of the previously agreed-upon timetable in the North American Free Trade Agreement. Also, the government did not consider the possibility of imposing controls on capital movements. This was, in part, due to its own experience of failure with capital controls in response to the 1982 crisis. In fact, at that time, controls could not prevent the hemorrhage of reserves.[19] Also, the intensification of controls on outflows in Spain, Ireland, and Portugal following the ERM crisis failed to prevent a change in the exchange rate. This reinforced the view that capital controls were not an appropriate response to financial stress (Chwieroth 2008).

---

[18] Salinas cited France's Crédit Lyonnais, privatized in 1997, as an illustration of the failures of other bank privatizations (2000: 452). President Salinas also referred to the cases of Thailand and Malaysia to argue that high rates of domestic savings are not a guarantee against financial crisis (2000: 1072). Overall, President Salinas seems to have used foreign experiences to defend himself rather than to learn from them.

[19] As Jesús Silva-Herzog (first finance minister under de la Madrid) recalls, the imposition of capital controls could not prevent a massive hemorrhage of capital. He explains: "despite the exchange controls, or maybe because of them capital flight during the months of September to December 1982 was one of the most severe of our history" (2007: 71).

162   *Learning and Capital Account Liberalization*

Apart from this previous experience, political accounts have empha-sized that governments may have no choice over whether to impose capi-tal controls in the event of a financial crisis (Haggard and Maxfield 1996; Lukauskas and Minushkin 2000). Countries that have a long-standing reputation for macroeconomic stability can afford to impose controls without scaring off investors (say, South Korea). However, countries with a less credible macroeconomic record (for instance, Mexico) may not be able to impose controls if they want to signal a credible commitment to policies that investors value.[20]

Finally, the top-down convergence mechanism of coercion seems not to have been relevant in the Mexican case. IFIs did not impose financial liberalization. Rather, they found that the Mexican economic team was aligned with their views. As Finance Minister Pedro Aspe openly stated, he saw "no contradiction between Mexican sovereignty and respect for IMF guidelines..." (quoted in Santín 2001: 53). The relationship between IFIs and the Mexican economic team was one of "learning through tech-nocratic alignment with transnational epistemic communities" rather than one of imposition (see also Centeno 1994; Santín 2001: 50).

To summarize, according to Kessler (1999: 89), different accounts agree that the "liberalization [of the financial system] was the most viable eco-nomic response to the obvious failure of traditional inward-oriented economic policies, changes in global financial markets, and the pressing need for capital in the wake of the debt crisis." The experience of other countries inspired particular reforms, notably the opening of the *Bolsa* and the privatization of the banking sector. However, despite using it to justify some of its mistakes, the Mexican team did not learn all the lessons from the ERM crisis. Had they learned from it, the Mexican gov-ernment might have been more cautious in regulating capital inflows, as other countries were – notably Chile. Also, had Salinas and his team learned from the ERM crisis, they would have devalued earlier to avoid the depletion of international reserves, but domestic political calculations prevailed. Devaluing with elections coming up was inconceivable. How-ever, the decision to remain open in the aftermath of the crisis is partly

---

[20] Moreover, as other analyses have shown, the imposition of capital controls in the event of crises may not accord with leaders' desire to ameliorate the pain imposed on the citizenry. Interestingly, Johnson and Mitton (2001) show that the controls imposed in Malaysia benefited primarily Mahathir's cronies.

explained by the country's previous experience with capital controls and the experience of European countries following the ERM crisis. In addition, there was the need to restore credibility and, with it, the return of capital. Agreement on views rather than imposition characterized the communication between the Mexican economic elites and the IFIs.

The next section tests the roles that learning, capital competition, and IMF agreements played in the decision to liberalize the capital account using data from many countries. All these mechanisms turn out to be relevant in explaining capital account openness, but their impact on the probability of opening is small.

5.4. Learning and Capital Account Liberalization: The Results

Did governments liberalize the capital account in view of the relatively better growth performance of the countries that had already liberalized? Also, did other mechanisms of diffusion, such as coercion or the spread of global norms, influence the decision to lift capital controls? Finally, are domestic conditions significant in explanations of the decision to open the capital account?

Regarding learning, and in view of the inconclusive theoretical and empirical discussion linking this policy to performance, I remain agnostic as to whether the experience of others was a relevant motive in the drive for liberalization. There seems to be a strong theoretical case for liberalization as long as prudence is present and the sequencing is correct: Liberalization should be accomplished in a stable macroeconomic environment and it should follow rather than precede trade liberalization (Wahba and Mohieldin 1998; World Bank 2005). Capital account openness seems to promote growth when things go well; but it is debatable whether controls should be reimposed in the event of crisis (Mishkin 2000; Corbo 2000).

The impact of learning is measured as previously explained. Own, regional, and world experience with and without an open capital account are compared. It is expected that the greater the growth believed to follow capital account openness as compared with closure after learning from experience, the more likely a switch to that policy will be. I also expect governments to be risk averse – that is, to be less prone to open the capital account the greater the volatility of results is among those

164   *Learning and Capital Account Liberalization*

with an open capital account, and conversely more prone to open the greater the volatility of results among those with closed capital accounts. The same is expected regarding the probability of sustaining a capital account policy: Countries will be more likely to sustain an open capital account the greater their expectations of growth if they sustain this policy as opposed to the growth they expect if the capital account is closed. Concerning the volatility of results, the probability of sustaining an open capital account is expected to be positively related to believing that economic performance will be less volatile with an open capital account after observing own experience and the experience of others. This holds as long as governments are risk averse.

The results of the estimations are shown in columns (1) and (2) of Table 5.2. The results, including the three mechanisms of policy convergence considered in this study (learning, coercion, and emulation), are shown in columns (3) and (4). Consistent with the dynamic probit model explained in Chapter 2, columns (1) and (3) refer to the probability of making a transition *from a closed to an open* capital account. Columns (2) and (4) give information about the probability of it *remaining open* after a switch to that policy. The variable COERCION indicates whether a country, in a particular year, was under an IMF agreement (Vreeland 2003). The variable EMULATION measures the total number of other countries with an open capital account in a particular year. As discussed in the introductory chapter, EMULATION is a measure of unchanneled diffusion that emphasizes global norms. It entails that policies diffuse not because they are understood to be better but because they are thought to be more highly regarded. It is the symbolic rather than the utilitarian value of the policy that motivates its adoption.

I concentrate on the discussion of results that are robust across the two model specifications. Regarding OWN experience, governments adopted risk-prone behavior in their decision to switch. In other words, a high variability in observed performance under an open capital account was not a deterrent to adopting this policy. In fact, it is related to a greater likelihood of opening. Also, the risk-prone behavior entails that highly volatile performances under capital account closure did not prompt governments to abandon this policy and switch to capital account openness. This behavior, which is actually not matched by beliefs about own growth with and without an open capital account (the average results

5.4. Learning and Capital Account Liberalization: The Results 165

Table 5.2. *Probability of launching and sustaining an open capital account (1968–1996)*

Dependent variable: capital account position	Baseline model		Baseline model and alternative diffusion mechanisms	
	Launching (1)	Sustaining (2)	Launching (3)	Sustaining (4)
CONSTANT	−2.00***	0.99***	−2.01***	2.29***
	(−9.41)	(4.26)	(−6.65)	(3.40)
OWN EXPERIENCE				
AVERAGE RESULTS	−0.003	0.02	−0.01	0.03
	(−0.18)	(0.78)	(−0.79)	(1.21)
VARIABILITY OF RESULTS	0.12***	−0.15**	0.14***	−0.13*
	(2.95)	(−2.07)	(3.26)	(−1.75)
REGIONAL EXPERIENCE				
AVERAGE RESULTS	0.01	−0.09	−0.001	0.007
	(0.50)	(−1.07)	(−0.07)	(0.08)
VARIABILITY OF RESULTS	0.06	−0.16**	0.06	−0.15*
	(1.37)	(−2.14)	(1.22)	(−1.84)
WORLD EXPERIENCE				
AVERAGE RESULTS	0.38***	0.57***	0.26**	0.77***
	(3.72)	(3.28)	(2.08)	(3.71)
VARIABILITY OF RESULTS	−0.08	−0.22**	−0.17*	−0.11
	(−0.92)	(−2.22)	(−1.71)	(−1.02)
EMULATION			0.34**	−0.47*
			(2.18)	(−1.90)
COERCION			0.31**	−0.33
			(2.13)	(−1.52)
Log Likelihood	−278.27		−270.90	
LR Chi-Squared	2216.04		2230.78	
p-value for F	0.000		0.000	
Observations	3049		3049	

$^*p < .10$; $^{**}p < .05$; $^{***}p < .01$; z-scores in parentheses; all variables lagged one year.
The Pseudo R^2 is 0.79 and 0.80 respectively. 97% percent of correctly predicted 1s and 0s

are not significant), hints at nonrational behavior related to unfounded expectations about performance under capital account openness. However, as I show in the simulations that follow, the impact of these beliefs is robust but very small in magnitude.

In the models that refer to the probability of *sustaining* the policy (2 and 4), countries do behave in the expected risk-averse way: The probability of sustaining an open capital account was negatively related to the volatility of outcomes under this policy as concluded from own experience with it. The result also holds for the relative volatility observed in a country's region. Countries are less likely to keep the capital account open the greater the volatility of results under capital account openness is expected to be.

A robust result across models is that LEARNING FROM AVERAGE EXPERIENCE, WORLD (excluding own and regional experience) affected the decision to lift controls and the decision to sustain this policy. Countries were more likely to open the capital account and to keep it open if, according to their posterior beliefs based on the experience in the world, the expected growth was higher with an open capital account. It could well be that the aggregate experience in the world made up for the lack of sufficient and relevant experience in quite a few regions. It is thus rational for a government wanting to learn about the expected impact of capital account openness on economic growth to look beyond the scant information available in its neighborhood.

Finally, the IMF played a significant role in the decision to liberalize: As expected, countries under an IMF agreement were more likely to open. However, being under an IMF agreement is not related to the probability of sustaining an open capital account. The number of other countries with an open capital account in the world (EMULATION) is also significant, with the expected sign. But, unexpectedly, a large number of other countries was negatively related to the probability of keeping the capital account open. All in all, the decision to *sustain* an open capital account appears positively related to observing a better performance in the world and negatively related to a higher volatility of performance under capital account openness in own and the regional results.

Some simulations of the impact of the significant variables on the probability of opening the capital account show that the role neither of the learning variables nor of the alternative diffusion hypotheses should be overstated, though. Variation in one standard deviation around the mean of variables VARIABILITY OF RESULTS, OWN; AVERAGE RESULTS, WORLD; and EMULATION increases the probability of opening the capital account by barely 2, 0.6, and 1 percentage points respectively. Going from not being to being under an IMF agreement increases a country's probability of opening the capital account by a meager 0.7 percentage points.

In the next section, I subject these results to further international and domestic controls. I also entertain the hypothesis that the weak results of learning from experience with this policy may have to do with the averaging problems identified by Eichengreen and Leblang (2003). If capital controls have different effects on growth in crisis and noncrisis periods, models that do not explicitly take economic shocks into account are likely to provide misleading results regarding the relationship between capital controls and growth and, therefore, between learning from experience and subsequent policy decisions.

I model the shocks by increasing the uncertainty attached to the beliefs that politicians hold regarding capital account positions and economic growth. Although the intervention makes them more attentive to actual data, the intervention does not artificially impose policy switches in light of strongly contradictory evidence.

Learning and Financial Crises

Are the results just discussed robust to the inclusion of other control variables such as competitive pressures or domestic characteristics? Columns (1) and (2) in Table 5.2 show the results of a model with several controls in addition to the two alternative diffusion mechanisms (COERCION and EMULATION). REGIME (Gandhi 2004) and OPENNESS (exports and imports as a percentage of GDP, World Development Indicators) capture two domestic characteristics: Are democracies more likely to open, and are countries that are more open to trade more likely to have liberal capital accounts? As explained, democratically elected governments may have an interest in providing the general population with better access to credit instead of using the financial system as a tool of patronage to distribute benefits. Regarding the impact of trade openness, capital account liberalization is considered a side effect of the liberalization of trade. Nations that conduct multilateral trade require financing and therefore cannot forgo their reliance on the international financial system. Simmons and Elkins (2004) report a positive answer for both questions. The authors also find that the capital account position of countries that

168   *Learning and Capital Account Liberalization*

are capital and trade competitors is crucial to explaining the decision to open the capital account. Pressed by the need to remain competitive, countries adopt the same policies as in their network of competitors (CAPITAL COMPETITION and TRADE COMPETITION).[21]

The same is true for countries that share the same religion (RELIGION PARTNERS). Surprisingly, religion is the only "cultural" trait of the many that Simmons and Elkins consider that seems to influence the decision to liberalize.[22] Finally, and importantly for this discussion, the authors find that currency crises increase the probability of the capital account being liberalized (CURRENCY CRISES). Simulations of the impact of this variable show that the probability of maintaining a restrictive capital account is lower for countries and years experiencing a currency crisis, but the impact of this variable is small. To test the relevance of this factor, I borrow the indicator used by Leblang (2003), which measures abnormally strong market pressures for currency depreciation with a dummy variable.

As can be seen in Model 1, none of the learning variables is significant in explaining the decision to liberalize the capital account once controls were included in the specification, although learning from the volatility of own results is close to being statistically significant ($p = 0.11$). The number of other countries in the world with an open capital account loses significance, whereas the IMF continues to be associated with the decision to eliminate controls. Simmons and Elkins's results regarding trade competition, capital competition, and the degree of openness hold. The capital account policies of both trade and capital competitors are positively related to the decision to liberalize. However, these authors'

---

[21] Simmons and Elkins (2004) measure diffusion using a set of spatial lagged variables (see also Franzese and Hays 2006; Swank 2006). Spatial lags weigh the value of the dependent variable (in this case, capital account liberalization) along possible channels of influence, be they geographic distances among countries, networks of trade or capital competitors that may alter the material payoffs of policies, or shared affiliations. For instance, concerning trade competition, the spatial lag was calculated by measuring "distances" among countries that trade the most and that trade similar exports. Concerning capital competition, the spatial lag measures "distances" among countries with similar risk ratings. Those distances are then used to weigh the capital account positions of the tenth of the sample "closer" to the country in question in terms of trade relations or competition for capital. I am grateful to Zach Elkins for sharing the data and the weights.

[22] The authors also considered shared colonial heritage and language besides other affiliation data.

5.4. Learning and Capital Account Liberalization: The Results   169

results regarding political regime, currency crises, and shared religion as a channel of diffusion do not hold in this specification and estimation model. According to the results, democracies were more likely to have an open capital account, currency crises reduced rather than increased the probability of removing controls, and sharing religion increased the probability of liberalizing. However, none of the three results reached statistical significance.

These variables are surprisingly weak in explaining the decision to *sustain* an open capital account (Model 2). One learning variable – own experience with and without controls – is significant and signed as expected. Again, it seems that observing good growth results from financial opening was crucial for countries to pursue capital account openness in a sustained way. Yet, this variable is statistically significant only in this specification. The policy stance of trade competitors was also significant, but reverses its sign: The probability of keeping an open capital account is negatively related to the policies of trade competitors.[23] Overall, the explanatory model of the decision *to remove* capital controls seems to be a poor explanatory model of the decision *to sustain* the policy.[24]

Thus, after competition and other domestic characteristics are controlled for, learning loses the little explanatory power that it had in the baseline model. One result is robust so far, though: Being under an IMF agreement was positively related to the probability of opening the capital account. Chwieroth's (2007) study of capital account liberalization in emerging economies backs the results of this chapter. What it is not possible to discern in the statistical approach is when the views of the IMF were and were not shared by domestic elites, as the case of Mexico showed.

The last model specification (columns 3 and 4) in Table 5.3 adds a twist to the story of the adoption of an open capital account: Do these results differ if learning from the financial crises of the 1990s is modeled? Did governments learn from these crises, and did the learning affect their decisions concerning this policy? I model policy makers' beliefs about what outcomes to expect from financial openness as conveying more

---

[23] Interestingly, Simmons and Elkins find a similar result: The capital account position of trade competitors is negatively (not positively) related to the decision to adopt a restrictive policy, although, in their model, this result is not statistically significant.

[24] Brune and Guisinger (2007) report similar results for their model specification concerning the probability of sustaining an open capital account in developing countries using a dynamic logit estimation.

Table 5.3. *Probability of launching and sustaining an open capital account. Financial crises (1968–1996)*

Dependent variable = capital account position	Competition and domestic controls		Financial crises and intervention	
	Launching (1)	Sustain (2)	Launching (3)	Sustain (4)
CONSTANT	**−3.26*****	3.61	**−3.34*****	**2.53****
	(−2.71)	(1.28)	(−3.46)	(2.12)
OWN EXPERIENCE				
AVERAGE RESULTS	−0.03	**0.14****	−0.02	0.05
	(−1.07)	(2.39)	(−0.87)	(1.33)
VARIABILITY OF RESULTS	0.10	−0.17	**0.11***	**−0.20***
	(1.60)	(−1.18)	(1.76)	(−1.67)
REGIONAL EXPERIENCE				
AVERAGE RESULTS	0.02	−0.22	−0.1E-2	−0.02
	(0.43)	(−0.94)	(−0.02)	(−0.15)
VARIABILITY OF RESULTS	0.10	0.18	0.07	−0.08
	(1.25)	(0.71)	(1.01)	(−0.63)
WORLD EXPERIENCE				
AVERAGE RESULTS	0.31	−0.49	**0.33***	**0.98*****
	(1.39)	(−0.63)	(1.83)	(3.18)
VARIABILITY OF RESULTS	−0.07	0.08	−0.12	−0.06
	(−0.34)	(0.15)	(−0.91)	(−0.41)
EMULATION	−0.25	−0.30	−0.23	**−0.90***
	(−0.55)	(−0.29)	(−0.61)	(−1.92)
COERCION	**0.53****	−0.46	**0.55****	−0.19
	(2.25)	(−1.21)	(2.53)	(−0.72)
REGIME	−0.10	−0.04	0.02	−0.07
	(−0.44)	(−0.12)	(0.12)	(−0.23)
OPENNESS	**0.005****	0.005	**0.004****	**0.01*****
	(2.25)	(0.94)	(2.10)	(2.72)
CAPITAL COMPETITION	**0.18***	−0.02	**0.21****	0.04
	(1.94)	(−0.29)	(2.35)	(0.52)
TRADE COMPETITION	**0.18****	**−0.46****	**0.16****	−0.14
	(2.48)	(−2.20)	(2.53)	(−1.33)
CURRENCY CRISES	−0.13	0.10		
	(−0.51)	(0.25)		
RELIGION PARTNERS	0.16	0.14	0.07	0.05
	(1.41)	(0.43)	(0.76)	(0.36)
Log Likelihood	−140.74		−181.10	
LR Chi-Squared	1526.48		1669.33	
p value for F	0.000		0.000	
Observations	2037		2307	

*$p < .10$; **$p < .05$; ***$p < .01$; z-scores in parentheses; all variables lagged one year. The Pseudo R^2 are 0.84 and 0.82 respectively. 96% percent correctly predicted 1s and 0s.

5.4. Learning and Capital Account Liberalization: The Results 171

uncertainty. The greater uncertainty makes decision makers more attentive to actual performance under an open and a closed capital account.

As mentioned earlier, during the 1990s, several countries experienced severe speculative attacks. The ERM was the first victim in 1992–93, although, in this case, the currency crisis did not translate into fully fledged financial crises. Mexico was next in 1994–95. In 1997–98, several Asian countries experienced similar attacks, starting with the baht in Thailand. The "Asian flu" soon affected Malaysia, the Philippines, and Indonesia. This flu proved to be capable of transatlantic travel, forcing the flotation of the Brazilian real in 1999. Similar episodes include the financial crisis in Russia in 1998 and Argentina's traumatic abandonment of the currency board in late 2001–early 2002 (Mishkin 1996, 2000; Mussa 2002).

Unlike previous financial crises caused by sharp macroeconomic imbalances, the new crises could not be explained in terms of big macroeconomic disequilibria. On the contrary, these crises were the consequence of financial panics that led investors en masse to try to dump the currency in question. The ex post reading of these financial panics was related to credit booms and imprudent behavior on the part of investors following the process of financial liberalization undertaken in the 1990s.[25] Basically, many countries contracted short-term debt, frequently denominated in U.S. dollars, in a proportion that made investors worry about the capacity of governments to honor those debts given the countries' levels of international reserves. Thus, there was a maturity mismatch: Short-term international liabilities were far greater than short-term assets. This mismatch caused the financial panics and the subsequent runs on the currencies.[26]

Two issues are relevant to the lessons that can be learned from the financial turmoil. First, there is general agreement that mistakes in the

---

[25] Chang (1999) is an excellent account of financial crises in emerging markets. Mishkin (2000) offers an interesting discussion of the relationships among banking crises, currency crises, and financial crises. It was the weakness of the banking system, in turn related to the mistakes of the liberalization process, that turned currency crises into fully fledged financial crises in a good number of emerging markets.

[26] As shown in the Mexican case, the crises had also a political side. Governments in countries such as South Korea, Indonesia, or Malaysia used the financial sector actively and as a political instrument to favor parts of the private sector. In these countries, the lack of transparency in business–government relations and of political checks on business was reflected in the perverse influence of owners of financial institutions (Haggard 2000).

172   *Learning and Capital Account Liberalization*

process of financial liberalization encouraged the imprudent behavior just described. The unconditional promotion of capital account liberalization downplayed issues of sequencing and prudential regulation, which proved catastrophic. Second, there is little agreement about what to do in the face of these crises. Does the reimposition of capital controls help ameliorate the economic recession or, on the contrary, does it deepen the crisis? Some authors claim that, once reimposed, capital controls tend to stay, which sends a very negative signal to investors. Thus, using capital controls only delays the very much needed return of capital inflows, postponing economic recovery. Against this, some authors argue that imposing capital controls, as long as they are temporary, helps countries to muddle through the crisis without having to increase interest rates, which would only worsen the recession. Finally, other authors contend that controls on capital inflows, but not on capital outflows, help prevent and overcome financial crises, and even the former should be subject to caveats (Krugman 1998; Edwards 1999; Corbo 2000; Mishkin 2000; Stiglitz 2002; Eichengreen and Leblang 2003).[27] Unfortunately, empirical research going beyond particular cases is scarce, and, overall, many aspects of financial liberalization and the appropriate reaction to financial crises remain obscure (Srinivasan 2000).

Thus, in principle, learning could have been about (1) the risks of a too-rapid and too-imprudent financial liberalization, and (2) the convenience of closing the capital account in the event of a run against one's currency in order to minimize the subsequent recession. However, given the prevailing lack of consensus, particularly about point (2), I do not expect learning from these financial crises to have been a major cause of financial openness. On the contrary, it makes more sense to stipulate that financial crises may have affected views and beliefs about the preceding decision to liberalize the capital account and, therefore, about whether to reimpose controls or keep the account open. Hence, learning from financial crises may have been consequential in the decision to *sustain* an open capital account rather than the decision to adopt it.

---

[27] The experience of Malaysia under Mahathir in 1998 seems to support this view. China and Venezuela are two other frequently cited examples of the successful imposition of capital controls to fend off contagion in the face of financial crises. However, some authors argue that positive results from closure, particularly in China, are exceptions to the rule. A fierce attack on the policies pursued by the IMF in response to the financial crises can be found in Stiglitz (2002).

5.4. Learning and Capital Account Liberalization: The Results   173

I modeled the financial crises by introducing an intervention in the learning process in two years: 1993 (following the ERM crisis) and 1995 (following the Mexican tequila hangover).[28] The intervention, which consists in attributing more uncertainty to politicians' beliefs about the growth rates of opening as opposed to closing the capital account, makes policy makers more attentive to actual performances. Thus, providing governments choose policies rationally, whether or not they change policy course will be closely related to learning from experience under alternative policies observed around those years.

Columns (3) and (4) provide the results of the estimation after the intervention is included. Several issues stand out: First, CAPITAL COMPETITION, TRADE COMPETITION, OPENNESS and agreements with the IMF continue to be significant in explaining countries' decisions to open the capital account. These variables have the expected positive sign. In particular, being under an IMF agreement was a significant predictor in every specification I tried. Interestingly, some of the learning variables regain statistical significance after the financial crises of the 1990s are modeled. Second, governments were risk prone despite the high variability of results with an open capital account given own experience. Moreover, both for the *decision to open* the capital account and for the *decision to keep it open*, observing the experience under alternative policy stances (open and closed) in the WORLD was important. In other words, policy makers' posterior beliefs about average growth with an open capital account as compared with their beliefs about performance without it were related to a greater probability of opening and remaining open.

Some simulations may help to clarify the impact of learning. All simulations are based on Models 3 and 4 (those that consider financial crises) and with the rest of the variables set at their mean values. As can be

---

[28] In one of the models I estimated, I included an intervention for the year 1983, following the debt crisis. Note that, because, in principle, that crisis was not related to financial liberalization but to macroeconomic imbalances, the impact it may have had on the reassessment of the desirability of financial liberalization should be small. In fact, the effect that learning has when only the financial crises of the 1990s are considered vanishes completely when the 1982 debt crisis is also modeled. This may also be explained by the fact that most countries' immediate response to the 1982 debt shock was capital closure rather than openness, as the Mexican story indicated. Results are available from the author.

174 *Learning and Capital Account Liberalization*

Table 5.4. *Change in predicted probability of launching and sustaining an open capital account (percentage points)*

Predictors	Switch to capital account openness	Sustaining capital account openness
VARIABILITY OF EXPERIENCE, OWN	0.8	−3
AVERAGE RESULTS, WORLD	0.6	8
COERCION	0.1	
EMULATION		−5
CAPITAL COMPETITION	0.4	
TRADE COMPETITION	0.5	
TRADE OPENNESS	0.4	19

Note: Changes in predicted probabilities of moving one standard deviation around the mean of the relevant predictors, based on Models 3 and 4. All other variables were set at their mean values. For IMF agreements, the relevant change is from 0 to 1.

seen in Table 5.4, the impact of learning is of a higher magnitude when it comes to explaining the probability of sustaining an open capital account rather than the probability of opening it in the first place. This result is in line with lesson (1) presented previously: The decision to open the capital account preceded the financial crises, and, thus, learning from the crises and its impact on economic growth could hardly be a motivation for engaging in its adoption in the first place.

Of the significant predictors in the story of *opening* the capital account, being under an IMF agreement appears as the most robust and relevant determinant. Yet, the magnitude of the impact is small: The probability that a country under an IMF agreement opens its capital account is only one percentage point greater than that of a country without it. The small impact applies equally to the other significant predictors of capital account liberalization.[29] By contrast, concerning the decision *to sustain* an open capital account, it is possible to see that learning from own volatility of outcomes and learning from the experience in the world

[29] The positive impact of learning from the results in the world and of the competition variables in the decision to adopt an open capital account is relevant in magnitude for very high values of the variables (excluding outliers). It seems that, for these predictors to have relevant impact, it is necessary to have learned from the world experience that capital account openness is substantially superior to capital account closure and from a network of capital competitors in which openness is predominant.

5.4. Learning and Capital Account Liberalization: The Results   175

were significant, with the expected signs. In particular, governments' risk-prone behavior applied to the decision to adopt capital account liberalization, but not to sustaining it. Also, after the financial crises are modeled to make policy makers more attentive to the impact of the capital account stance on growth in the years following the crises, learning from the experience in the world was consequential to *sustaining* an open capital account.[30] Thus, these crises seem not to have questioned the desirability of capital account openness, although a debate (which intensified at the end of the 1990s) was initiated about the correct speed of, and the preconditions for, "good" capital account openness.

A significant counterintuitive result is that the network of other liberal countries reduces the probability that a country will remain open. Recall that, in this study, the number of other countries that have adopted a policy was taken to be a proxy of the extent to which a particular policy is considered to be a social norm, with intrinsic value for symbolic reasons. It may be that the heated controversy concerning the too-imprudent liberalization of capital flows, which included a confrontation among IFIs, had very prestigious economists as vocal actors, and was widely aired by the press, threw some doubt on the international legitimacy of a big bang approach to capital account liberalization. Note, however, that, despite the moderate impact of (negative) emulation on the probability of sustaining the policy, it was the extent to which a country is embedded in the international economy that exerts the strongest pressure on the capital account stance. The more a country trades, the more likely it is to sustain an open capital account.

In sum, the story of capital account liberalization seems to be one in which countries learned, and responded to their degree of openness and to the policies of their competitors. The fact that governments adopted the policies of their capital competitors and liberalized if the latter did is not a tenable explanation unless governments strongly believed that attracting capital, and thus competing for it, is a good thing for their economies. Hence, it is reasonable to wonder whether governments learned from experience that this is the case. After several variables are controlled for, it seems that the experience of others mattered, but mostly

---

[30] In Latin America, Brooks and Kurtz (2007) find that the 1995 year dummy to account for the Mexican tequila effect is positively related to capital account openness.

176 Learning and Capital Account Liberalization

to the decision *to sustain* a capital account and only after financial crises were taken into account. Despite mounting criticisms, the calls to remain open in the event of a crisis seem to have allowed growth to resume relatively quickly on average (World Bank 2005), although with dramatic social costs (Haggard 2000). The role of the IMF cannot be disregarded in view of the results. In a rather counterintuitive way, recent studies hold that being under IMF conditionality is, if anything, negatively related to the degree of capital account openness.[31] However, simulations of the impact of this variable on the probability of opening suggest that being under an IMF agreement increases the probability of opening only by between one and two percentage points depending on model specification. Note also that the impact of the IMF may be overdetermined in the model: Some countries faced so many credibility problems that they simply could not afford not to be even more orthodox than the IMF required (Weyland 2002). That Mexico would have experienced a milder recession had it imposed restrictions on capital flows in response to the 1994 attack is a reasonable assumption. For some, it is also a reasonable assumption that investors would have interpreted this decision as a lack of commitment to sound policies, delaying the return of much-needed investment.

Finally, note two negative findings of the empirical tests. First, the number of others in the world or herding on the views of many others carrying out that policy either was rarely significant in explaining the decision to liberalize or was significant with the opposite sign. It seems that in quite a few regions the number of other countries with an open capital account never reached the stipulated minimum threshold to make others herd on that decision. However, this finding may also have to do with the controversy that surrounded this policy in the postcrisis environment and that may have questioned its international legitimacy. The second negative finding is that the political regime appears inconsequential in explaining capital account liberalization. In particular, democracies were not more likely to liberalize their capital accounts.

Overall, the analysis backs the idea that, since the impact of capital account liberalization on growth seems not to be unconditional,

---

[31] For instance, in a recent World Bank Report (2005: 205) it is openly stated that African countries turned to financial liberalization in the 1990s "often in the context of stabilization and reform programs supported by International Monetary Fund and World Bank."

distinguishing between crisis and noncrisis contexts is the appropriate way to assess whether learning from experience had any relevance for the decision to liberalize the capital account in the 1990s. Note that these results are preliminary. A more definitive account of the impact of financial crises on learning and policy choices would require extending the analysis to model the shocks in East Asia, Russia, Brazil, Turkey, and Argentina. These were the crises that most deeply questioned the big bang approach to capital account liberalization. However, it seems that the consensus on the long-run desirability of this policy remains solid (Chwieroth 2008).

5.5. Discussion

Is learning a plausible explanation of countries' decisions to open the capital account? It seems hard to give a clear-cut and unambiguous answer to this question, as it is hard to answer the many questions concerning the relationship between capital account liberalization, financial crises, and economic growth. Developed countries are completely open to capital flows, and many developing countries followed this trend. Important regional differences remain, however, and many countries still resort to capital controls. Indeed, at the end of the period analyzed in this chapter (1997), only thirty percent of the 129 countries included were classified as open.

There is a strong theoretical case in favor of financial liberalization. Especially in developing countries, incoming flows of capital can make up for scarce local savings, thus helping to finance the process of economic development. However, these inflows may have important destabilizing effects. As the Mexican narrative showed, when financial openness is not tilted in favor of long-term capital and when the regulatory framework does not punish excessive risk taking, capital is likely to flee as soon as investors' confidence is shaken, with or without good reason. Thus, analysts insist that financial liberalization is not unconditionally good. Correct sequencing and prudential regulation are essential if countries are to fully grasp the benefits of financial openness.

Two possible lessons could have been learned regarding growth and financial liberalization. One lesson is related to the fact just mentioned: Capital account openness is good for growth only if certain prerequisites are met. Thus, unconditional adoption of financial liberalization does not make sense. The second lesson relates to whether a temporary resort to capital controls is advisable when countries confront currency crises. In this case, theory and empirics are less conclusive. Moreover, it seems that, from a credibility and reputation point of view, countries are not completely free to choose which way to go. As the Mexican narrative illustrated, countries with a bad record for macroeconomic stability may be unable to choose policies that could question their credibility. Moreover, previous experience may indicate that establishing controls on capital movements is not the solution.

In the view of such an inconclusive case for the liberalization of capital controls, why did governments increasingly liberalize in the 1990s? According to this study and others, countries opened their capital accounts because greater integration demanded it, because their competitors had already done so, and because the IMF advocated it. Yet, the magnitude of all these effects is small. Thus, this leaves open the question as to why countries embraced capital account openness. According to recent research (Stiglitz 1998, 2000; Chwieroth 2007, 2008), part of the answer may be the prevalence of an idea that, despite being hotly debated in academic circles, made its way into policy circles in its most radical incarnation.

Learning from the experience of others mattered only when financial crises were taken into account. Adopting capital account openness and sustaining this policy were positively related to learning from the experience with capital controls in the world. Given the meager experience that most countries and regions had had with capital account openness, this result is not surprising. It is important to emphasize that learning played a more relevant role in the decision to sustain rather than to initiate capital account liberalization. Learning from the responses to financial crises, and from the consequences of those responses for economic growth in the world, was crucial to staying open. But, most prominently, the international economic context in which a particular country operated dictated which capital account stance was to be sustained.

All in all, the results of this chapter add up to a call for further inquiry beyond anecdotes about whether countries that do not impose capital controls in the face of crises resume growth faster, conditional on their past macroeconomic performance and hence on their bargaining position vis-à-vis IFIs and private investors.

APPENDIX

Table A5.5. *Prior parameters, capital account openness*

	Openness		Closure	
Year	Mean	Variance	Mean	Variance
1968	1.65	16	1.81	25
1969	2.67	36	3.27	25
1971	2.73	16	3.86	64
1972	3.06	9	4.68	100
1973	1.35	25	2.97	36
1974	5.54	16	2.72	49
1976	−0.64	16	1.7	64
1978	3.09	16	3.09	49
1979	1.79	36	2.73	36
1980	3.46	16	1.74	64
1981	1.79	25	0.78	64
1982	1.39	36	0.69	100
1985	1.04	16	0.04	64
1986	0.5	36	0.95	36
1987	0.7	25	1.71	36
1990	2.59	16	0.72	49
1991	2.21	25	0.1	25
1993	1.78	9	−0.28	36

Note: Based on observed average and variance of growth results in the world the year before entry in the database.

Table A5.6. *Descriptive statistics, capital account openness*

	Mean	s.d.	Minimum	Maximum
Beliefs Average Growth, Own	−.43	4.13	−30.00	40.61
Beliefs Variability Growth, Own	−2.04	2.47	−14.91	3.03
Beliefs Average Growth, Region	−.88	2.47	−19.22	9.98
Beliefs Variability Growth, Region	−1.63	1.49	−9.17	4.46
Beliefs Average Growth, World	−.24	.72	−2.45	4.04
Beliefs Variability Growth, World	−2.06	.80	−6.44	1.37
Policies of Capital Competitors	2.27	1.36	0	10
Policies of Religion Partners	2.24	1.08	0	8.57
Policies of Trade Competitors	1.92	1.35	0	6.36
Regime	.56	.49	0	1
Number of Other Countries	1.84	.48	1	3.3
IMF Agreement	.34	.47	0	1
Exports plus Imports/GDP	63.84	42.34	6.32	423.41
Currency Crises	.17	.38	0	1

Table A5.7. *List of countries, capital account openness*

Sub-Saharan Africa	Latin America	Advanced Countries	Pacific Islands	North Africa, Middle East	South Asia	Eastern Europe	South East Asia	Caribbean, Non-Iberian America
Angola	Costa Rica	Austria	Fiji	Morocco	Bangladesh	Georgia	Indonesia	Belize
Benin	Dom. Republic	Denmark	Papua N Guinea	Israel	India	Latvia	Laos	Santa Lucia
Botswana	El Salvador	Finland	Solomon	Jordan	Nepal	Romania	Malaysia	Bahamas
Burundi	Guatemala	France	Vanuatu	Syria	Pakistan	Poland	Philippines	Barbados
Cameroon	Honduras	Greece	Western Samoa	Turkey	Bhutan	Hungary	Singapore	Grenada
Cape Verde	Mexico	Iceland	Kiribati	Algeria	Maldive	Bulgaria	Thailand	Haiti
CAR	Nicaragua	Ireland		Egypt	Sri Lanka			Jamaica
Chad	Panama	Italy		Tunisia				Trinidad and Tobago
Comoro	Argentina	Malta		Iran				Guyana
Congo	Bolivia	Netherlands		Irak				Suriname
Djibuti	Brazil	Norway						Dominica
Namibia	Chile	Portugal						St. Kitts/Nevis
Ethiopia	Ecuador	Spain						St. Vincent
Gambia	Colombia	Switzerland						
Gabon	Paraguay	Sweden						
Ghana	Peru	Australia						
Guinea	Uruguay	United Kingdom						
G-Bissau	Venezuela	Japan						
Côte d'Ivoire		New Zealand						
Kenya		United States						
Lesotho		Canada						
Liberia								
Madagascar								
Malawi								
Mali								
Mauritania								
Mauritius								
Mozambique								
Níger								
Nigeria								
Rwanda								
Senegal								
Seychelles								
Sierra Leone								
Somalia								
Sudan								
Tanzania								
Togo								
Uganda								
Zaire								
Zambia								

SIX

Learning and IMF Agreements

The degree of confidence that governments have in IMF conditionality depends in part on the effects that it has had in the past.

Bird (1996b: 495)

In this final empirical chapter, I explore whether governments entered into agreements with the International Monetary Fund as a result of learning from the performance of these agreements.

The standard view of IMF activities is as follows. Countries confronting balance-of-payment (BoP) problems can weather them by resorting to IMF loans. Because the existence of a lender of last resort may create moral hazard problems, the IMF exchanges loans for conditions. Conditionality entails several austerity measures aimed at removing basic macroeconomic imbalances (stabilization) and creating the conditions for sustainable growth (adjustment). Typically, these measures involve fiscal austerity (cutting government spending and increasing taxes), a tight monetary policy (raising interest rates and reducing credit creation), and currency devaluation (Taylor 1993: 41–42; Bird 1996a; Bordo and James 2000; Dreher 2002; Lee 2002; Vreeland 2003). As Guitián (1995) pointed out, there is a high degree of coincidence between IMF policy prescriptions and the package of policies envisaged in the Washington Consensus.[1]

---

[1] According to Guitián (1995: 812), "there are significant areas of common ground between this economic policy consensus [the Washington Consensus] and the policy framework underpinning IMF conditionality practices, both in concept and in practice."

Because these measures are unpopular, it is assumed that governments turn to the IMF only when they *need* a loan – that is, only when they face an acute BoP crisis or when they run out of foreign reserves. Yet, a closer look shows that governments may turn to the IMF even if, on those criteria, they do not need loans. Participation in IMF programs is also surprising given that IMF programs do not result in a better growth performance (Vreeland 2003).

Studying whether entering into IMF agreements has anything to do with learning from the experience of others is interesting for at least one reason: IMF conditionality includes (among others) the policies that I have surveyed so far. Learning was relevant to explaining privatization, trade liberalization, and capital account liberalization. In the last two cases, learning was significant only after the 1982 debt crisis and the early 1990s financial crises, respectively, were modeled. In the case of capital account liberalization, the impact of learning was very small, at least on the decision to adopt the policy. The relevant question is whether IMF packages are a mere aggregation of these policies or, alternatively, IMF programs have costs other than the policies they prescribe. Besides, exploring the decision to enter into IMF agreements is illuminating from the point of view of adding nuisance to the coercion mechanism. As recent studies have shown, there is more to IFIs' participation in market reforms than blatant coercion suggests (Thacker 1999; Stone 2002; Vreeland 2003).

As I show, learning from the world experience with IMF agreements is significant to explaining the signing of agreements. This result is robust in three different model specifications: One that considered only learning, a second that looked into the effects of domestic economic and political controls in the decision to sign, and a third that explored the impact of learning after the 1982 debt crisis was modeled. However, despite this positive result for learning, it is important to emphasize that domestic economic and political factors did prevail over learning in the decision to switch.

In the different model specifications, several results suggest that IMF packages are not a mere aggregation of the policies they advocate. For instance, the baseline model of learning reveals a quite persistent willingness to take risks. This may have to do with the bad economic prospects faced by the governments that turned to the IMF. Also, recall that, for the adoption of development strategies and capital account liberalization, learning from experience was significant only after the impact of several shocks was modeled on policymakers' beliefs. It was learning from the shocks, rather than learning during normal times, that, in part, explained the switches.[2] Contrary to this finding, modeling the shock as an increase in the uncertainty about what to expect from IMF programs following the 1982 crisis reduces, rather than increases, the leverage of learning as a motive to sign contracts. This result is easy to reconcile with the fact that, even after initial conditions are controlled for, IMF agreements have been proven not to be good for growth.

As for the decision to sustain the programs, another counterintuitive finding suggests that IMF agreements are not equivalent to the policies they endorse: Being under an IMF agreement is not a situation that governments like to prolong. The probability of remaining under an agreement with the IMF is negatively related to performance at all levels of experience, although only the regional experience is significant at conventional levels. In other words, the probability of remaining under an IMF agreement is negatively related to expecting a better performance under an IMF agreement. Thus, in line with Bird (1996a), this finding may be understood in terms of governments' willingness to escape IMF agreements as soon as the economic situation improves.

All in all, these results suggest that governments do not regard IMF packages as routine economic policy making.

6.1. Explaining IMF Agreements[3]

The IMF was created in 1944 under the umbrella of the Bretton Woods Conference. Its initial mandate, as specified in the original Articles of

---

[2] Recall that IMF agreements were influential in the decision to open the capital account, but with little impact. Most of the liberalization took place in the 1990s, a period that is not covered in this chapter. Being under an IMF agreement was also relevant for the adoption of EO in the Development Strategies Database. In none of these illustrations was the IMF influential on policy sustainability.

[3] Unless otherwise stated, this section and Section 6.2 are based on Bird (1996a, 1996b), Thacker (1999), Bordo and James (2000), Stone (2002), Lee (2002), Dreher (2002), Vreeland (2003), and Barnett and Finnemore (2004).

184   *Learning and IMF Agreements*

Agreement, limited the Fund to promoting international monetary cooperation and stability, and facilitating international trade by providing short-term financial assistance to members facing BoP problems. Short-term assistance would prevent countries from resorting to competitive devaluations and other nationalistic solutions to BoP maladjustments (beggar-thy-neighbor policies), which were regarded as the major cause of the collapse of international trade and international monetary cooperation in the interwar period. The Bretton Woods monetary regime established a system of fixed but adjustable exchange rates, the surveillance of which was also delegated to the IMF.

In the IMF, voting is a function of the quota that countries contribute to the organization. The quota, in turn, is a function of the size of a country's economy. Thus, wealthy countries (the United States, Germany, Japan, France, and the United Kingdom) control the agenda of the Fund through direct representation on the Fund Executive Board. In particular, the United States alone has some seventeen percent of the voting power of the institution. Given that the most important decisions of the Fund require an eighty-five percent agreement, the United States can veto them. Thus, the Fund cannot de facto act against the interests of the United States in the Fund's most important matters.[4]

The collapse of the par value system in 1973 and the rise of private capital markets willing to finance the external deficits of troubled economies caused an "existential crisis" for the Fund. With two of its most important functions gone, the Fund started to look for alternative ones. It found them in the dramatic increase in its membership from the original 29 countries to the current 185.[5] More importantly, the new members were low-income developing countries and transition economies that found it especially difficult to access private capital markets.

The sudden reversal of private capital flows that took place in the early 1980s as a result of the debt crisis revealed that private capital was capricious and may be scarce in times of crisis. Under those circumstances, some authority was seen as desirable to allay creditors' fears that they would not be repaid. Thus, the IMF acquired two new functions:

---

[4] For instance, the appointment of the Fund Managing Director and quota revisions (thus, voting power) require eight-five percent of the vote.
[5] As of July 2007.

6.1. Explaining IMF Agreements 185

It became (1) a development financer and (2) a crisis manager for the emerging economies. However, the Fund has faced mounting criticisms of its performance of these new functions.

Regarding its role as development financer, it is a widely shared view that the Fund became an aid agency prescribing the same (and unique) recipe for development to its members. The recipe was a blend of stabilization and adjustment policies à la Washington Consensus. Stabilization policies (restrictive fiscal and monetary policies, and devaluation) were supposed to solve the problem of excessive aggregate demand, in turn considered to be the cause of fiscal and external imbalances. Adjustment policies, however, are defined as policies designed to set countries on the path to sustained growth. These policies included privatization, tax reform, trade liberalization, and deregulation, among other things.

Regarding its role as crisis manager, the Fund is considered to have made crucial mistakes in the East Asian (1997), Russian (1998), Brazilian (1999), and, above all, Argentine (2001–02) financial crises. First, enthusiastic advocacy of financial liberalization during the 1990s in countries without adequate regulatory frameworks, as well as the existence of the IMF as a lender of last resort, encouraged private investors to assume excessive risk in the expectation that they would be bailed out in the event of a crisis. Thus, conditionality did not deter private investors from engaging in risky behavior, or emerging countries from accumulating debt.[6] Second, it is agreed that the IMF failed to anticipate and prevent these crises. And, finally, the IMF persevered in the promotion of the same old package of austerity measures even though the recent financial crises were not caused by classic macroeconomic imbalances

---

[6] A convincing explanation of the failure of conditionality can be found in Conway (2003). The author models the conditions as an outcome of a bargaining process between the IMF and the participating country. If conditions are not met, lending is suspended, but both the IMF and the country bargain over the conditions so disbursements can be made. To achieve this goal, there are two options: Introducing an IMF program immediately after another with less restrictive conditions or canceling the current program and introducing a new one with more lenient conditions. As Stone (2002) shows, this pattern is more common between the Fund and important (big) countries. On IMF conditionality, its content, and evolution see the detailed work by Dreher (2002). See also Martin (2002).

(Strang 1999).[7] As a result of the failed extension of the Fund's activities as de facto development aid, voices were raised demanding that the Fund restore its original activities of surveillance and providing information, reliable data, and technical advice, and also demanding enhanced IMF transparency and independence from politics.

Against this background, why do countries and the Fund sign agreements? The straightforward answer is that countries enter into agreements because they *need* loans and the IMF gives loans to countries that *need* them, conditional on the adoption of certain policies. Yet, recent research demonstrates that need (defined in terms of restrictive criteria such as reserves or the state of the BoP) is not a sufficient explanation.[8] For instance, neither does the IMF give funds to all countries that need them, nor do all countries that need loans turn to the Fund. Moreover, not all countries that fail to meet IMF conditionality are denied new programs (Thacker 1999; Stone 2002; Vreeland 2003).

Concerning the IMF, it has been demonstrated that it is not a technocracy that acts purely on the basis of economic indicators; rather, it is a bureaucracy that seeks to maximize its power and resources (Vaubel 1991). The Fund's posture is more permissive toward those countries whose external imbalances may be especially destabilizing for international trade. Also, the prominent position of the United States in the Fund has, on quite a few occasions, involved the use of the Fund's resources to attend the geopolitical interests of that country. Thacker (1999), for instance, shows that the United States uses the IMF to reward friends, and particularly to reward (punish) countries that move closer to (further from) the policies favored by the United States. This is a reality that has survived the end of the Cold War. Several authors point out that countries such as Russia or Turkey received more lenient treatment from the IMF for security reasons. As Bordo and James put it (2000: 36), Russia was "too nuclear to fail." As a consequence of such differential treatment of

---

[7] See Rogoff (2003) for a defense of the Fund against these criticisms.

[8] Vreeland's criterion of need is foreign reserves worth less than 2.4 times monthly imports. This cut-off point is the average level of reserves of countries participating in agreements, according to his data. In his data, forty percent of countries had either high reserves and an agreement or low reserves and no agreement with the IMF. See also Trudel (2005).

6.1. Explaining IMF Agreements

countries for economic or security reasons, the Fund suffers from a credibility problem: It cannot credibly threaten to punish large countries for noncompliance. Large countries are punished more frequently but for shorter periods. In turn, as I explain subsequently, the credibility problem has economic consequences (Stone 2002). Finally, Vreeland (2003) shows that the Fund is constrained by its budget: Its negotiation posture is tougher the tighter its budget constraint. Moreover, since dictatorships' commitment to public opinion is less binding, dictators seem to be better negotiation partners for the Fund. Overall, it is clear that the IMF is far from being a neutral institution acting exclusively on the basis of economic need.

As for national governments, it is equally unclear why they enter into agreements with the IMF. The policies that the agreements entail are unpopular. Not only do governments usually face the accusation of selling out to international powers; the programs typically entail austerity measures that have a severe impact on labor and the poor (Pastor 1987; Garuda 2000; Vreeland 2003).

Most empirical research on the determinants of program participation has focused on economic factors alone. The standard explanation for decisions to enter into agreements with the IMF is that governments sign amid severe BoP deficits – that is, countries enter into agreements because they need them. However, research on the impact of need on the decision to sign is inconclusive (Bird 1996b; Vreeland 2003). The same disagreement exists regarding the role of inflation and the terms of trade in determining participation. However, it seems that high levels of public debt and large budget deficits make IMF agreements more likely. The same is true of low levels of development, an overvalued exchange rate, and low reserves.[9]

Economists' stories of country participation in IMF agreements have generally disregarded the role of political factors. Only the impact of past participation in IMF agreements has been considered (recidivism), and it has been interpreted in different ways: The longer governments are under IMF agreements, the less the sovereignty costs they face (Vreeland

---

[9] See the works of Bird (1996a,b); Vreeland (2003: 12–13); and Sturm, Berger, and J. de Haan (2005) for a review of explanatory variables and results.

2003); the longer governments are under IMF agreements, the more they learn how to negotiate with the Fund (Bird 1996a). In any case, the effect of this variable on the probability of signing is also ambiguous (Conway 1994; Sturm, Berger, and de Haan 2005).

Purely economic explanations cannot account for the fact that not all countries that need foreign reserves turn to the IMF. Conversely, countries with a sound BoP and no need of foreign reserves enter into agreements. For instance, Nigeria faced its worst economic crisis ever in 1983. This crisis persisted for another three years, yet only in 1987 did the government turn to the IMF. Conversely, countries such as Uruguay, Turkey, or Portugal signed agreements despite not needing currency. It is important to highlight that Vreeland's definition of need is restrictive, referring only to the level of foreign reserves (see Footnote 8).

The cluster of "victims without a program" reveals that governments in need of a loan may not seek an agreement if sovereignty costs are high and if elections are close. Sovereignty costs are high when a country has no previous history of IMF agreements; they are also higher the smaller the number of countries under agreements at any point in time. Thus, governments are more likely to enter into agreements with the IMF if many other countries are in the same situation. However, given that the IMF budget is limited, the probability that a particular country will get a loan is smaller the more countries are under an agreement. Finally, since conditionality implies austerity, governments minimize the political risks of approaching the IMF by taking advantage of honeymoons at the beginning of their terms of office.

The "non-victims with a program" illuminate other interesting political aspects of the decision to sign agreements. Sometimes currency is not needed, but unpopular measures need to be adopted – in particular, a cut in government expenditure – amid domestic political opposition. One way to overcome resistance is to invoke a third party to "do the dirty work." Domestic opposition is more likely to comply with this maneuver the greater is the cost of rejecting an IMF program. Typically, rejecting an IMF agreement sends a bad signal to creditors and investors. Domestic opposition may acquiesce precisely to avoid sending that negative signal. Thus, the greater the debt and the lower the investment, the greater is the cost of rejecting an agreement with the IMF (Vreeland 2003).

Hence, governments sign agreements when they need resources, when they want conditions, or when they want both the money and the conditions. Vreeland's work also shows that hardly any of the factors that induce governments to enter into agreements with the IMF influence governments' decisions to remain under a contract. In fact, only the number of other countries participating seems to be relevant to decisions to remain under agreements. This result could be interpreted to mean that governments are more likely to remain under IMF surveillance the lower the sovereignty costs they have to pay.

In sum, the decision to enter into agreements with the IMF involves two parties that confront economic and political constraints and motivations. Governments decide to enter into agreements with the IMF when they need them or when they want to adopt certain measures but face domestic obstacles. The decision to sign an agreement is subject to rejection and to sovereignty costs.

Also, governments may want to bring the IMF in because its policies enhance growth, even if this happens at the cost of short-term recessions. After all, this is what the logic behind IMF policies entails: Swallowing a bitter pill is a prerequisite for resuming growth. However, are IMF policies good for growth?

6.2. Consequences of IMF Agreements

In the words of Michael Camdessus, "[o]ur primary objective is growth. In my view, there is no longer ambiguity about this. It is toward growth that our programs and their conditionality are aimed" (Przeworski and Vreeland, 2000: 385).[10]

---

[10] Regarding other economic variables, some studies report improvements in the balance of payments whereas others report no effects at all. As for inflation, results vary along the whole spectrum: Most studies report no impact and, exceptionally, some reduction in inflation. Stone (2002) shows that the credibility problem of the Fund when it comes to punishing large or important countries results in more inflation than in smaller countries in which the Fund does not face the same credibility constraint. Thus, the capacity of IMF conditionality to enforce anti-inflationary policies is asymmetric: The smaller the country, the more credible the threat of punishment by the Fund, and, thus, the more effective are its policy recommendations. The impact of IMF programs on the current account is inconclusive.

190   *Learning and IMF Agreements*

Most empirical studies report no effects of IMF agreements on growth; an isolated study reports a worsening in the short run and an improvement thereafter (Conway 1994). Empirical research on the impact of IMF agreements on growth has suffered from an important methodological flaw. As explained in the previous section, there are particular factors that influence governments' decisions to sign an agreement with the IMF. Because those factors can actually influence the results of the program, it is necessary to isolate the impact of the program from the impact of the factors that determine participation. Moreover, selection is caused not only by observable factors but also unobservable ones such as a "visionary leader" or "political will." Controlling only for observable conditions, as is the usual procedure, yields biased results.

Using the appropriate tool, Vreeland (2003) found that IMF programs reduce growth rates while countries remain under them, and this occurs regardless of whether these countries face good or bad initial conditions. When countries leave the agreements, they grow faster than under the program but more slowly than if they had not participated. This result appears unrelated to the length of the spell under contracts. Hence, IMF agreements are not well designed to meet the long-term objective of growth that Camdessus prescribed. Whereas this study is indeed a step forward in understanding the cause and the effects of IMF agreements, it is based on an assumption that may be heroic: That all the programs signed are actually implemented. Eventually, what we do not know is whether bad performance is due to IMF policies or, on the contrary, to their partial or nonimplementation.[11]

According to Vreeland (2003, 2007) and Bird (1996a), the main drawback of IMF programs is that they entail particular conditions but no specification as to how those conditions should be met. For instance, governments are requested to reduce their budget deficits; but it is left to governments to decide how. Governments may choose to cut public investment or public wages and benefits. Cutting public wages and benefits is clearly more unpopular. Thus, governments generally cut public investment, which hinders long-run growth. Also, a tight monetary

---

[11] Bird (1996b) reports the results of a study of 266 programs negotiated with the IMF over 1980–90. The study shows that the majority of these programs broke down.

6.2. Consequences of IMF Agreements

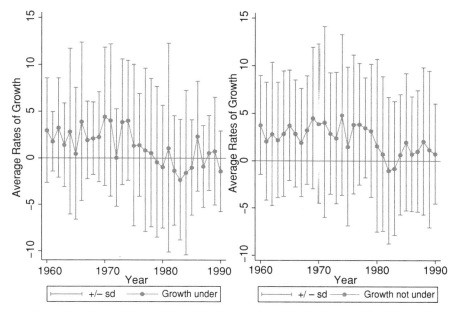

Figure 6.1. Average Rates of Growth and Volatility of Results (+/− s.d.) Under and Not Under an IMF Agreement, 1960–1990. Data on rates of growth taken from the ACLP Political and Economic Database, 1997. Growth is the annual rate of growth of real per capita GDP, 1985, international prices, chain index.

policy typically results in higher interest rates that affect firms in an indiscriminate way. Efficient firms may shut down along with inefficient ones. Finally, advocating the implementation of a package of economic policies without reference to proper sequencing may result in bad policy decisions with perverse outcomes. A misuse of Fund resources in the hands of corrupted politicians is another explanation for the poor results of IMF agreements in particular and of international aid in general (Easterly 2003).

Figure 6.1 shows the average rates of growth with and without IMF agreements in developing countries. Although this is purely a descriptive exercise very likely affected by the selection problem mentioned earlier (namely, that countries under IMF agreements perhaps grow less due to the bad circumstances under which they enter them rather than the IMF program itself), the figure shows that countries participating have grown

192   *Learning and IMF Agreements*

more slowly than countries not participating, particularly after the first oil crisis.

If IMF programs do not enhance growth and their impact on other economic variables is controversial, why do governments sometimes actively seek to have IMF conditions imposed – as the political story of selection in countries that are non-victims with a program entails?

This is an intriguing question and one that most authors only speculate about. For Vreeland (2003), governments may approach the IMF simply seeking short-run financial stability, without concerns about long-term growth. However, this argument would apply only to the subset of governments that do face financial constraints. Governments' motives may be more insidious. Manuel Pastor found that, from the mid-1960s to the mid-1980s, IMF agreements decreased the labor share of income in Latin America (Pastor 1987). One may argue that governments bring in the IMF to redistribute income away from labor. Vreeland's research (2002, 2003) also confirms that labor and the poor are worse off as a result of IMF agreements whereas the owners of capital increase their share of national income (see also Garuda 2000).[12]

Another story of participation could lie behind the large number of countries under programs, along the lines of the research in the present study. One may contend that such a high number of participants is indicative of a favorable opinion toward IMF policies. On this interpretation, countries participate in IMF programs not only because the large number of other countries participating reduces the sovereignty costs of signing, but also because governments want to live up to policies regarded as good. Thus, governments may sign IMF agreements for the sake of their reputation and their international legitimacy and credibility. In fact, some governments exceeded the Fund's conditions in the radicalism of their adjustment, apparently seeking international favor, credibility, and creditworthiness (Weyland 2002).

A different account, and the one that I test next, is that governments want IMF policies because they have learned from the experience that IMF programs have a positive effect on growth (relative to not having a

---

[12] As Vreeland acknowledges, he uses data about labor only in manufacturing, which is problematic given that this sector represents a minor share of the economies of quite a few developing countries. His data are for 110 countries in the period 1961 through 1993.

program). Conversely, governments may not want to sign agreements if they believe the opposite after observing the experience of others. The estimation reveals this to be the case. Two results are interesting. First, the baseline model that considers only the learning variables reveals quite significant risk-prone behavior in the decision to enter into IMF agreements. Second, after several political and economic variables are controlled for, learning from the experience in the WORLD with IMF agreements is a robust explanation of the decision to enter, and its impact on the probability of signing or not signing is nonnegligible. However, unambiguously, domestic economic and political conditions rather than policy diffusion were responsible for the decision to enter into contracts with the IMF. Thus, as explained in Chapter 1, the peak in IMF agreements around the 1982 crisis appears, if at all, a case of bottom-up policy convergence.

6.3. Learning and IMF Agreements: The Data

The statistical test of the learning model is based on data from Vreeland (2003). This database provides information on IMF agreements for 135 countries between 1950 (or year of independence) and 1990.

There are four types of IMF agreements, which differ in their conditions, timing, and size of the loan disbursements. They are known as the Standby Arrangement, the Extended Fund Facility, the Structural Adjustment Facility, and the Enhanced Structural Adjustment Facility. Standby agreements address temporary BoP deficits. These agreements, which constitute eighty-eight percent of total agreements in the database, aim to have results in the short run, generally within 12 to 18 months. However, a common practice has been to sign consecutive agreements, that is, a spell of agreements.[13] During the period 1952–90, the average spell under IMF contracts lasted 4.7 years. Between 1971 and 1990, it lasted 5.3 years.

The dependent variable was coded 1 if a particular country in a particular year had an agreement with the IMF regardless of type of agreement. It was coded 0 otherwise. I limited the scope of my research to

---

[13] For instance, South Korea spent thirteen years under consecutive agreements, Zaire spent fourteen years, and Liberia fifteen. Peru participated for eighteen years and Panama for twenty. Argentina borrowed money from the IMF in thirty-four of the past forty-five years (Lee 2002: 295).

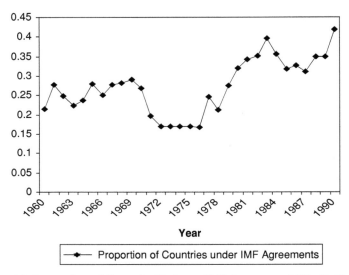

Figure 6.2. Proportion of Countries Under an IMF Agreement, 1960–90. Data on IMF participation for 135 developed and developing countries taken from Vreeland (2003).

135 countries between 1960 and 1990.[14] For this period, there are a total of 3,623 country-year observations, of which 1,002 are observations under IMF agreements and 2,621 are observations not under agreements. Figure 6.2 shows the proportion of countries under IMF agreements for the period 1960–90. As can be seen, this proportion gradually increased, reaching a peak in 1983, decreasing thereafter, and reaching another peak at the end of the decade. Clearly, the jump in participation coincided with the onset of the debt crisis in 1982.

I grouped the 135 countries into ten regions.[15] The list of countries in the database is provided in the Appendix. To understand the results discussed subsequently and particularly the relevance of learning from the experience in the region in one of the specifications, it is important

---

[14] Prior to 1960, there are only seventeen country-year observations under IMF agreements.
[15] Africa (1,155), South Asia (139), East Asia (98), South East Asia (185), Pacific Islands and Oceania (63), Middle East and North Africa (323), Latin America (558), Caribbean and Non-Iberian America (177), Eastern Europe and Soviet Union (186), and Industrial Countries (739).

6.3. Learning and IMF Agreements: The Data 195

Table 6.1. *Average rates of growth by region under and not under an agreement*

Region	Annual rates of growth under agreements (%)	N	Annual rates of growth not under agreements (%)	N
Africa	−0.60	341	1.57	814
South Asia	**2.73**	64	1.33	75
South East Asia	**6.23**	24	4.78	74
East Asia	2.39	51	4.66	134
Pacific/Oceania	−0.42	11	1.31	52
Middle East/North Africa	2.20	71	3.15	252
Latin America	1.13	290	1.77	268
Caribbean and Non-Iberian America	−0.57	70	2.55	107
Eastern Europe and Soviet Union	1.77	32	4.07	154
Industrial Countries	2.55	48	3.26	691
TOTAL	0.85	1002	2.61	2621

to note than all ten regions had considerable experience under IMF agreements.[16]

Overall, annual rates of growth for countries participating and not participating under IMF agreements were 0.85% and 2.61% respectively. As Table 6.1 shows, by region, and with the exception of South Asia and South East Asia, rates of growth in countries *not* under IMF agreements were greater than those in countries under IMF programs.[17] However, learning may be from specific cases rather than from average experience. South Korea remained under IMF surveillance between 1965 and 1977 and again between 1980 and 1987. During the first period, the average rate of growth was 8.11%. In 1970, the growth rate reached a peak of 15%. It was an average of 6.07% during the second period. Chile is another emblematic case of success accomplished under successive

---

[16] In Africa, thirty-six of forty-five countries had some experience under IMF agreements, eleven of twenty-four advanced countries, four of five in Oceania and Pacific, six of ten in the Caribbean and Non-Iberian America, nine of eleven in the Middle East and North Africa, four of six in Eastern Europe, two of four in South East Asia, and five of seven in East Asia. All Latin American and South Asian countries had experience with IMF agreements.

[17] In East Asia, higher rates of growth under IMF agreements relate to South Korea. In South Asia, Bangladesh grew by 27.93% in 1974. In 1977, Nepal grew by 34.47%, and in 1965, Pakistan grew by 18.65%. The three countries were under IMF agreements in those years.

196   *Learning and IMF Agreements*

agreements with the IMF. Between 1984 and 1990, Chile was under a spell of agreements and growing at an average rate of 4.47%. It grew by 9.20% in 1989. For some governments, the South Korean and Chilean experiences might have proved that the Fund's austerity policies were not incompatible with growth and could even promote it.

6.4. Learning and IMF Agreements: The Results

In order to test whether learning explains countries' decisions to enter into agreements with the IMF, I proceed in the usual manner, relating the observed path of agreements with the difference in posterior beliefs about average growth under and not under IMF contracts. Starting with some prior beliefs about growth under and not under an IMF agreement (see Appendix), governments update those beliefs with the information provided by the experience of participants and nonparticipants. They compare those posteriors and choose the policy that yields the best expected outcome. The question is: Does such rational behavior predict the policy choices observed? The answer, in brief, is "barely."

To control for proximity and shared characteristics, I structured the available information at the levels of the country, the region, and the world. Information is about both average growth and the variability of results under alternative status. Using a dynamic version of probit, I estimate the impact of learning on the probability of *signing* an IMF agreement and on the probability of *remaining* under an IMF agreement.

Baseline Model

Columns (1) and (2) of Table 6.2 give the results of the baseline model, one in which only the learning variables were included. Column (1) refers to the probability of *entering* into an IMF program whereas column (2) refers to the probability of *remaining* under a program. I expected that the higher the anticipated growth rate in posterior beliefs under IMF participation in comparison with nonparticipation, the greater the probability that a program will be adopted. Also, under the assumption that governments are risk-averse, the greater the expected variability of results of being under an IMF program compared with not being

6.4. Learning and IMF Agreements: The Results 197

under one, the less likely it is that an approach will be made to the IMF. However, if governments are not risk averse, a high variability of results, which entails observing very bad but also very good performers under IMF programs, may not deter countries from entering into IMF agreements.

As column (1) of Table 6.2 shows, governments entered into agreements with the IMF as a result of learning from their own experience and from world experience under alternative policies. Also, and interestingly, governments were willing to take risks and to enter into agreements with the IMF on the basis of experience with IMF programs in their region and in the world. Regarding permanence under IMF agreements, column (2) shows that governments were willing to take risks and remain under IMF contracts after observing experience in the world; but the probability of remaining is negatively related to high growth rates under IMF agreements in the region. Note that, although the coefficients of own and world average experience are not significant, they are also negative. Hence, the probability of remaining under IMF programs is negatively related to growth under these programs. A likely explanation for this result is that governments abandoned IMF agreements as soon as growth resumed. It seems that being under an IMF agreement is not a situation that governments on average sought to prolong. Improving rates of growth made agreements economically less necessary and politically less justifiable, and thus more costly. Note as well that three significant coefficients refer to attitudes toward risk and that all three coefficients picture governments as willing to assume them. Overall, it seems that the decision to enter into agreements with the IMF was characterized by a willingness to take risks that I did not find in previous applications of the learning model.

Why this willingness to run risks? I hinted at one possible explanation earlier: Even if it seems that IMF programs are not good devices to spur growth, there are emblematic cases of economic success that achieved outstanding rates of growth under IMF programs. Other governments might have observed these good outcomes and might have concluded that IMF austerity policies were the secret of their success. Hence, governments were not deterred by the high volatility of outcomes and were willing to run the risk of adopting them. Another explanation has to do with governments' willingness to run risks – in the sense of adopting policies the outcomes of which are highly volatile – when confronted with very bad economic prospects (Kahneman and Tversky 1988; Weyland 1998). In fact, the BoP and the state of foreign reserves may be too strict a description of economic need. Confronted with an *overall* deteriorating economic situation, governments make the choice to adjust.[18]

For example, Uruguay epitomizes the case of a non-victim with a program. When, in 1990, President Lacalle signed an agreement, the country was in no need of foreign currency. Foreign reserves amounted to 7.7 times the average monthly import requirements, double the average amount in the region. However, in 1990, inflation had reached 112.5%. In 1989, foreign debt was rising again after a peak in 1985 (89.7% of GNP) and the public deficit had reached its highest figure since 1984. Also, rates of growth had been negative in 1988 and 1989. In 1989, they reached their lowest level since 1984. Moreover, although the level of foreign reserves was higher than the regional average, reserves had been declining since 1987. Hence, by several economic criteria, Uruguay was a "victim." Confronted with a latent crisis and gloomy prospects, a "reform-oriented" government with hardly any mandate for reform took the risk of bringing in the IMF to have the reforms it wanted imposed upon the country.

Portugal is another case of a non-victim with a program. The Portuguese government signed an agreement in 1977 with a strong reserve position. But, as Vreeland acknowledges, the current account was negative in the three preceding years and the year of the agreement. Hence, a need for reserves might have been developing before the government turned to the Fund. This was not the only problem. In 1974, annual inflation had reached 27.96%. It declined in 1975 and 1976 but increased to 27.11% in 1977. In 1984, inflation reached a peak of 29.3%. In precisely that year, and despite having extremely high reserves, Portugal was under an IMF agreement.

The Uruguayan and Portuguese cases show that a static picture of the external accounts or foreign reserves may be a partial indicator of the need

---

[18] Note that Vreeland (2003) uses RESERVES as an indicator of the need for a loan, which is different from the need for a program in that the program entails a loan plus conditions.

6.4. Learning and IMF Agreements: The Results

for a program. Other economic indicators may confront governments with the prospect of big losses and cause a shift in their willingness to take risks and adopt austerity measures with highly uncertain outcomes. It is true that not all countries facing bad economic conditions turn to the IMF. Sometimes they delay the adjustment and sometimes they introduce austerity measures on their own initiative.[19] But it is also true that all countries that turn to the IMF seem to have something in common: They do not have good economic prospects or they face a problem on some macroeconomic indicator even if a one-shot look at their external accounts or foreign reserves indicates the opposite.

This willingness to run risks should not be overstated, though. As the model that controls for economic and political determinants of participation shows, such behavior practically vanishes when alternative explanations of IMF participation are included in the analysis. Domestic circumstances carried most of the weight in the story of participation.

Extended Model

Columns (3) and (4) of Table 6.2 give the results of the model that controls for alternative mechanisms of selection into IMF programs. Apart from learning, this model includes four sets of explanations, which all proved to be significant in Vreeland's account of IMF participation. EMULATION and YEARS UNDER refer to the sovereignty costs of signing an agreement. Note that I treat the number of other countries currently under an IMF agreement as EMULATION, consistent with how this variable has been treated in other chapters. I do not consider that my interpretation of this variable contradicts Vreeland's: Most likely, emulating the policies of many others is a good way to appease domestic opposition. Countries are expected to be more likely to enter into agreements with the IMF the longer their history of IMF participation and the more countries contemporaneously participating. However, the latter effect is likely to be more complex: In Vreeland's model, which is a bivariate version of dynamic probit, the number of other countries under an IMF agreement

---

[19] For instance, when Nigeria finally entered into an agreement in 1987, the Fund was willing to sign because the country had already accomplished most of the conditions ex ante (Vreeland 2003).

is positively related to the probability of *governments* entering into an agreement and negatively related to the probability of the *IMF* signing agreements. The logic behind these contrasting effects is that the more countries are under an IMF agreement, the less the sovereignty costs that governments confront but the tighter the budget constraint the IMF faces. To capture these opposed effects in the univariate and dynamic version of probit I employ, I introduce a quadratic term expecting that the probability of entering into agreements with the IMF will increase up to a particular number of countries under agreements, beyond which the probability of getting an agreement will decrease due to the budgetary pressures of the Fund. I also included the variables REGIME (with value of 1 for dictatorships, Przeworski, Alvarez, Cheibub, and Limongi 2000) to account for the likelihood that democracies, in which politicians are held accountable, faced greater sovereignty costs than did autocracies.[20]

RESERVES (World Development Indicators) tell the story of economic need: In principle, countries are more likely to sign agreements with the IMF when their reserves are low. BUDGET (World Development Indicators) and ELECTIONS (Przeworski, Alvarez, Cheibub, and Limongi 2000) tell the story of political capabilities (Dreher 2003). Governments whose budgets are in the red are more likely to bring in the IMF to have austere fiscal policies imposed on them, but they are more likely to do so after elections. Finally, DEBT SERVICE (World Development Indicators) and INVESTMENT (World Development Indicators) capture the costs of saying "no" to the IMF. A country that is highly indebted or needs foreign investment but rejects an IMF austerity package is likely to send a very bad signal to creditors and investors. Thus, the higher the debt and the lower the investment, the more likely countries are to enter into IMF programs.

As can be seen in Table 6.2, columns (3) and (4), learning from own and world experience survives the introduction of controls into the model. The three variables that refer to learning from average results under versus not under IMF agreements have the expected positive sign. As for the

---

[20] In Vreeland's model, REGIME appears in the equation that concerns the IMF's decision to lend. In his model, the result shows that the IMF is more likely to lend to dictatorships, probably because this type of regime, being less accountable, makes a better negotiating partner than does a democracy.

Table 6.2. *Probability of entering and remaining under an IMF agreement (1960–1990)*

Dependent variable: IMF agreement	Entering (1)	Remaining (2)	Extended model entering (3)	Extended model remaining (4)
CONSTANT	−1.19***	0.72***	−2.87***	−0.67
	(−11.2)	(5.07)	(−2.64)	(−0.63)
OWN EXPERIENCE				
AVERAGE RESULTS	0.02***	−0.01	0.03*	−0.0009
	(3.09)	(−0.92)	(1.83)	(−0.05)
VARIABILITY OF RESULTS	−0.02	−0.03	−0.02	−0.05
	(−0.79)	(−1.19)	(−0.69)	(−1.26)
REGIONAL EXPERIENCE				
AVERAGE RESULTS	−0.02	−0.08***	0.10*	−0.09*
	(−0.98)	(−2.64)	(1.79)	(−1.76)
VARIABILITY OF RESULTS	0.05*	0.68	0.10	0.09
	(1.72)	(1.43)	(1.51)	(1.27)
WORLD EXPERIENCE				
AVERAGE RESULTS	0.21***	−0.03	0.77**	−0.05
	(2.66)	(−0.37)	(2.44)	(−0.15)
VARIABILITY OF RESULTS	0.19***	0.14*	0.05	−0.06
	(3.32)	(1.91)	(0.27)	(−0.29)
EMULATION			1.82***	0.88
			(2.64)	(1.25)
EMULATION^2			−0.25**	−0.11
			(−2.54)	(−1.13)
YEARS UNDER			0.001	−0.16
			(0.99)	(−1.15)
RESERVES			−1.13***	−0.34
			(−3.07)	(−0.93)
BUDGET			−0.25***	0.14
			(−2.80)	(1.20)
ELECTIONS			0.43***	−0.007
			(2.59)	(−0.04)
DEBT SERVICE			0.79***	0.25
			(3.89)	(1.25)
INVESTMENT			−2.76**	0.56
			(−2.10)	(0.43)
REGIME			0.06	0.09
			(0.35)	(0.49)
Log Likelihood	−1099.58		−369.28	
LR Chi-Square	1949.22		670.81	
p-value for F	0.000		0.000	
Observations	3488		1024	

*$p < .10$; **$p < .05$; ***$p < .01$; z-scores in parentheses; all variables lagged one year.
Pseudo R^2 is 0.47 with 89% of correctly predicted 1s and 0s (Model 3).

willingness to take risks found in the baseline model, only the result concerning regional experience is close to being statistically significant ($p = 0.13$). Thus, in this smaller sample, it is not possible to reject the hypothesis that countries entered into IMF agreements due to learning from all levels of experience (own, region, and world) with IMF programs.

Economic need, political opportunity, and rejection costs are statistically significant with the expected signs. Thus, governments signed agreements with the IMF when their foreign reserves were low, when the fiscal budget was pressing, and when they were highly indebted and in need of investment. Governments signed after elections, a result also reported by Sturm, Berger, and de Haan (2005).[21] However, concerning sovereignty costs, it is interesting that, when learning is considered as an explanation of IMF participation, the number of years under IMF agreements is not significant.[22] As I show in Figure 6.3, the number of other countries under IMF programs has the expected two-way effect. The probability of entering into agreements with the IMF does increase with the number of other countries under IMF agreements. However, when more than thirty-five countries are already under IMF agreements, the probability of entering decreases. The likely explanation for the reversal in the effect has to do with the pressure on the finances of the IMF as more and more countries receive loans. The more customers, the less lenient the conditions that the IMF is willing to offer in exchange for loans and, consequently, the less likely governments are to agree with the

---

[21] Given that in Vreeland's argument the lack of political capacity of governments to carry out reforms is central to invoking the IMF, the author included in an alternative model specification the number of veto players, which has the expected sign. The more veto players, the more difficult it is for a government wanting to adopt reforms to have them passed, and thus, the more likely the government is to resort to the IMF to tame domestic opposition.

[22] The usual variable to capture the effect of having been under agreements with the IMF is precisely a lagged variable of past participation. If I use this proxy and run a probit, the lagged participation is strongly related to the probability of participation and continues to be so after the introduction of the learning variables. However, the alternative operationalization of recidivism that I employ following Vreeland (the cumulative number of years under IMF agreements) is not statistically significant in the presence of the lagged variable of participation. All in all, I find it hardly impressive that the lagged participation variable turns out to be so relevant in a probit estimation. Note also that the lack of significance of the variable "Cumulative number of years under IMF agreements" may be due to the different estimation method employed in this study.

6.4. Learning and IMF Agreements: The Results   203

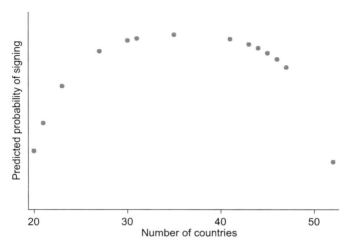

Figure 6.3. Predicted Probability of Signing by Number of Countries Under IMF Agreements.

demands of the Fund. Finally, dictatorships were more likely to enter into agreements with the IMF, but this effect was not statistically significant.

To facilitate the interpretation of the results and to compare the relative impact of the different significant variables, I simulate the change in the predicted probability of entering into an agreement with the IMF after moving one standard deviation around the mean of the significant predictors. The graph in Figure 6.3 shows the change in predicted probability and the 95% confidence interval. As can be seen, the volume of RESERVES has the greatest impact on the probability of signing IMF agreements. Variation in one standard deviation around the mean of the volume of reserves reduces the probability of entering into an agreement by thirteen percentage points. Variation from the minimum NUMBER OF COUNTRIES under an IMF agreement (nineteen) up to the median of the distribution (thirty-six countries), where the effect of this variable changes sign, increases the probability of entering into agreements in eleven percentage points. The impact of LEARNING FROM THE EXPERIENCE IN THE WORLD is of the same magnitude as the impact of DEBT SERVICE. A one-standard-deviation increase in posterior beliefs about growth under versus not under an IMF agreement and in debt service increases the probability of entering into agreements in about

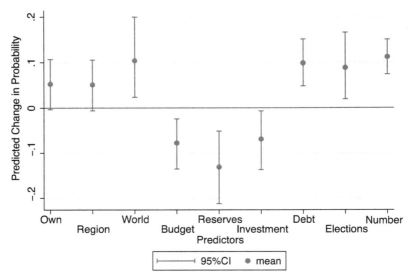

Figure 6.4. Change in Predicted Probabilities and 95% Confidence Intervals of Moving One Standard Deviation Around the Mean of the Predictors. All other variables were set at their mean values. Note that for the coefficients that were significant at 10%, the 95% confidence interval does include zero.

ten percentage points. Having held ELECTIONS in the previous year increases the probability of signing an IMF program by nine percentage points. Finally, a two-standard-deviation improvement in the BUDGET and in INVESTMENT decreases the probability of entering into agreements in eight and seven percentage points respectively. The graph includes the impact of learning from OWN and REGIONAL experience. In both cases, the estimated change in the predicted probability of a one standard deviation around the mean of these variables increases the probability of being under an IMF agreement by about five percentage points.[23] However, as I show below, these two latter variables are no longer significant when learning is altered to test for the role of learning about an "abnormal policy" during "abnormal" times.

As happens in Vreeland's model, these variables are mainly irrelevant in explaining why countries *remain* under IMF programs (column 4).

[23] Alternative model specifications (not shown) report a nonsignificant coefficient for own experience, which suggests that this coefficient is hardly robust. Alternatively, in other specifications, the variance of results in the region became significant but with a very weak impact on the probability of signing.

6.4. Learning and IMF Agreements: The Results 205

Whereas, in his model, the number of other countries participating is the only significant variable in that decision, that is not the case after learning is included in the model specification. Again, in the extended model, we observe that the probability of remaining under an IMF agreement is negatively related to performance under IMF agreements in the REGION. The more countries are expected to grow under IMF programs, the less likely a government is to remain under them. Note that the sign is also negative for own and world experience, although these coefficients are not statistically significant. Most likely, governments are willing to abandon IMF programs as soon as the economic situation allows them to do so. Conway (1994), for instance, found that rapid economic growth in the previous year reduced the time spent in IMF programs. This indicates that, contrary to "policy as usual," governments do not seek to remain under IMF agreements when they do well under them. A one standard variation around the mean of the variable LEARNING FROM EXPERIENCE, REGION reduces the probability of remaining under an agreement with the IMF by six percentage points.

In sum, the model indicates that governments did look at the experience of other countries, they learned from it, and they decided to enter into agreements with the IMF if they believed that growth under IMF agreements would be greater than economic performance without it after learning from experience. Yet, as I show subsequently, learning from own and regional experience is not robust, whereas domestic political and economic conditions prevail in the decision to sign.

Learning from the 1982 Crisis and IMF Agreements

In general, IMF agreements are not normal economic policy making, and economic crises are not normal times.[24] As Figure 6.2 showed, the IMF became more prominent following the 1982 debt crisis and the subsequent cut in private capital flows to developing countries. In the years following the crisis, there was a peak of victims turning

---

[24] Africa may constitute an exception to this generalization. In this region, a permanent economic crisis made international aid and loans from IFIs an equally permanent fact of policy making. However, international aid helped sustain the very policies responsible for the state of economic disarray that justified the aid in the first place. See Van de Walle (2001, chapter 5) for a critique of the role of international financial assistance in Africa.

to the IMF. A policy maker wanting to learn about the consequences of IMF agreements on growth would have been especially attentive to the performance of those countries pursuing IMF policies following the increase in participation. Recall, however, that IMF agreements entail visible sovereignty costs, and the government that signs them may suffer a severe loss of popularity. Therefore, contrary to other policies embraced on a country's own initiative, it is less convincing to hypothesize that governments signed contracts and sustained contracts if, according to several pieces of evidence, agreements delivered faster growth.

As can be seen in Table 6.3, increasing uncertainty about the growth that is expected to follow an IMF agreement – which, in turn, makes policy makers more attentive to actual performance in the years after the shock – implies that learning is no longer significant as an explanation for signing and sustaining contracts. Learning from the experience in the WORLD under and not under an IMF agreement is the only learning effect that survives. Although its impact continues to be relevant, it is smaller than before: A one standard deviation change in the difference in posterior beliefs about growth under and not under an IMF agreement increases the probability of signing in eight (0.04) percentage points (versus ten percentage points before).

Modeling the 1982 debt shock as an increase in uncertainty reinforces the finding that the decision to enter into IMF agreements was fundamentally an independent response driven by local circumstances. Being in dire straits, having previously held elections, experiencing a bad budgetary situation, and the number of other countries under IMF agreements explain (up to a point) why governments entered into negotiations with the Fund. The latter factor also explains why governments sustained such agreements: Seeing many other countries under an IMF agreement was positively related to the probability of remaining under one.[25] Note also that governments are now risk averse in light of own experience. A one standard deviation around the mean of posterior beliefs about OWN growth under versus not under an IMF agreement

---

[25] Interestingly, in this particular specification, the burden of debt service is very close to reaching statistical significance ($p = 0.12$). Thus, the greater the burden of debt service and the greater the number of countries simultaneously under an IMF agreement, the more likely a particular country was to sustain a contract.

Table 6.3. *Probability of entering and remaining under an IMF agreement, 1982 shock*

Dependent variable: IMF agreement	Extended model crisis, enter (5)	Extended model crisis, remain (6)
CONSTANT	−2.66**	−0.92
	(−2.46)	(−0.86)
OWN EXPERIENCE		
AVERAGE RESULTS	0.01	−0.009
	(0.85)	(−0.51)
VARIABILITY OF RESULTS	−0.02	−0.11*
	(−0.45)	(−1.80)
REGIONAL EXPERIENCE		
AVERAGE RESULTS	−0.03	−0.01
	(−0.59)	(−0.36)
VARIABILITY OF RESULTS	0.08	0.002
	(1.39)	(0.04)
WORLD EXPERIENCE		
AVERAGE RESULTS	0.40**	0.05
	(2.07)	(0.29)
VARIABILITY OF RESULTS	0.16	−0.12
	(0.99)	(−0.81)
EMULATION	1.39**	1.11*
	(2.06)	(1.66)
EMULATION^2	−0.20**	−0.14
	(−2.03)	(−1.47)
YEARS UNDER	0.08	−0.14
	(0.63)	(−1.02)
RESERVES	−1.04***	−0.43
	(−2.88)	(−1.21)
BUDGET	−0.24***	0.10
	(−2.79)	(0.89)
ELECTIONS	0.41**	−0.006
	(2.53)	(−0.03)
DEBT SERVICE	0.78***	0.29
	(3.79)	(1.53)
INVESTMENT	−3.64***	0.46
	(−2.84)	(0.37)
REGIME	0.08	0.17
	(0.47)	(0.93)
Log Likelihood	−371.19	
LR Chi-Square	666.99	
p-value for F	0.000	
Observations	1024	

$^*p < .10; ^{**}p < .05; ^{***}p < .01$; z-scores in parentheses; all variables lagged one year. 86% of correctly predicted 1s and 0s.

208   *Learning and IMF Agreements*

reduced the probability of sustaining an agreement by six percentage points.

These findings contrast with the effect that modeling shocks had in previous illustrations. Modeling several crises increased the leverage of learning in the decision to adopt an EO development strategy and in the decision to sustain an open capital account. However, learning from the relative performance of countries under and not under IMF agreements is practically inconsequential for the decision to sign. One may want to pursue a policy that, on average, is shown to have performed better in comparative terms, but adopting and sustaining these policies on a country's own initiative is not the same as having them imposed as packages of conditions that, on average, have been shown to be bad for growth. After modeling the shock and in the view of negative evidence in favor of IMF agreements, learning was less rather than more consequential.[26]

6.5. Discussion

IMF programs are the cross that countries have to bear in exchange for loans. These programs are packages of economic policies aimed at stabilizing and adjusting economies in the way, so we are told, that best guarantees growth. These packages frequently include the policies (privatization, trade liberalization, and capital account opening) studied in previous chapters. Yet, there are reasons to believe that IMF packages are more than an aggregation of those policies and that they impose additional political costs that the policies taken individually and implemented on a country's own initiative do not entail. Hence, they deserve to be studied in their own right.

Did governments enter and remain under IMF agreements as a result of learning from experience with these programs? In the baseline learning model that did not include any domestic controls, I could not reject the hypothesis that entering into IMF agreements had to do with a willingness to take risks that seems specific to this policy choice. Both in the baseline model and in the extended model, governments were less likely

---

[26] Further, this exercise shows that modeling a shock as an increase in governments' uncertainty about what to expect from policies is not a statistical artifact that makes learning significant.

to continue under IMF programs the better their performance under such agreements. This makes sense in that, most likely, the Fund is unwilling to go on lending money to countries that are growing, and countries are unwilling to remain under programs that are widely unpopular. Modeling the 1982 crisis as an increase in policy makers' uncertainty concerning growth under versus not under an IMF agreement made learning practically inconsequential for explaining entrance into agreements. Of all the learning effects, only learning from world experience is robust in all model specifications. These three results back up the idea that IMF agreements are not policy making "as usual."

Domestic economic and political conditions, rather than international factors, were robust and strong drivers of agreements signed with the IMF. Most variables that are usually included in political economy models of IMF agreements (the burden of debt service, the volume of reserves, and the level of investment) continued to be significant and important.

In line with previous studies, the number of other countries under IMF agreements reduced the sovereignty costs of bringing in the IMF and, therefore, increased the probability of signing agreements; but the effect held up to a certain number of countries, beyond which the budgetary pressure of the IMF reduced the likelihood of getting a loan. Electoral honeymoons also increased the probability of signing. Interestingly, after learning is included in the model, the impact of sovereignty costs on the decision to sign agreements partially held. One effect that was robust to samples and specifications in previous studies – namely, recidivism – is not significant in this specification. The cumulative years of experience under IMF agreements had the expected positive sign but it was not statistically significant. It could well be the case that the different estimation method caused the difference in results. However, there could also be an interesting substantive explanation for this finding. When learning is included in the model – that is, when the model somehow controls for the outcomes of agreements (not only whether or not previous agreements existed) the cumulative number of years per se no longer is significant. This is a hypothesis that scholars working on the political economy of IMF agreements should further explore. Finally, in all model specifications, dictatorships were more likely to enter into agreements with the IMF; but this relationship was never statistically significant.

To summarize: Concerning the decision to sign and to sustain IMF agreements, evidence of policy convergence caused by a process of horizontal policy diffusion is small. Despite the fact that the existence of a large number of other countries under an IMF agreement helped governments present these policies as desirable and reduced sovereignty costs, the decision to enter into agreements with the IMF is, for the most part, a case of bottom-up convergence driven by domestic conditions.

APPENDIX

Table A6.4. *Prior beliefs, IMF*

	Under IMF		Not under IMF	
Year	Mean	Variance	Mean	Variance
1960	−0.95	13	3.74	18
1961	3.19	30	4.57	22
1962	1.87	14	3	32
1963	3.32	25	3.05	42
1964	2.24	21	2.5	31
1965	3.33	72	3.42	34
1966	0.75	45	3.94	26
1968	1.68	17	2.23	27
1970	2.35	22	4.89	34
1971	4.39	51	4.37	56
1974	3.86	45	3.15	38
1975	4.05	39	4.12	58
1976	0.88	66	1.05	60
1977	1.29	28	3.88	44
1978	1.03	69	3.5	35
1980	−0.24	60	3.23	38
1981	−0.95	44	1.68	62
1984	−2.31	42	−0.16	37
1985	−1.59	76	1.35	31

Note: Based on data on growth and variability the year before a country's entry in the database.

Appendix

Table A6.5. *Descriptive statistics, IMF*

	Mean	s.d.	Minimum	Maximum
Beliefs Average Growth, Own	−1.54	4.62	−14.58	28.17
Beliefs Variability Growth, Own	−.40	1.78	−6.31	12.00
Beliefs Average Growth, Region	−1.37	1.51	−5.91	3.82
Beliefs Variability Growth, Region	.18	1.11	−3.88	3.30
Beliefs Average Growth, World	−1.33	.36	−3.27	.26
Beliefs Variability Growth, World	.38	.45	−1.19	1.91
Budget Surplus	−.62	.78	−7.07	2.64
Number of Other Countries	3.61	1.05	1.9	5.2
Years Under Agreements	.69	.62	.0	2.5
Reserves	.29	.29	−.01	1.77
Elections	.19	.39	.0	1
Debt Service	.51	.44	.0	3.03
Investment	.13	.06	−.045	.45
Regime	.73	0.44	.0	1

212   *Learning and IMF Agreements*

Table A6.6. *List of countries, IMF*

Sub-Saharan Africa	Latin America	Advanced Countries	Oceanía/Pacific Islands	North-Africa Middle East	South Asia
Angola	Costa Rica	Austria	Fiji	Morocco	Bangladesh
Benin	Dom. Republic	Denmark	Papua New Guinea	Israel	India
Botswana	El Salvador	Finland	Solomon	Jordan	Nepal
Burkina Faso	Guatemala	Canada	Vanuatu	Yemen	Sri Lanka
Burundi	Honduras	France	Western Samoa	Syria	Pakistan
Cameroon	Mexico	Greece		Turkey	
Cape Verde	Nicaragua	Iceland		Algeria	
CAR	Panama	Ireland		Egypt	
Chad	Argentina	Italy		Tunisia	
Comoros	Bolivia	Malta		Iran	
Congo	Brazil	Netherlands		Iraq	
Djibuti	Chile	Norway			
Ethiopia	Ecuador	Portugal			
Gambia	Colombia	Spain			
Gabon	Paraguay	Switzerland			
Ghana	Peru	Sweden			
Guinea	Uruguay	Australia			
G-Bissau	Venezuela	UK			
Ivory Coast		Japan			
Kenya		New Zealand			
Lesotho		United States			
Liberia		Belgium			
Madagascar		Germany			
Malawi		Luxembourg			
Mali					
Mauritania					
Mauritius					
Mozambique					
Níger					
Nigeria					
Rwanda					
Senegal					
Seychelles					
Sierra Leone					
Somalia					
South Africa					
Sudan					
Swaziland					
Tanzania					
Togo					
Uganda					
Zaire					
Zambia					
Zimbabwe					

Caribbean/ Non-Iberian America	Eastern Europe	East Asia	South East Asia
Belize	Soviet Union	Indonesia	China
Bahamas	Yugoslavia	Laos	South Korea
Barbados	Romania	Malaysia	Mongolia
Haiti	Poland	Philippines	Taiwan
Jamaica	Hungary	Singapore	
Trinidad	Bulgaria	Thailand	
and Tobago	Czechoslovakia	Myanmar	
Suriname	East Germany		
Grenada			
Guyana			

SEVEN

Conclusions

> If we can achieve a sense of balance, if we can learn the lessons from the failures
> of the reform agenda of the past, there is at least a glimmer of hope.
> Stiglitz (2000: 580)

This book started out with a question: *Did governments adopt market-oriented reforms in the 1980s and 1990s as a result of learning?*

This question is important, for several reasons. From a substantive point of view, at least two theoretical issues needed to be tackled. First, the argument that the switch to more liberal economic policies during the last two decades of the twentieth century was motivated by a process of learning from past mistakes is prevalent in the literature on market-oriented reforms. Yet, it remained untested. Second, beyond the specific topic of market-oriented reforms, the claim that policies change because policy makers learn from policy failures and successes is hardly questioned in many public policy arenas, both domestic and international; however, it is much more frequently assumed than actually demonstrated. Thus, whether learning actually happens matters for public policy and international relations in general, and for understanding the switch to liberal economic policies at the end of the twentieth century in particular.

In large part, debates about learning have remained in the realm of speculation because of methodological difficulties involved in, first, testing arguments about learning and, second, convincingly demonstrating that policy switches are caused by learning. Thus, the central task of this book has been to test learning in a way that makes it possible to answer

Conclusions

my substantive question and similar questions that other researchers may pose.

Finally, the contribution of this book is not only substantive and methodological. Important normative issues are involved, too. As I shall reiterate later, I tested a model of learning that presumes that policy makers scan for information around the world, draw conclusions about what works and what does not, and finally make policy choices consistent with what they have learned from the available evidence. Thus, if policy makers are rational they will always be attentive to the performance of policies, and will select policies on that basis. In other words, the policy choices made by a rational learner will be optimal from an economic point of view. However, if, as I have demonstrated, rational learning is not the only factor that explains policy switches, and coercion or emulation also play a role, then we need to speculate about the consequences of choosing policies on the basis of these alternative mechanisms. As Elkins and Simmons suggest (2005), deviating from learning when making policy choices is likely to result in suboptimal policy choices. If that is the case, a clear policy recommendation follows: Governments and international organizations should be encouraged to institutionalize the process of diagnosis and policy response. I explore the sense in which rational learning and rational choice can be made realistic enough so that this model can be used as a guiding principle in real policy making.

This final chapter proceeds as follows: First, I summarize and discuss the main lessons of the book. I devote some space to discussing what we have learned about the role of economic crises in spurring learning and policy change. Next, I discuss the main results for the alternative hypotheses. In particular, I discuss whether the switches to liberal economic policies had to do with coercion, with imitating the behavior of others, or with domestic factors. This book is a first attempt at tackling very complex substantive and methodological issues, and so it poses as many questions as it answers. Thus, in the last section, I discuss the substantive and normative issues that remain unresolved. Among these questions, I stress the prospects for economic reform in the post–Washington Consensus era.

7.1. Lessons about Learning

I argued that the first step in testing whether learning caused the shift toward market-oriented reforms was to come up with a working definition of learning. In this book, I assumed that policy makers are rational learners, meaning that they process all information in the same way. Starting with some initial beliefs that reflect the uncertainty about the outcomes of policies, policy makers use the evidence provided by their own and other countries' experience to update their initial beliefs about outcomes. The value given to the observed experience is directly related to the quantity of information it provides and also to its quality – that is, to how reliable the information is as an indicator of the true impact of policies on outcomes. In fact, if policy makers are very uncertain in their prior beliefs, and observed experience is overwhelming in quantity and quality, all policy makers will converge in their posterior beliefs. In addition, if they choose policies rationally on the basis of posterior beliefs, they will make the same policy choices.

I operationalized the quality of the information regarding policy outcomes by including in the model specification a variable measuring learning about the volatility of those outcomes. Here the presumption was that, if the results of policies vary widely, it would be more difficult for policy makers to draw clear conclusions about the link between a particular policy and the observed outcome; it would also be more difficult to anticipate the consequences of adopting a particular policy.

Because policy making is frequently a choice among at least two alternative courses of action (the status quo and an alternative policy), and because narratives suggested that policy makers learn both from the mistakes of particular policies and from the successes of alternative ones, I modeled the learning process as a comparative exercise: Governments learn from different policy status, compare what they have learned, and make decisions in the light of what they have learned. This, I argued, is an advance on the very few tests of learning that have been undertaken to date in cross-national research.

Because the acquisition of information is costly even for a rational learner, I assume that governments may learn from three different sources of information: Their own past experience with policies, the experience of the region they belong to, and the experience of other countries in the world. I distinguished rational learning from rational choice. In other words, I did not assume that rational learning is necessarily accompanied by a policy switch. Policy makers may actually learn rationally from experience, but the experience may not be conclusive. Thus, a switch may not be justified. Moreover, the experience may be conclusive in pointing to a clearly superior policy, and yet a policy switch may not be observed, for a host of political reasons. Finally, a policy switch may be observed but rational learning may not be the explanation, or the only explanation, for it.

Note that my analysis has been deductive but also exploratory. Starting with a specific hypothesized model of policy learning and policy choice, the question asked was how well this model predicts what we observe. My initial expectations were clear regarding the fact that governments are more likely to change policies if they learn from evidence showing that an alternative policy leads to better outcomes than the status quo. Yet, regarding attitudes toward risk and regarding how a rational learner would process information coming from different sources, my priors were weaker. Under the assumption of risk aversion, I expected governments to prefer policies that deliver good outcomes with little volatility. Under the assumption that the cost of acquiring information is low, I expected governments to prefer more evidence to less. Thus, in principle, information coming from the world should have a greater impact on policy decisions than information based on the country's own past experience or the experience in the region.

Before evaluating the results provided by this approach to learning and to policy choice, it is worth examining the pattern of policy choices regarding the illustrations I surveyed in the book. As it is possible to see from Figure 7.1, in all cases there was an increase in the proportion of countries liberalizing their trade and capital accounts, privatizing, and adopting IMF agreements. However, the trend was not steady across policies, and the proportion of countries that adopted each of these liberal policies at the end of the period varied greatly. Whereas, in the case of privatization and trade liberalization, the proportion is about eighty percent of countries in the sample under that policy at the end of the period under study, it is no more than forty percent for the other

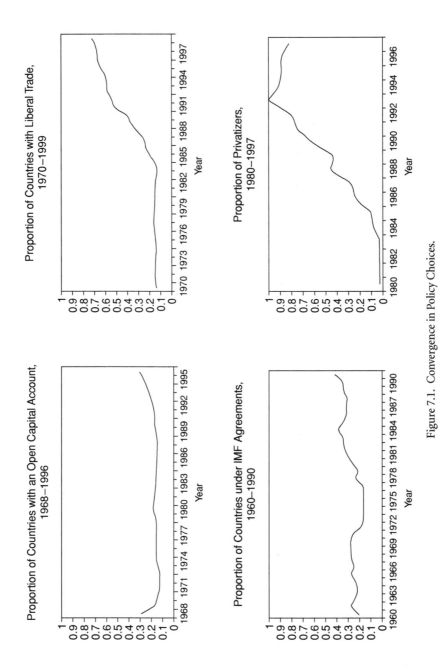

Figure 7.1. Convergence in Policy Choices.

7.1. Lessons about Learning

policies. Also, recall that the regional coverage differed among policy cases. The study of development strategies and trade liberalization looked at developing countries only. The analysis of IMF agreements and capital account liberalization covered both developed and developing countries. Finally, the study on privatization focused on Latin America and the OECD.

How much does this model of rational learning and rational choice help our understanding of the wave of market reforms? In commenting on the findings, I shall focus on the results that proved robust to the inclusion of controls. For development strategies and trade liberalization, capital account liberalization, and IMF agreements, the models took several external shocks into account. Table 7.1 and Figure 7.2 provide a summary of results for the decision *to adopt* these policies. Numbers in bold refer to changes in the predicted probabilities of *sustaining* them. The table shows the sign, significance, and simulated change on the predicted probability of adoption of moving one standard deviation above and below the mean of the relevant predictors.

Recall the main expectations of this study as spelled out in Chapter 2: (1) Under the assumption of risk aversion, rational learning from the volatility of results was expected to have a negative impact on the probability of policy adoption: The greater the expected variability of results of, say, privatizing vis-à-vis not privatizing, the less likely a switch to privatization. (2) Rational learning from average results was anticipated to have a positive impact on the probability of switching and sustaining reforms: The greater the posterior belief about growth privatizing versus not privatizing, the more likely a switch to privatization. (3) Under the assumption of rationality, learning based on the experience in the world, that is, on more observations, was expected to have the greatest impact on the probability of switching. Finally (4) rational learning was expected to be more consequential in explaining the probability of *adopting* than of *sustaining* market reforms. This is because the premise of autonomous change teams whose learning crucially shapes economic decision making is less defensible in the mid- and long term. The introduction of some of the aforementioned reforms, such as reducing or eliminating barriers to trade, can be achieved by a few key actors and by administrative decree. However, eventually, whether reforms are sustained depends, among

220   *Conclusions*

Table 7.1. *Summary of results. Change in predicted probabilities of adopting and sustaining policies (percentage points)*

Change in the predicted probability of switching and sustaining	Development strategies 1964–90 (a)	Trade liberalization 1970–99 (b)	Privatization 1980–97 (c)	Capital account liberalization 1970–96 (d)	IMF agreements 1960–90 (e)
OWN EXPERIENCE					
AVERAGE RESULTS	1 (*)	2 (**)			
VARIABILITY OF RESULTS				0.8 (*) −3 (*)	−6 (*)
REGIONAL EXPERIENCE					
AVERAGE RESULTS			9 (*)		
VARIABILITY OF RESULTS					
WORLD EXPERIENCE					
AVERAGE RESULTS			12 (**)	0.6 (*) **8 (***)**	8 (**)
VARIABILITY OF RESULTS	−7 (***)	−3 (**)			
COERCION	3 (**)			1 (**)	
EMULATION	4 (***)	3 (***)	17 (***)	−5 (*)	10 (**) *(f)* **7 (*)**
REGIME		−5 (***)			

Note: The coefficients were significant at 10%; **significant at 5%; ***significant at 1%.
Changes in predicted probabilities of one standard deviation above and below the mean, all other variables set at their mean values.
For the dichotomous variables (COERCION and DEMOCRACY), the simulated changes correspond to moves from 0 to 1.
Numbers in bold correspond to the changes in the predicted probability of *sustaining* the policies.
Predictions in (a) are based on Model 3, Table 3.3.
Predictions in (b) are based on Models 3 and 4, Table 3.4.
Predictions in (c) are based on Model 2, Table 4.1.
Predictions in (d) are based on Model 3 and 4, Table 5.3.
Predictions in (e) are based on Model 5 and 6, Table 6.3.
(f) The number reported is the simulated change in the probability of moving from the minimum to the median of the distribution.

other things, on whether they bear fruit and thus gather the support of the general public, but also on whether the losers from reforms are compensated, and whether the political opposition and other potential veto players agree to support the reforms. Thus, following Hall (1993), learning has to be social for reforms to be sustained.[1]

The most interesting way to look at Table 7.1 is to compare the results by rows – that is, among policies. The table shows that rational learning

[1] Jacoby (2000) makes a similar point in his study of successful and failed imitations.

7.1. Lessons about Learning

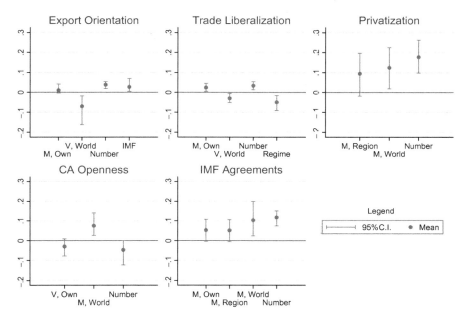

Figure 7.2. Predicted Change in the Probability of Adopting Several Market Policies and 95% Confidence Interval, with all other variables set at their mean values. The figure for capital account openness refers to changes in the probability of *sustaining* that policy. V refers to learning from volatility, M refers to learning from average results, and Number is the number of other countries carrying out the policy in question.

played a significant role in the adoption of all policy decisions. Yet, when it comes to comparing the magnitude of the effects, it is clear that rational learning was particularly relevant in the adoption of privatization (Chapter 4). It was marginal in the decision to liberalize the capital account (and less so in the decision to keep it open) (Chapter 5), and it fell somewhere in between in the decisions to change development strategies and to liberalize trade (Chapter 3) and in the decision to enter into agreements with the IMF (Chapter 6).

Figure 7.2 is another way of depicting the main findings of this study. The figure shows the mean predicted change in probability of adoption and the 95% confidence interval of moving one standard variation around the mean of the significant predictors. The further away the mean prediction is from the zero line, the stronger the impact of the variable in question. However, the effect is ambiguous (at least at the 95% confidence level) when the confidence interval includes zero.

222   *Conclusions*

There are two strong, consistent and, unambiguous results: Learning from the experience of each of these policies in the WORLD and the number of other countries under a particular policy did significantly affect the probability of adopting these policies. Learning and emulation turned out not to be exclusive phenomena. Indeed, governments learned as much as they imitated the policies previously embraced by others.

The findings closely match the initial expectations as spelled out earlier. In general, rational learning was more relevant to explaining policy switches than in accounting for policy continuity. Recall, however, that, due to data constraints, I estimated the probability only of sustaining an open capital account and of entering into agreements with the IMF.[2] On average, the signs are as expected: Positive for mean results and negative for the volatility of results. In addition, when it comes to comparing the different geographic sources of information, the WORLD appears to be the most relevant in frequency and magnitude (significant in the five policy illustrations). I found weaker and more ambiguous evidence in favor of learning from the other geographic sources of information. This finding matches the expectations of rational learning: Provided the information is readily available, a rational learner prefers more information over less.

Interestingly, regional experience turned out to be significant in explaining the adoption of the only policy innovation in the sample of policies: Privatization. This may be related to the fact that, being an *innovation*, the amount of experience available to learn from was initially scant and geographically concentrated (Weyland 2007). In particular, the impact of rational learning from regional experience on the decision of Latin American countries to privatize was the strongest in the study. However, it is important to keep in mind that the sample used for this illustration was the least random of all: Only Latin American and OECD countries were considered; the two reform pioneers (Britain and Chile) belonged to these regions; and privatization was widely practiced in both of them.[3]

---

[2] I also estimated the probability of sustaining privatization but in a model without controls. In that model, only the variability of results from own experience mattered (see Chapter 4).

[3] The other peculiarity of this illustration is that, for each of the regions, world experience is confined to experience in the other region.

7.1. Lessons about Learning

The lack of significance of regional experience in most illustrations may be surprising, but it is less so when one analyzes both the narratives and the data. In fact, this study gave multiple examples in which policy makers explicitly referred to experiences outside their regions as sources of inspiration. The narrative on Mexican financial reforms revealed that learning from experience outside Latin America was not infrequent.[4] Extensive learning from the East Asian experience epitomizes this phenomenon, too. For instance, Leszek Barcerowicz, who was responsible for the Polish shock therapy stabilization program, asserted that "[a]nother important lesson was that, in the absence of competition, import substitution and the heavy regulation of the economy are sufficient to cause low efficiency and widespread rent-seeking; private property cannot remedy this situation. These were the negative conclusions I drew from the experiences of many Latin American countries and India . . ." (in Blejer and Coricelli 1995: 65). He added, "I was especially attracted to the cases of radical policy shifts leading to what were called, after the event, 'economic miracles'. So I studied in depth the experience of South Korea . . ."

Interestingly, another Eastern European reformer, Peter Bod of Hungary, downplayed the inspiring role played by his most obvious neighbors. He stated that "[i]t is evident that countries facing similar historic tasks should learn from one another's successes and mistakes. Nevertheless, I could not say that the countries of the former Soviet empire should have paid much attention to one another. External coercion had forced peoples of different natures and different cultures into the Soviet sphere of interest, and, in spite of the similarities, the ways and means of making the break have also been different" (in Blejer and Coricelli 1995: 65). Thus, this sort of statement, widely documented in the introductory chapter together with the results of this study, points to two facts: First, at least in the realm of economic policy reforms, policy makers do pay attention to distant experiences as long as they find them relevant. In other words, in the arena of first-generation economic reforms availability is not as constraining as the defenders of the bounded learning approach claim. Second, the "regional" category, which is widely used in international and comparative political economy, may be more fictional than real. Under the regional umbrella, many different experiences coexist.

---

[4] See Chapter 5.

224   *Conclusions*

In fact, a closer look at the data revealed that there was a wide variation in both interregional and intraregional adoption of reforms (World Bank 2005; Guisinger, 2005; Simmons, Dobbin, and Garrett 2006). Latin America ranks as a dynamic reformer in any interregional comparison. At the other extreme, Sub-Saharan Africa appears as a perpetual failed reformer (Van de Walle 2001), which, however, contributes about one third of the country-year observations in the capital account and IMF case studies, and about half the country-year observations in the trade case study. In this region as much as in South Asia and the Middle East, reforms were mostly confined to a few isolated countries, thus making "average regional experience" a largely uninformative category.

Finally, I should stress an important finding: Even when rational learning seems particularly powerful, it was not the most important factor causing politicians to change and to sustain policies – except in the Development Strategies case study. In the case of privatization, emulation outstripped rational learning; in the case of IMF agreements, domestic conditions (not reported in the table) told the bulk of the story; and for trade liberalization in the database that covers the period 1970–99, being a democracy seems to predict the decision to liberalize better than does learning. In sum, rational learning, specifically from the world experience, was unambiguously an important variable to explain the switch in policies, but always in conjunction with other explanations.

Taken together, these results demonstrate that policy makers' stories and scholars' frequent claims about the relevance of learning in shaping the content of market reforms amount to more than isolated anecdotes: On average, governments did learn, and on average governments did switch policies as a result of that learning.

Learning and Economic Shocks

Most of the time, policy making happens in a context of continuity. To use Hall's (1993) terminology, normal policy making entails either first- or second-order changes, the latter meaning just marginal changes in the policy instruments or in the levels at which those policy instruments are set. However, shifts in policy paradigms – that is, changes in the ultimate goals of economic policy – sometimes happen and are intimately related to the fact that a particular economic model no longer works. In common with other authors, I considered that the shift in policy that took place in the 1980s and 1990s can be depicted as a paradigm shift (Kahler 1990, 1992; Biersteker 1995). Fighting inflation became the primary goal of economic policy. Markets gained prominence over the state when it came to promoting economic development. If the state was to be active in any area, it would be so precisely in creating the conditions for the good performance of markets.

The narrative stories suggested that major economic disruptions brought into question the validity of the model, leading to a revision of the cause and effect relationships that characterize a particular paradigm. In order to test the impacts of crises on learning and of crises and learning on policy switches, I assumed that deep crises affect the learning process because they increase the uncertainty attached to policy makers' beliefs about policies. A mild economic recession may not bring into question the validity of the economic model. The same can be true of a shock due to exogenous factors. Yet, a major economic disruption attributed to bad management is very likely to increase uncertainty about the validity of previous policy ideas. This is the intuition: When a crisis takes place, uncertainty about the "correct" model of the world and about what to expect from alternative policies increases. Policy makers react by observing the experience of other countries with alternative policies in an attempt to gain information and to reduce the uncertainty caused by the crisis. This is, I believe, a very compelling description of how economic shocks may affect the way in which policy makers revise their beliefs about the expected outcomes of policies. Note that modeling the effect of crises as an increase in uncertainty about the parameters of the model did not entail policy switches.[5] It imposed more attention on actual data on the part of policy makers, but, if the data on alternative policies are inconclusive, then policy switches may not occur.

This study shows that the impact of the 1982 debt crisis on learning from alternative development strategies was important to explain the shift toward more open trade regimes. The model of learning from the financial crises of the 1990s did not explain the adoption of

[5] See Chapter 2.

226   *Conclusions*

capital account openness; but it partly explained the decision to keep the capital account open,[6] in the sense that (imprudent) liberalization was a cause of financial crises, not vice versa. Thus, the financial turmoil provided lessons concerning the desirability of sustaining a policy that had been previously adopted. Note, however, that learning was not the most important determinant of the decision to sustain an open capital account: Trade flows significantly conditioned the decision to stay open.[7] Since the impact of the allegedly more influential financial crises was not covered in the analysis, this finding should be taken as suggestive but also as preliminary.

Whereas this approach to modeling the impact of crises on learning is substantively persuasive and empirically interesting, it is not without problems. Most obviously, this approach does not fully capture the impact of political shocks that, despite not having major disruptive consequences for global growth figures, may deeply affect policy makers' beliefs about the validity of alternative economic models. For instance, the fall of the Berlin Wall in the late 1980s was a political watershed that, despite not translating into a major international economic recession, had worldwide consequences in terms of the assessment of the feasibility of alternative economic models. To some extent, I confirmed this point in a different way. At least in Latin America, the decision to privatize was positively related to the events that took place in Eastern Europe and the former Soviet Union in the late 1980s and early 1990s.

7.2. Alternative Hypotheses

Learning is just one possible mechanism causing policies to converge. As explained in the introductory chapter, there are other horizontal diffusion mechanisms, such as *emulation*, that may have generated the same outcome. Policy convergence may have been *imposed* by a third party (top-down convergence). Alternatively, convergence might have been the result of independent but coincidental responses to the same

---

[6] Both for capital account openness and for trade liberalization, learning was significant only after the crises were modeled as an increase in the uncertainty of governments' beliefs about the outcomes of policies (Chapters 3 and 5).

[7] See Chapter 5.

environmental conditions (bottom-up convergence). I expected policy switches to have resulted from a blend of these different mechanisms, with neither domestic factors nor international factors exclusively telling the whole story. This research, like other recent studies, reveals that previous work that did not pay detailed and systematic attention to diffusion processes was missing an important part of the picture (see the contributions in Levi-Faur and Jordana 2005; Knill 2005; Simmons, Dobbin, and Garrett 2006; Weyland 2007).

Imposition and Emulation

Imposition refers to the adoption of particular policies as the outcome not of choice but of coercion. Some supranational or international entity may use its position of power to impose policies on national governments that have no alternative but to submit to its demands. This is the crudest portrayal of how external imposition may cause policies to converge, and the crudest representation of this crudest imposition is epitomized by IMF conditionality.

Quantitative and aggregate research of the type I carried out operationalizes imposition by including in empirical models variables that measure the amount of money received from international financial institutions – World Bank, IMF, affiliation with international organizations that imply a commitment to particular policies – GATT/WTO, or the presence of an agreement with the IMF. These, however, are only rough indicators of imposition, let alone of the likelihood of the policies prescribed actually being implemented. However, even if the indicators are rough proxies, in principle likely to overstate the role played by these organizations, the truth is that support for the coercion hypothesis in recent studies is either poor or contradictory (see the contributions in Simmons, Dobbin, and Garrett 2006).

Admittedly, measuring imposition in this way, which is typical of big N research designs, is bound to capture only the most partial and probably uninteresting aspects of the role that international powers may play in causing particular policy choices to be adopted. From recent research on this topic, we know that IFIs rarely coerce; instead, they persuade. Programs are adopted out of consensus and coincidence of

228 *Conclusions*

views rather than out of external imposition. We also know that national governments have actively sought to have policies that they privately want imposed on them in order to help them deal with domestic opposition. We know that IFIs are not purely technocratic institutions and that this has consequences for the outcomes of the policies they prescribe. We also know that, on occasion, funding from IFIs has been used to delay reforms and to finance the neo-patrimonial policies of corrupt governments (Stallings 1992; Kahler 1992; Haggard and Webb 1994; Thacker 1999; Van de Walle 2001; Stone 2002; Easterly 2003; Vreeland 2003, 2007). The complexity of these relationships cannot be fully captured by rough operationalizations, and we ought to be cautious about how much we can say when we proceed in this way.

In this research, being under an agreement with the IMF was positively related to two of the policies surveyed: Liberalizing the capital account and adopting an export-oriented development strategy. However, the effects were small. Moreover, the impact of IMF agreements on trade liberalization vanished in the (1970–1999) sample. Overall, and in accordance with the established literature on economic reforms and on the diffusion of economic policies, governments enjoyed considerable latitude in their decisions about which reforms to undertake.

Emulation is the other horizontal diffusion mechanism that I considered. The line that separates learning from emulation is subtle but nonetheless real. Whereas learning, be it of the rational or the bounded type, entails a purposive search for information about what works and a more or less sophisticated understanding of what causes what outcome, emulation does not entail a reflection on causal paths relating policies to outcomes (Holzinger and Knill 2005; Meseguer 2005; Elkins and Simmons 2005; Weyland 2005, 2007). Seeing many others adopting a particular policy stance is taken by the emulator as a sign that the policy is good. Adoption by many others also serves the purpose of making the policy choice more legitimate if opposition to a policy exists. A policy is adopted not because it has been understood to be superior but because the sheer number of others adopting it makes it good, and enhances its legitimacy in the eyes of the emulator.

It seems that learning does not preclude emulation; that is, policy makers may adopt policies already embraced elsewhere both because they have learned that they are better policies and because a large number of previous adoptions reinforce policy makers' belief that the policies are good. Indeed, and again according to the results, we observe that when one mechanism is significant so is the other. Thus, the results suggest that the two mechanisms are likely to operate in tandem. Emulating the behavior of others proved the most important thrust to privatize. It was also significant and with the expected sign in decisions concerning development strategies and trade liberalization, and, up to a point, the number of other countries under IMF agreements substantially increased the probability of participating in, and of remaining under, IMF contracts.[8] However, the number of other countries with an open capital account reduced rather than increased the probability of *sustaining* this policy. This counterintuitive result is significant after several factors are controlled for and after the 1990s financial crises are modeled. One possible explanation is that, over the period of study, capital account openness was far from being a consensual policy. Indeed, capital controls were first advocated and later questioned, to be vindicated again in the aftermath of the financial crises (Chwieroth 2008). On the whole, in theory and practice, capital account openness was the most controversial of the market reforms in this study.

Domestic Politics and Economics

Beyond a descriptive account of the results, there is a substantive issue concerning domestic politics that deserves closer inspection. In all model specifications, I controlled for the political regime. Rivers of ink have been spilled on the compatibility between democratization and the adoption of market reforms (Nelson 1990a; Przeworski 1991; Pereira, Maravall, and Przeworski 1993; Haggard and Kauffman 1992, 1995; Haggard and Webb 1994; Williamson 1994; Geddes 1994; Weyland 2002). On the one hand, many scholars thought it unlikely that such unpopular policies could be accepted and implemented in a context in which people were allowed to vote. During the 1960s and 1970s the fact that some

---

[8] After a certain point, an excess of customers reduced the probability of getting a loan via the requirement of more stringent conditions (see Chapter 6).

230   *Conclusions*

of the most radical and successful market reforms were accomplished under brutal dictatorships that repressed any opposition seemed to back the view that dictatorships were better equipped to make their citizens swallow the bitter pill. However, in the 1980s and 1990s, a wave of democratization preceded and accompanied the adoption of market reforms. Surprisingly, in quite a few cases, radical reforms even boosted the popularity of democratically elected leaders, against all odds, albeit temporarily (Stokes 2001b). To be sure, in some of the new democracies, governments resorted to *quasi*-dictatorial means to pass the reforms where there was opposition to them (O'Donnell 1994). However, it is also true that other new democracies that could rely on broad majorities built popular consensus among contending social groups by compensating the losers, and, relying on a gradual approach to reform, were able to pass them at the same time as their young democracies were being consolidated (Bresser, Maravall, and Przeworski 1993; Maravall 1997).

If economic policies are to be adopted under democracy, the crucial datum is what the median voter wants. In other words, to make compelling the argument that democratization is compatible with economic reforms entails demonstrating that the median voter preferred liberal economic policies, and particularly that there was a shift in the position of the median voter, who, in other periods of history, voted for interventionist policies.

Some of the economic policies surveyed in this study were clearly designed to gain the support of the median voter. The case of privatization and popular capitalism is paradigmatic: Let us transform the median voter into a small shareholder with a stake in the privatization process. For other economic policies, such as trade liberalization, economic theory suggests that abundant factors operated. At least in developing countries, where the median voter is an unskilled worker and, in turn, the abundant factor, democratization should be accompanied by greater demands for liberalization.[9] Thus, in LDCs, democracy would be perfectly compatible with trade liberalization. This is precisely the result that Milner and

---

[9] It is well known that the predictions of economic theory regarding who will benefit from particular policies can tell us little about actual outcomes independently of the capacity for collective action of the potential beneficiaries and of those hurt by the reforms (see, for instance, Rudra 2002).

Kubota (2005) and Guisinger (2005) report and that I also found. The same logic would apply to democracy, developed countries, and capital account liberalization in that cluster of countries.

Being democratic did increase the likelihood of opening up to trade in developing countries. Moreover, democracies also appeared to be more attentive to the world around them. Democracies were significantly more likely than dictatorships to jump on the trade liberalization bandwagon even if the number of other countries doing so was not overwhelming. The political regime mattered also in Latin America and for privatization, but the result was that less democratic regimes were more likely to privatize. Overall, I did not find support for the hypothesis that dictatorships are better equipped than democracies to engage in and to sustain market reforms. In fact, regime type appeared inconsequential for the most part.

7.3. What Remains To Be Learned?

This research is a novel approach to a long-standing question in political science: Do policy makers learn? In the discipline, no matter whether the research question is concerned with democratic transitions, economic reforms, particular public policies, or institution building, the argument that policies or institutions change because politicians and citizens learn is pervasive. I addressed this question with a particular model of learning that allowed me to test the role of rational learning in the adoption of liberal economic policies. This empirical strategy provided new insights, and above all, posed new questions and challenges that should motivate additional research. I comment next on the theoretical and normative issues that deserve further consideration.[10]

[10] The operationalization of learning used a Bayesian approach. The empirical strategy was a combination of Bayesian updating and classical statistical analysis. Several comments and caveats apply to this methodological approach: First, Bayesian updating is based on quite strong assumptions, in particular regarding the independence of observations gathered over time. Also, sample information is assumed to be independent – that is, the average rate of growth of Chile at time t is assumed to be independent of the average rate of growth of Peru also at t. These are strong assumptions, which make the analysis tractable. Yet, further research should explore the consequences of altering these assumptions and carefully modeling the time series component of the sequential updating process.

232 *Conclusions*

About Theory

Several substantive issues have not being addressed or resolved in this research. To recall, I modeled learning exclusively from economic results. To increase the comparability among policies, I assumed, in line with research on economic reform, that the main economic result policy makers cared about was economic growth. However, it could be argued that different policies are evaluated in terms of different economic results. Governments may privatize because they care about reducing public deficits or because they want to improve the performance of the privatized firms. Governments may reduce barriers to trade in the context of a stabilization program aimed at reducing inflation. Note that, as long as good and comparable data on these economic alternative variables exist, the Bayesian updating model can be easily adapted to take learning from these specific variables into account.

Obviously, policy makers care about things other than economic results. To be sure, I took domestic politics into account, at least controlling for some political variables such as the political regime, the proximity of elections, and the political leanings of the government.[11] Some policies have been very popular whereas others have attracted significant opposition. This is a piece of information that politicians are unlikely to ignore and that the model does ignore. For instance, case studies show that some governments felt attracted to privatization after seeing the high level of popularity that this policy achieved in the United Kingdom. Politicians may be concerned about this short-term popularity rather than the long-term objective of generating economic growth – although economic prosperity will very likely boost their popularity too.[12] The

---

[11] Focusing mainly on the political regime was justified by the heterogeneity of the regions included in this study, particularly in terms of political development. Other political variables such as party politics, political ideology, or veto players were bound to turn out to be of little significance in such a heterogeneous setting (see Guisinger 2005).

[12] There also seems to be a learning process concerning not only the outcomes of reforms, but also the politics of the reform process. Václav Klaus, a Czech reformist leader, asserted that "we learned from the experience of these countries [Poland and Hungary] that economic reforms measures must be systemic, consistent and quick, that social consent is indispensable, and that the reform process must be led by a strong right-wing political party that has the support of the majority of citizens" (in Blejer and Coricelli 1995: 67). In a telling statement, Polish reformer Balcerowicz acknowledged that "[w]hat I had in mind as a warning was the fate of Raúl Alfonsín in Argentina

7.3. What Remains To Be Learned?

question, then, is how to integrate learning from political results into the decision-making rule. This seems far from simple but it is certainly worth thinking about. What piece of information should we look at in modeling learning from political results? Should we look at data on re-election rates? On government popularity? On voting intentions? Perhaps other data concerning public opinion on specific policies? Would it be possible to find comparable and reliable data on these indicators of popular support so as to carry out cross-national research such as that undertaken for this book? These questions are certainly challenging, and addressing them is likely to result in a fascinating research program.

Another major issue is that the effect of learning has been tested in a linear fashion – that is, without conditioning on relevant factors such as the passage of time or domestic politics. For instance, the way learning takes place has been proved to evolve over time, with rational learning being gradually more relevant (Gilardi, Flüglister, and Luyet 2008). This suggests that policy makers may be temporarily bounded, but in the long run, rational learning prevails.

Besides, whether learning occurs may be conditional on other factors such as whether the regime is a well-functioning democracy with a capable bureaucracy. This is implied by Van de Walle's (2001: 170–77) research on African economic reform. This region is portrayed by the author as an example of non-learning in a context of a permanent crisis. According to the author, an ambivalent, if not hostile, ideological view of neo-liberal reform, coupled with the absence of a clear success story in the region, precluded learning. However, countries such as Ghana, Mauritius, South Africa, Botswana, and, more recently, Uganda, Tanzania, and Mozambique are often cited as cases of relative success. Arguably, these cases could have inspired reforms in other countries for which the status quo was not any better – at least for the general public. The author suggests that "relative" success was not enough to spur learning, though.

who started a radical stabilization programme as a very popular politician and who lost both the popularity and the stabilization. This is why I tended to prefer those policy options which were associated with a higher risk of being rejected by society but which, if implemented, promised to bring better economic results than those that were socially less risky but economically also less promising" (in Blejer and Coricelli 1995, 96). Note, then, than the gamble was political rather than economic: Market reforms were adopted because they were expected to deliver better outcomes.

Learning was, in part, precluded by dogmatism. Translated into the jargon of this study, dogmatism entails having little uncertainty about the beliefs one holds. This, in turn, makes the incentives to look around and learn minimal. However, it is sensible to hypothesize that dogmatism should be better explained by particular political conditions. Politicians may not learn and stick to policies that do not deliver if they are not held accountable for what they do and, at the same time, inaction is compatible with preserving their rents (Van de Walle 2001). Thus, in authoritarian regimes – particularly of the neo-patrimonial type (Kohli 2004) – and malfunctioning democracies, rational learning may not happen or may happen more slowly than in stable democracies that enjoy bureaucracies of the rational–legal type and a well-organized civil society. This is just an example of how conditioning posterior beliefs on particular political characteristics may throw light on why some governments in some regions appear to be faster learners than others.

Normative and Policy Questions: The Prospects for Market Reform in Developing Countries

This book looked into the change in policy paradigm that took place in the 1980s. This change translated into a whole set of policies that were implemented – with different degrees of zeal and coherence – in much of the developing world during the 1990s. I enquired whether learning from alternative development strategies was a relevant explanation for that switch, and concluded that, along with other domestic and international factors, it was. However, the results also revealed that there was a considerable amount of symbolic emulation. This may be of concern in that governments adopted policies that were perceived as increasing their status, but that may have been ill-fitted to their particular contexts (Elkins and Simmons 2005; Weyland 2007).

In this last section, I briefly review the reform experience of the 1990s and the lessons that are being learned after two decades of reforms. As much as governments were proved to have acted as Bayesian learners in the paradigm switch that took place in the 1980s, scholars now anticipate that governments will question the desirability of market reforms in the light of their partial success. For instance, discussing the reforms in

7.3. What Remains To Be Learned? 235

Eastern Europe and Russia, Stiglitz (2000: 567, emphasis added) states that:

There are externalities to the reform process: failures in one country convey lessons for others. Today, not only is there virtually no support in Russia for the form of reforms that characterized the 1990s there, but the perceived failures in Russia have also discredited the entire reform strategy. To be sure, the reasons for the failure may be many and only partly related to the reform strategy; yet *as good Bayesians*, those in other countries draw the inference that the form of the reforms was at least partly to blame.

I discuss how these lessons are affecting the thinking about development in academic and policy circles. I also speculate about what the lessons may imply for reformist governments in developing countries.

The balance sheet of more than a decade of reforms is in the eye of the beholder. The World Bank 2005 Report openly recognized several unmet expectations concerning the pace of development in countries that supposedly "did their homework." Despite notable variation, Latin America as a continent was probably the most enthusiastic reformer, but only recently has it started to reap the fruits of its diligence. In Eastern Europe and Russia, the recession that accompanied the transition was longer than expected, and the transformation of socialist economies into capitalist ones was mired in corruption (Tornell 2000). The economies of Sub-Saharan Africa remain stagnant.[13] And the financial crises of the late 1990s cast doubt on the unconditional promotion of capital mobility. When it happens, growth seems not to translate into better standards of living for the majority: Poverty and inequality remain a problem in many LDCs.

On the positive side, some countries managed to break the vicious circle of stagnation and poverty and seem now on the road to faster growth – Bangladesh, Botswana, China, and Tunisia, among others. Also, many countries have successfully stabilized their economies and macroeconomic mismanagement is much less a problem today than it was before. These are no small accomplishments. Indeed, any criticism of the decade of reforms will be more balanced and constructive if the likely outcome of the counterfactual (indeed the factual) of partial reform is

---

[13] Chinese investment and conditional debt relief may be bringing about a turnaround in the region, though (El País, 12/03/2007).

borne in mind, too. Van de Walle's (2001) excellent study of Africa is an example.

There are two alternative interpretations of these mixed results. One contends that reforms failed because their implementation was partial. From this perspective, the obvious corollary is that more commitment to reforms is needed, rather than a profound revision of ideas on economic development (Krueger 2000). A more critical interpretation is that the prevalent economic development paradigm consisted of a set of too-broad economic principles packaged in a single-minded approach to development. To be sure, the now widely criticized Washington Consensus came with no instructions as to its "correct" implementation. As the father of the term forcefully claims, it is probably unfair to blame what was meant to be a generic set of principles for what was made out of it in practice (Williamson 2000).

It is worth discussing a couple of issues concerning the shift in views that the reckoning just outlined has provoked. The first is the extent to which the mixed outcomes of reforms, and particularly the financial crises of the late 1990s, constitute a deep questioning of the underlying economic paradigm. Are we witnessing a shift in economic paradigm of the sort I explored in this study? In my view, the answer is no. The mixed record of the reforms suggests that some of the means were taken to be goals in themselves. One should not privatize or liberalize trade for the sake of it, but because privatization and trade liberalization are means to achieve greater efficiency and greater economic growth. Yet, however controversial the effect of these policies is taken to be, no one (or almost no one) would seriously think today that "looking only inward to support growth or . . . become deeply pessimistic about foreign markets [and] negligently manage short-term macroeconomic policies" is the way to go (Iglesias 1992: 70). The amendments being proposed are compatible with the view that the neoclassical paradigm is still alive (Rodrik 2007).

Second, the partial success of reforms also questions, in an important way, the would-be role of state policies in economic development. The most successful episodes used to illustrate the virtues of the orthodox approach indeed deviated considerably from the alleged orthodoxy. In particular, the role played by the state was prominent in East Asia in the 1960s and 1970s. It has been prominent in the China of the 1980s and

7.3. What Remains To Be Learned? 237

1990s, too (Rodrik 1996, 2003, 2006; Gore 2000). Today, a new group of policy advisers of the neo-statist type (as depicted by Stark and Bruszt 1998) advocates a more visible role for the state.

The fundamental lesson of a decade of market reforms, and more specifically of the financial crises, is that reforms are not unconditionally good. For them to bear fruit, reforms require a correct sequencing and institutional preconditions that are hardly met in most developing countries. Thus, the lesson goes, get your institutions right (rule of law, regulatory capacity, a capable and honest civil service) before anything else. This is, of course, easier said than done. Getting a Korean rational-legal bureaucracy is far more complicated than eliminating quotas. In particular, these transformations require resources and capable states in the first place, which are a scarce commodity in the poorest developing countries. Moreover, for good or ill, there is no blueprint about how to get institutions right. Thus, developing countries appear more than ever to be locked into a sort of inverse "orthodox paradox" (Kahler 1990): Whereas, in the 1980s and 1990s, big but weak states were required to withdraw from economic management, in the early twentieth century, weak states are required to become strong to be able to accomplish reforms successfully.

After these paradigm revisions, what is left for the reformist policy maker in LDCs? Is there anything more than confusion after the consensus (Naím 1999; Rodrik 2006)? On the one hand, policy makers could try to identify the particular constraint(s) on growth in their particular countries (Rodrik 2003, 2007).[14] It is a lesson of the decade of reforms that undertaking them without a clear focus on what needs to be changed is a sure recipe for failure. One should not privatize SOEs if SOEs are not a binding constraint on growth. One should not reform the financial sector if the financial sector is not an obstacle to growth. One should not undertake institutional reforms if institutions are not the problem. What may work in one country may not work in others because the constraints on growth are not universally the same. However, although certainly appealing, this type of approach requires a deep knowledge of many aspects

---

[14] See also Rodrik, Hausmann, and Velasco. 2005. Growth Diagnostics. Web site: http://ksghome.harvard.edu/~drodrik/papers.html.

238   *Conclusions*

of the economy in question. Further, diagnosing growth, designing a policy accordingly, and institutionalizing the reform – which, indeed, entails institutionalizing learning – appears even more demanding on frequently nonexistent or weak indigenous technical and administrative capabilities.

On the other hand, reformist governments of the populist type may find in the vocal criticisms to the reform agenda not new ideas for action, but valuable ammunition to justify a backlash and undertake reforms that have already failed and caused much harm. In Latin America, a few cases of this sort of unlearning, feeding on reform fatigue, are of concern. Moreover, it is doubtful that the revision of the paradigm – and the policy recommendations that follow from it – will be enough to break the impasse in countries comfortably set in the type of nonlearning equilibrium described by Van de Walle (2001): One of dogmatism and clientelism. I am more optimistic than Van de Walle that the expansion of democracy could put a high bar on permanently failed policies. However, this may not happen in the short run, especially if democracy is mere window dressing.

One final reflection refers to the learning process undergone by IFIs during the 1990s. In particular, the East Asian financial crises and their consequences opened an internal debate about several aspects of capital mobility and more generally about the "one-size-fits-all" type of formula. The crises questioned the validity of the beliefs endorsed by the most radical approach to capital account openness. As a result of this internal battle of ideas, the gradualist approach to financial liberalization became dominant and the official appreciation of the role of capital controls (on inflows) somewhat more sympathetic. As Stanley Fischer recognized (1998), "there is no denying that each of these [financial] crises has been difficult – especially for the IMF members most adversely affected. In each case, we, the IMF and the international community as a whole, learned from our experiences."[15] However, this learning has translated into less official enthusiasm for rapid liberalization, but without

---

[15] Address by Fischer, First Deputy Managing Director of the IMF, Washington, 22 January 1998.

7.3. What Remains To Be Learned? 239

questioning the overall desirability of liberalization in the long run (Chwieroth 2008).

The debate on the would-be role of the IMF and other IFIs has also transcended the walls of the institutions themselves. In its active advocacy of rapid liberalization, the IMF prescribed policies for which there was little academic consensus, a multitude of qualifications, and contradictory evidence (Stiglitz 1998, 2000, 2002). The general view of its activities is that, in its role as development manager, the Fund made painful mistakes. As a result, a new role is being demanded of the Fund – one much more in line with its original mandate[16]: To focus on improving data gathering, surveillance, and disseminating the best data possible so that national governments can make the best policy choices. The IMF should contribute to reducing the biases in the processing of information and help countries with strong limitations in data gathering to reduce those biases, without alienating local expertise. This is a practical attempt to improve the rationality of decision-making processes and should be welcome. This is also an interesting demonstration that the rational perspective is not an academic abstraction but a template that can, in principle, inspire institutional reform. Likely, all the changes suggested here will have the greatest impact in so far as they de facto improve the policy advice function of IFIs.

All in all, the revisions that are being made to the paradigm that inspired the reforms of the 1980s and 1990s are substantial and important; yet they represent an emphatic reminder of what the goals of reform were rather than a change in the goals themselves. In my view, the lessons learned do not, by themselves, constitute an alternative policy paradigm. True, the state is being vindicated as a positive and necessary development tool; however, this vindication refers to means, and it should not be taken to be, itself, a goal. In the end, a politician who has learned the lessons spelled out earlier will carry out the same policies, albeit with more prudence and perhaps with more imagination.

Discussing the balance of reforms in Latin America, a commentator stated that "[t]he Latin American curse does not exist. There are deep

---

[16] See Chapter 6.

240 *Conclusions*

problems with solutions that require perseverance with policies and the intelligence to learn from our mistakes and the mistakes of others, recent mistakes and historical ones."[17] But it should not be forgotten that learning requires, first of all, incentives to doubt one's own beliefs, and second, analytical capacity to understand the lessons of the past and what is at stake. Countries and regions in which both requisites are present will go on learning, as they have in the past. However, in other countries and regions, improving mechanisms of political accountability, accumulating talent, and bureaucratic reform will probably have to be accomplished first.

[17] José Juan Ruiz, El País, 10/07/2005, p. 50, my translation.

References

Adler, Emanuel and Peter M. Haas. 1997. Conclusion: Epistemic Communities, World Order and the Creation of a Reflective Research Program. In *Knowledge, Power and International Policy Coordination*, edited by Peter M. Haas (Columbia, SC: University of South Carolina Press), 367–90.

Alvarez, Michael, José Cheibub, Fernando Limongi, and Adam Przeworski. 1997. *World Political and Economic Database*.

Amemiya, Takeshi. 1985. *Advanced Econometrics* (Cambridge, MA: Harvard University Press).

Appel, Hillary. 2000. The Ideological Determinants of Liberal Economic Reform: The Case of Privatization. *World Politics* **52**: 520–49.

Ardito, Nicolás. 1994. Panel Discussion. In *The Political Economy of Policy Reform*, edited by John Williamson (Washington, DC: Institute for International Economics), 457–466.

Arriagada, Genaro and Carol Graham. 1994. Chile: Sustaining Adjustment during Democratic Transition. In *Voting for Reform: Democracy, Political Liberalization, and Economic Adjustment*, edited by Steven B. Webb and Stephan Haggard (Oxford: Oxford University Press), 242–89.

Aspe, Pedro. 1993. *El Camino Mexicano de la Transformación Económica* (México: Fondo de Cultura Económica).

Bagheri, Fatholla M. and Nader Habibi. 1998. Political Institutions and Central Bank Independence: A Cross Country Analysis. *Public Choice* **96** (1–2): 187–204.

Baker, Andrew. 2003. Why Is Trade Reform so Popular in Latin America? A Consumption Based Theory of Trade Policy Preferences. *World Politics* **55**: 423–55.

Balassa, Bela. 1980. The Process of Industrial Development and Alternative Development Strategies. *Essays in International Finance*, No 141 (Princeton, NJ: Princeton University Press).

Balassa, Bela. 1989. Outward Orientation. *Handbook of Development Economics*, vol II, edited by Hollis Chenery and T. N. Srinivasa (New York, NY: Elsevier Science Publishers), 1645–89.

242 *References*

Barnett, Michael and Martha Finnemore. 2004. Expertise and Power at the International Monetary Fund. In *Rules for the World. International Organizations in Global Politics* (Ithaca, NY: Cornell University Press), 45–72.

Bates, Robert and Anne Krueger. 1993. *Political and Economic Interactions in Economic Policy Reform: Evidence from Eight Countries* (Oxford; Cambridge, MA: Blackwell).

Beck, Thorsten, Philip Keefer, and George Clarke. 2000. *Database on Political Institutions* (World Bank, 2000 version).

Bennett, Colin. 1991. What Is Policy Convergence and What Causes It? *British Journal of Political Science* **21** (2): 215–33.

Bennett, Colin and Michael Howlett. 1992. The Lessons of Learning: Reconciling Theories of Policy Learning and Policy Change. *Policy Sciences* **25**: 275–94.

Berger, James O. 1985. *Statistical Decision Theory and Bayesian Analysis*, 2nd edition (New York, NY: Springer–Verlag).

Berk, Richard, Alec Campbell, Ruth Klap, and Bruce Western. 1992. The Deterrent Effect of Arrest in Incidents of Domestic Violence: A Bayesian Analysis of Four Field Experiments. *American Sociological Review* **57**: 698–708.

Bermeo, Nancy. 1990. The Politics of Public Enterprise in Portugal, Spain and Greece. In *The Political Economy of Public Sector Reform*, edited by Ezra Suleiman and John Waterbury (Boulder, CO: Westview Press), 113–36.

Bhagwati, Jagdish. 1985. Trade Regimes. In *Dependence and Interdependence. Essays in Development Economics*, vol II, edited by Gene Grossman (Oxford: Blackwell Basil) 123–37.

Biersteker, Thomas. J. 1995. The Triumph of Liberal Economic Ideas in the Developing World. In *Global Change, Regional Response: The New International Context of Development*, edited by Barbara Stallings (New York, NY: Cambridge University Press), 174–96.

Bird, Graham. 1996a. Borrowing from the IMF: The Policy Implications of Recent Empirical Research. *World Development* **24** (11): 1753–60.

Bird, Graham. 1996b. The International Monetary Fund and Developing Countries: A Review of the Evidence and Policy Options. *International Organization* **50** (3): 477–511.

Birsch, Melissa and Jerry Haar, eds. 2000. *The Impact of Privatization in the Americas* (Miami, FL: University of Miami Press).

Bjork, James. 1995. The Uses of Conditionality: Poland and the IMF. *East European Quarterly* **29** (1): 89–120.

Blejer, Mario and Fabio Coricelli. 1995. *The Making of Economic Reform in Eastern Europe. Conversations with Leading Reformers in Poland, Hungary, and the Czech Republic* (London: Edward Elgar).

Blyth, Mark. 1997. Any More Bright Ideas? The Ideational Turn of Comparative Political Economy. *Comparative Politics* **29** (2): 229–50.

Blyth, Mark. 2002. *Great Transformations: Economic Ideas and Political Change in the Twentieth Century* (New York, NY: Cambridge University Press).

Boix, Carles. 1998. Political Parties, Growth, and Equality (New York, NY: Cambridge University Press).

References 243

Boix, Carles. 2003. *Democracy and Redistribution* (New York, NY: Cambridge University Press).

Bollard, Allan. 1994. New Zealand. In *The Political Economy of Policy Reform*, edited by John Williamson (Washington, DC: Institute for International Economics), 73–110.

Bordo, Michael and Harold James. 2000. The IMF: Its Present Role in Historical Perspective. *NBER Working Papers* 7724, June.

Braun, Dietmar and Fabrizio Gilardi. 2006. Taking Galton's Problem Seriously: Towards a Theory of Policy Diffusion. *Journal of Theoretical Politics* **18** (3): 298–322.

Bresser, Luiz C., José María Maravall, and Adam Przeworski. 1993. *Las Reformas Económicas en las Nuevas Democracias* (Madrid: Alianza Editorial).

Brinks, Daniel and Michael Coppedge. 2006. Diffusion Is No Illusion. Neighbor Emulation in the Third Wave of Democracy. *Comparative Political Studies* **39** (4): 463–489.

Broad, Robin and John Cavanagh. 1999. The Death of the Washington Consensus. *World Policy Journal* **16** (3): 79–88.

Brooks, Sarah M. 2005. Interdependent and Domestic Foundations of Policy Change: The Diffusion of Pension Privatization around the World. *International Studies Quarterly* **49**: 273–94.

Brooks, Sarah M. and Marcus Kurtz. 2007. Capital, Trade, and the Political Economies of Reform. *American Journal of Political Science* **51** (4): 703–20.

Broz, Lawrence. 2002. Political System Transparency and Monetary Commitment Regimes. *International Organization* **56** (4): 861–87.

Brune, Nancy and Geoffrey Garrett. 2000. "The Diffusion of Privatization in the Developing World." Manuscript, Yale University.

Brune, Nancy, Geoffrey Garrett, and Bruce Kogut. 2004. The IMF and the Global Spread of Privatization. *IMF Staff Papers* **51** (2): 195–219.

Brune, Nancy and Alexandra Guisinger. 2007. "Myth or Reality? The Diffusion of Financial Liberalization in Developing Countries." Manuscript, University of Pennsylvania.

Bruton, Henry. 1989. Import Substitution. In *Handbook of Development Economics*, vol II, edited by Hollis Chenery and T. N. Srinivasan (New York, NY: Elsevier Science Publishers B.V.), 1601–44.

Bueno de Mesquita, Bruce, Alistair Smith, Randolph Siverson, and James Morrow. 2003. *The Logic of Political Survival* (Cambridge, MA: MIT Press).

Buttari, Juan J. 1994. A Review of Economic Policies and Strategies for Trade and Industrialization in Central America. In *Trade Integration and Industrialization in 20th Century Central America*, edited by Irma de Aloson (Westpoint, NY: Praeger), 223–36.

Celarier, Michelle. 1996. Privatization: A Case Study in Corruption. *Journal of International Affairs* **50** (2): 531–43.

Centeno, Miguel. 1994. *Democracy within Reason: Technocratic Revolution in Mexico* (Philadelphia, PA: Penn State University Press).

Chang, Roberto. 1999. Understanding Recent Crises in Emerging Markets. *Federal Reserve Bank of Atlanta Economic Review*, Second Quarter: 6–16.

244 *References*

Chiluba, Frederick. 1996. *Democracy. The Challenge of Change* (Lusaka: Multimedia Publications).

Chwieroth, Jeffrey. 2007. Neoliberal Economists and Capital Account Liberalization in Emerging Markets. *International Organization* **61**: 443–63.

Chwieroth, Jeffrey. 2008. Norm Adoption from Within. The International Monetary Fund's Approach to Capital Account Liberalization. *International Studies Quarterly* **52** (1): 129–58.

Clark, Mary. 2001. *Gradual Economic Reform in Latin America. The Costa Rican Experience* (Albany, NY: State University of New York Press).

Clifton, Judith, Francisco Comín, and Daniel Díaz-Fuentes. 2003. *Privatization in the European Union* (Dordrecht: Kluwer Academic Publishers).

Cohen, Benjamin. 1996. *The Geography of Money* (Ithaca, NY: Cornell University Press).

Collier, Ruth and David Collier. 1991. *Shaping the Political Arena. Critical Junctures, the Labor Movement, and Regime Dynamics in Latin America* (Notre Dame, IN: Notre Dame University Press).

Conway, Patrick. 1994. IMF Lending Programs: Participation and Impact. *Journal of Development Economics* **45**: 365–91.

Conway, Patrick. 2003. "Endogenous IMF Conditionality: Theoretical and Empirical Implications." Manuscript, Department of Economics, North Carolina-Chapel Hill.

Corbo, Vittorio. 2000. Economic Policy Reform in Latin America. In *Economic Policy Reform*, edited by Anne Krueger (Chicago, IL: University of Chicago Press), 61–98.

Coyle, R. G. 1972. *Decision Analysis* (London: Nelson).

De Groot, Morris. 1970. *Optimal Statistical Decisions* (New York, NY: McGraw–Hill).

De la Madrid, Miguel. 2004. *Cambio de Rumbo* (México D. F.: Fondo de Cultura Económica).

DiMaggio, Paul and Walter Powell. 1983. The Iron Cage Revisited. *American Sociological Review* **48** (2): 147–60.

Dolowitz, David and David Marsh. 2000. Learning from Abroad: The Role of Policy Transfer in Contemporary Policy-Making. *Governance* **13** (1): 5–24.

Domínguez, Jorge, ed. 1996. *Technopols: Freeing Politics and Markets in Latin America in the 1990s* (Philadelphia, PA: Penn State University Press).

Drazen, Allan. 2000. *Political Economy in Macroeconomics* (Princeton, NJ: Princeton University Press).

Drazen, Allan and William Easterly. 2001. Do Crises Induce Reform? Simple Empirical Tests of Conventional Wisdom. *Economics and Politics* **13** (2): 129–58.

Dreher, Alex. 2002. The Development and Implementation of IMF and World Bank Conditionality. *Discussion Paper* **165**. Hamburg Institute of International Economics.

Dreher, Alex. 2003. The Influence of Elections on IMF Programme Interruptions. *The Journal of Development Studies* **39** (6): 101–20.

Easterly, William. 2003. *The Elusive Quest for Growth. Adventures and Disadventures of Economists in the Tropics* (Cambridge, MA: MIT Press).

Edwards, Sebastian. 1989. Openness, Outward Orientaticn, Trade Liberalization and Economic Performance in Developing Countries, *NBER Working Papers* 2908.

Edwards, Sebastian. 1995. *Crisis and Reform in Latin America. From Despair to Hope* (Oxford: The World Bank and Oxford University Press).

Edwards, Sebastian. 1999. How Effective are Capital Controls? *Journal of Economic Perspectives* **13** (4): 65–84.

Edwards, Sebastian. 2001. Capital Mobility and Economic Performance: Are Emerging Economies Different? National Bureau of Economic Eesearch, *Working Paper* 8076.

Eichengreen, Barry. 1996. *Globalizing Capital. A History of the International Monetary System* (Princeton, NJ: Princeton University Press).

Eichengreen, Barry. 2001. "Capital Account Liberalization: Wʰat Do the Cross Country Studies Tell Us?" Manuscript, University of California-Berkeley.

Eichengreen, Barry and David Leblang. 2003. Capital Account Liberalization and Growth: Was Mr. Mahathir Right? *International Journal of Finance and Economics* **8**: 205–24.

Elkins, Zachary and Beth Simmons. 2005. On Waves, Clusters, and Diffusion: A Conceptual Framework. *The Annals of the American Academy of Political and Social Sciences* **598**: 33–51.

Elkins, Zachary, Andrew T. Guzman, and Beth Simmons. 2006. Competing for Capital: The Diffusion of Bilateral Treaties, 1960–2000. *International Organization* **60** (4): 811–46.

Esser, Josef. 1998. Privatization in Germany: Symbolism in tʰe Social Market Economy? In *Privatisation in the European Union*, edited by Eavid Parker (London: Routledge), 101–21.

Etheredge, Lloyd. 1981. Government Learning: An Overview. In *The Handbook of Political Behavior*, 2, edited by Samuel L. Long (New York, NY: Pergamon), 73–161.

Evans, Peter. 1995. *Embedded Autonomy. States and Industrial Transformation* (Princeton, NJ: Princeton University Press).

Finnemore, Martha. 1996. *National Interests in International Society* (Ithaca, NY: Cornell University Press).

Fishlow, Albert. 1990. The Latin American State. *Journal of Economic Perspectives* **4** (3): 61–74.

Frankel, Jeffrey and David Romer. 1999. Does Trade Cause Growth? *American Economic Review* **89** (3): 379–99.

Frankfurter, George and Herbert E. Phillips. 1995. *Forty Years ᴐf Normative Portfolio Theory: Issues, Controversies and Misconceptions* (London: Jᴇy Press Inc.).

Franzese, Robert and Jude Hays. 2006. Strategic Interaction among EU Governments in Active–Labor–Market Policymaking: Subsidiarity and Policy Coordination under the European Employment Strategy. *European Union Politics* **7** (2): 167–89.

Freeman, Richard. 2006. Learning in Public Policy. In *The Oxfoʳd Handbook of Public Policy*, edited by M. M. Rein Moran and R. Goodin (Oxford: Oxford University Press), 367–88.

246 *References*

Frieden, Jeffrey. 1991a. *Debt, Development and Democracy: Modern Political Economy and Latin America, 1965–1985* (Princeton, NJ: Princeton University Press).

Frieden, Jeffrey. 1991b. Invested Interests: The Politics of National Economic Policies in a World of Global Finance. *International Organization* **45** (4): 425–51.

Gandhi, Jennifer. 2004. "Political Institutions under Dictatorship"(PhD dissertation, New York University).

Gärdenfors, Peter and Nils Sahlin. 1988. *Decision, Probability and Uncertainty* (New York, NY: Cambridge University Press).

Gärdenfors, Peter and Nils Sahlin. 1988. Introduction: Bayesian Decision Theory Foundations and Problems. In *Decision, Probability and Utility*, edited by Peter Gärdenfors and Nils Sahlin (New York, NY: Cambridge University Press), 1–18.

Gärdenfors, Peter and Nils Sahlin. 1988. Unreliable Probabilities, Risk Taking and Decision Making. In *Decision, Probability and Uncertainty*, edited by Peter Gärdenfors and Nils Sahlin (New York, NY: Cambridge University Press), 313–34.

Garrett, Geoffrey. 1998. *Partisan Politics in the Global Economy* (New York, NY: Cambridge University Press).

Garrett, Geoffrey, Mauro Guillén, and Bruce Kogut. 2000. "Privatization around the World." Manuscript, Yale University.

Garrett, Geoffrey and Barry Weingast. 1993. Ideas, Interests and Institutions: Constructing the European Community's Internal Market. In *Ideas and Foreign Policy*, edited by Judith Goldstein and Robert Keohane (Ithaca, NY: Cornell University Press).

Garuda, Gopal. 2000. The Distributional Effects of IMF Programs: A Cross Country Analysis. *World Development* **28** (6): 1031–51.

Geddes, Barbara. 1994. *Politician's Dilemma* (Berkeley, CA: University of California Press).

Gelman, Andrew, John B. Carlin, Hal S. Stern, and Donald B. Rubin. 2004. *Bayesian Data* Analysis, 2nd edition (London: Chapman and Hall).

Gerber, Alan and Donal P. Green. 1998. Rational Learning and Partisan Attitudes. *American Journal of Political Science* **42** (3): 794–818.

Gereffi, Gary and Donald Wyman. 1991. *Manufacturing Miracles: Paths of Industrialization of Latin America and East Asia* (Princeton, NJ: Princeton University Press).

Ghosh, Bimal N., ed. 2000. *Privatisation. The Asean Connection* (New York, NY: Nova Science Publishers).

Gilardi, Fabrizio, Katherina Flüglister, and Stephan Luyet. Learning from Others: The Diffusion of Hospital Financing in OECD Countries. Forthcoming: *Comparative Political Studies*.

Gill, Jeff. 2002. *Bayesian Methods. A Social and Behavioral Sciences Approach* (Boca Raton, FL: Chapman & Hall/CRC).

Gill, Jeff and Lee Walker. 2005. Elicited Priors for Bayesian Model Specifications in Political Science Research. *Journal of Politics* **67** (3): 841–72.

Gleditsch, Kristian and Michael Ward. 2006. Diffusion and the International Context of Democratization. *International Organization* **60**: 911–33.

References

Goldstein, Judith and Robert Keohane, eds. 1993. *Ideas and Foreign Policy: Beliefs, Institutions and Political Change* (Ithaca, NY: Cornell University Press).

Goodman, John B. and Louis Pauly. 1993. The Obsolescence of Capital Controls: Economic Management in an Age of Global Markets. *World Politics* **46**: 50–82.

Gore, Charles. 2000. The Rise and Fall of the Washington Consensus as a Paradigm for Developing Countries. *World Development* **28** (5): 789–804.

Gowda, Rajeev and Jeffrey Fox. 2002. *Judgements, Decisions and Public Policy* (New York, NY: Cambridge University Press.)

Granovetter, Mark. 1978. Thresholds Models of Collective Behavior. *American Journal of Sociology* **83**: 1420–43.

Grindle, Merilee and John W. Thomas. 1991. *Public Choices and Policy Change* (Baltimore, MD: Johns Hopkins University Press).

Grossman, Sanford J. and Joseph Stiglitz. 1976. Information and Competitive Price Systems. *American Economy Review Papers and Proceedings* **66**: 246–53.

Guisinger, Alexandra. 2005. "Understanding Cross Country Patterns in Trade Liberalization" (Doctoral dissertation, Yale University).

Guitián, Manuel. 1995. Conditionality: Past, Present and Future. *IMF Staff Papers* **42** (4): 792–825.

Haas, Peter M. 1992. Introduction: Epistemic Communities and International Policy Coordination. *International Organization* **46** (1): 1–35.

Haas, Peter. M. 1997. Introduction: Epistemic Communities and International Policy Coordination. In *Knowledge, Power and International Policy Coordination*, edited by Peter M. Haas (Columbia, SC: University of South Carolina Press), 1–35.

Haas, Peter M. and Ernst B. Haas. 1995. Learning to Learn: Improving International Governance. *Global Governance* **1**: 255–85.

Hacking, Ian. 1988. Slightly More Realistic Personal Probability. In *Decision, Probability and Utility*, edited by Peter Gärdenfors and Nils Sahlin (New York, NY: Cambridge University Press), 118–35.

Haggard, Stephan. 1990. *Pathways from the Periphery: The Politics of Growth in the Newly Industrial Countries* (Ithaca, NY: Cornell University Press).

Haggard, Stephan. 2000. *The Political Economy of the Asian Financial Crisis* (Washington, DC: Institute for International Economics).

Haggard, Stephan and Robert Kaufman, eds. 1992. *The Politics of Economic Adjustment: International Constraints, Distributive Conflicts, and the State* (Princeton, NJ: Princeton University Press).

Haggard, Stephan and Robert Kaufman, 1995. *The Political Economy of Democratic Transitions* (Princeton, NJ: Princeton University Press).

Haggard, Stephan and Sylvia Maxfield. 1996. The Political Economy of Financial Internationalization in the Developing World. *International Organization* **50** (1): 35–68.

Haggard, Stephan and Steve B. Webb, eds. 1994. *Voting for Reform: Democracy, Political Liberalization and Economic Adjustment* (New York NY: Oxford University Press).

Hall, Peter. 1989. *The Political Power of Economic Ideas. Keynesianism Across Countries* (Princeton, NJ: Princeton University Press).

248 References

Hall, Peter. 1993. Policy Paradigms, Social Learning and the State: The Case of Economic Policy Making in Britain. *Comparative Politics* **25** (3): 275–96.

Harberger, Arnold. 1993. Secrets of Success: A Handful of Heroes. *American Economic Review* **83** (2): 343–50.

Harrington, Joseph E. 1993. Economic Policy, Economic Performance and Elections. *American Economic Review* **53** (1): 27–42.

Harrison, Ann and Ana Revenga. 1995. The Effects of Trade Policy Reform. What Do We Really Know? *NBER Working Paper* No 5225.

Heclo, Hugh. 1974. *Modern Social Politics in Britain and in Sweden* (New Haven, CT: Yale University Press).

Hodge, Graeme. 2000. *Privatization: An International Review of Performance* (Boulder, CO: Westview).

Holzinger, Katarina and Christopher Knill. 2005. Causes and Conditions of Cross–National Policy Convergence. *Journal of European Public Policy* **12** (5): 775–96.

Hood, Christopher. 1994. *Explaining Economic Policy Reversals* (Buckingham: Open University Press).

Horn, Karen and Romain Wacziarg. 2003. *Trade Liberalization and Growth: New Evidence. NBER Working Paper* 10152.

Howlett, Michael and M. Ramesh. 1993. Patterns of Policy Instrument Choices: Policy Styles, Policy Learning and the Privatization Experience. *Policy Studies Review* **12** (1/2): 1–24.

Hulsink, Willem and Hans Schenk. 1998. Privatization and Deregulation in the Netherlands. In *Privatization in the European Union*, edited by David Parker (London: Routledge), 242–58.

Iglesias, Enrique. 1992. *Reflections on Economic Development. Toward a New Latin American Consensus* (Washington, DC: Inter-American Development Bank).

Iglesias, Enrique. 1994. Economic Reform. A View from Latin America. In *The Political Economy of Policy Reform*, edited by John Williamson (Washington, DC: Institute for International Economics), 493–499.

Ikenberry, John. 1990. The International Spread of Privatization Policies: Inducements, Learning and Policy Bandwagoning. In *The Political Economy of Public Sector Reform and Privatization*, edited by Ezra Suleiman and John Waterbury (London: Westview Press), 88–110.

Iversen, Torben and Thomas R. Cusack. 2000. The Causes of Welfare State Expansion: Deindustrialization or Globalization? *World Politics* **52**: 313–49.

Jacobsen, John K. 1995. Much Ado About Ideas: The Cognitive Factor in Economic Policies. *World Politics* **47**: 283–310.

Jacoby, Wade. 2000. *Imitation and Politics. Redesigning Modern Germany* (Ithaca, NY: Cornell University Press).

Jervis, Robert. 1976. *Perception and Misperception in International Politics* (Princeton, NJ: Princeton University Press).

Johnson, Simon and Todd Mitton. 2001. Cronysm and Capital Controls: Evidence from Malaysia. *NBER Working Paper* 8521.

Kahler, Miles. 1990. Orthodoxy and Its Alternatives: Explaining Approaches to Stabilization and Adjustment. In *Economic Crisis and Policy Choice*, edited by Joan Nelson (Princeton, NJ: Princeton University Press), 33–62.

Kahler, Miles. 1992. External Influence, Conditionality, and the Politics of Adjustment. In *The Politics of Economic Adjustment*, edited by Stephan Haggard and Robert Kaufman (Princeton, NJ: Princeton University Press), 89–138.

Kahneman, Daniel, and Amos Tversky. 1988. Prospect Theory: An Analysis of Decision Under Risk. In *Decision, Probability and Uncertainty*, edited by Peter Gärdenfors and Nils Sahlin (New York, NY: Cambridge University Press), 183–214.

Katzenstein, Peter. 1985. *Small States in World Markets. Industrial Policy in Europe* (Ithaca, NY: Cornell University Press).

Kaufmann, Daniel and Paul Siegelbaum. 1996. Privatization and Corruption in Transition Economies. *Journal of International Affairs* 50 (2): 419–59.

Keeler, John T. 1993. New Perspectives on Democratic Reform. *Comparative Political Studies* 25 (4): 427–32.

Kelly, Margaret and Anne K. McGuirck. 1992. *Issues and Developments in International Trade Policy* (Washington, DC: International Monetary Fund).

Kessler, Timothy P. 1999. *Global Capital and National Politics. Reforming Mexico's Financial System* (Westport, CT: Praeger).

King, Gary, Michael Tomz, and Jason Wittenberg. 2000. Making the Most of Statistical Analyses: Improving Interpretation and Presentation. *American Journal of Political Science* 44 (2): 341–55.

Knight, Malcolm. 1998. Developing Countries and the Globalization of Financial Markets. *World Development* 26 (7): 1185–1200.

Knill, Christopher, ed. 2005. Cross–National Policy Convergence: Concepts, Approaches, and Explanatory Factors. In a special issue of the *Journal of European Public Policy* 12 (5): 764–74.

Kogut, Bruce and J. Muir Macpherson. 2008. The Decision to Privatize as an Economic Policy Idea: Economists, Palace Wars, and Diffusion. In *The Global Diffusion of Markets and Democracy*, edited by Beth Simmons, Frank Dobbin, and Geoffrey Garrett, (New York, NY: Cambridge University Press), 104–40.

Kohli, Atul. 2004. *State–Directed Development. Political Power and Industrialization in the Global Periphery* (New York, NY: Cambridge University Press).

Krauze, Enrique. 2004. *La Presidencia Imperial* 5th edition (Mexico: Fabula Tusquets).

Krueger, Anne. 1983. Trade Strategies, Growth and Employment. In *Trade and Employment in Developing Countries*, vol III, edited by Anne O. Krueger (Chicago, IL: University of Chicago Press), 30–54.

Krueger, Anne. 1984. Trade Policies in Developing Countries. In *Handbook of International Economics*, vol 1, edited by Ronald W. Jones and Peter B. Kenen (New York: Elsevier Science Publishers), 519–69.

Krueger, Anne. 1985. Import Substitution vs. Export Promotion. *Finance and Development* 22: 20–3.

Krueger, Anne and Ronal W. Jones. 1990. *The Political Economy of International Trade. Essays in Honor of Robert E. Baldwin* (Oxford: Basil Blackwell).

250 References

Krueger, Anne. 1990. Government Failures in Development. *NBER Working Paper W3340*.

Krueger, Anne. 1993. *Political Economy of Policy Reform in Developing Countries* (Cambridge, MA: MIT Press).

Krueger, Anne. 1997. Trade Policy and Economic Development: How We Learn? *American Economic Review* **87** (1): 1–22.

Krueger, Anne, ed. 2000, *Economic Policy Reform* (Chicago, IL: University of Chicago Press).

Krugman, Paul. 1998. "The Eternal Triangle." Manuscript, MIT.

Kuczynski, Pedro P. and John Williamson. 2003. *After the Washington Consensus. Restarting Growth and Reform in Latin America* (Washington, DC: Institute for International Economics).

Kyburg, Henry. 1988. Bets and Beliefs. In *Decision, Probability and Uncertainty*, edited by Peter Gärdenfors and Nils Sahlin (New York, NY: Cambridge University Press), 101–19.

Leamer, Edward. E. 1991. A Bayesian Perspective on Inference from Macroeconomic Data. *Scandinavian Journal of Economics* **93** (2): 225–48.

Leblang, David. 1997. Domestic and Systemic Determinants of Capital Controls in the Developed and Developing World. *International Studies Quarterly* **41**: 435–54.

Leblang, David. 2003. "Is Democracy Incompatible with International Economic Stability?" Manuscript. Department of Political Science. University of Colorado, Boulder.

Lee, Chang Kil and David Strang. 2006. The International Diffusion of Public–Sector Downsizing: Network Emulation and Theory-Driven Learning. *International Organization* **60** (4): 883–909.

Lee, Peter M. 1997. *Bayesian Statistics: An Introduction*, 2nd edition (London: Arnold).

Lee, Simon. 2002. The International Monetary Fund. *New Political Economy* **7** (2): 283–98.

Levi–Faur, David and Jacint Jordana. 2005. The Rise of Regulatory Capitalism: The Global Diffusion of a New Order. *The Annals of the American Academy of Political and Social Sciences* **598** (1).

Levy, Jack S. 1994. Learning and Foreign Policy: Sweeping a Conceptual Minefield. *International Organization* **48** (2): 279–312.

Lieberman, Ira W. 1994. Privatization in Latin America and Eastern Europe in the Context of Political and Economic Reform. In www.worldbank.org.

Long, John S. and Jeremy Freese. 2006. *Regression Models for Categorical Dependent Variables Using Stata*, 2nd edition (Texas: Stata Press).

Lora, Eduardo. 2000. What Makes Reform Likely? Timing and Sequencing of Structural Reforms in Latin America. *IADB, Working Paper* 424.

Lukauskas, Arvid. 1997. *Regulating Finance: The Political Economy of Spanish Financial Policy from Franco to Democracy* (Ann Arbor, MI: University of Michigan Press).

Lukauskas, Arvid and Susan Minushkin. 2000. Explaining Styles of Financial Market Opening in Chile, Mexico, South Korea, and Turkey. *International Studies Quarterly* **44**: 695–723.

Lupia, Arthur and Matthew McCubbins. 1998. *The Democratic Dilemma: Can Citizens Learn What They Need to Know?* (New York, NY: Cambridge University Press).

Maloney, William F. 1994. Privatization with Share Diffusion: Popular Capitalism in Chile, 1985–1988. In *Privatization in Latin America: New Roles for the Public and the Private Sectors*, edited by Werner Bear and Melissa H. Firch (London: Praeger), 135–62.

Manzetti, Luigi. 1999. *Privatization South America Style* (Oxford: Oxford University Press).

Maravall, José María. 1997. *Regimes, Politics and Markets: Democratization and Economic Change in Southern and Eastern Europe* (Oxford: Oxford University Press).

March, James G. 1978. Bounded Rationality, Ambiguity, and the Engineering of Choice. *Bell Journal of Economics* **9**: 587–608.

March, James and Johan P. Olsen. 1989. The Uncertainty of the Past: Organizational Learning Under Ambiguity. In *Decisions and Organizations*, edited by J. G. March (Oxford: Basil Blackwell), 335–58.

Mark, Mariusz. 1993. *The Political Logic of Privatization: Lessons from Great Britain and Poland* (Praeger: London).

Martin, Lisa. 2002. "Distribution, Information, and Delegation to International Organizations. The Case of IMF Conditionality." Manuscript, Department of Government, Harvard University.

Maxfield, Sylvia. 1997. *Gatekeepers of Growth: The International Political Economy of Central Banking in Developing Countries* (Princeton, NJ: Princeton University Press).

May, Peter. 1992. Policy Learning and Failure. *Journal of Public Policy* **12** (4): 331–54.

Meier, Gerald M. 1990. Trade Policy, Development and the New Political Economy. In *The Political Economy on International Trade*, edited by Anne Krueger and Ronald Jones (New York, NY: Basil Blackwell).

Meseguer, Covadonga. 2004. What Role for Learning? The Diffusion of Privatization in the OECD and Latin America. *Journal of Public Policy* **24** (3): 299–325.

Meseguer, Covadonga. 2005. Policy Learning, Policy Diffusion and the Making of a New Order. *Annals of the American Academy of Social and Political Sciences* **598**: 67–82.

Meseguer, Covadonga. 2006. Rational Learning and Bounded Learning in the Diffusion of Policy Innovations. *Rationality and Society* **18** (1): 35–66.

Meseguer, Covadonga and Fabrizio Gilardi. 2005. What Is New in the Study of Policy Diffusion? A Critical Review. *Working Paper, Department of International Studies, CIDE*, 115.

Meyer, Jack. 1987. Two Moment Decision Models and Expected Utility Maximization. *American Economic Review* **77** (3): 421–30.

Michaely, Michael, Demetrious Papageorgiou, and Armeane Choksi, eds. 1991. *Liberalizing Foreign Trade* (Cambridge, MA: Blackwell).

Milner, Helen and Keiko Kubota. 2005. Why the Move to Free Trade? Democracy and Trade Policy in the Developing Countries. *International Organization* **59**: 157–93.

Minushkin, Susan. 2001. "Opening the Floodgates" (PhD dissertation, University of Columbia).

252 References

Mishkin, Frederick. 1996. Understanding Financial Crises: A Developing Country Perspective. *NBER Working Paper* **5600**: 1–49.

Mishkin, Frederick. 2000. Financial Market Reform. In *Economic Policy Reform*, edited by Anne Krueger (Chicago, IL: University of Chicago Press), 511–47.

Mosley, Layna. *Global Capital and National Governments* (New York, NY: Cambridge University Press).

Murillo, Victoria. 2002. Political Bias in Policy Convergence: Privatisation Choices in Latin America. *World Politics* **54**: 462–93.

Murrell, Peter. 1991. Can Neoclassical Economics Underpin the Reform of Centrally Planned Economies? *Journal of Economic Perspectives* **5** (4): 59–76.

Mussa, Michael. 2002. *Argentina and the Fund: From Triumph to Tragedy* (Washington, DC: Institute for International Economics), 1–81.

Naím, Moisés. 1993. *Paper Tigers and Minotaurs: The Politics of Venezuela's Economic Reforms* (Washington, DC: Carnegie Endowment Book).

Naím, Moisés. 1999. Fads and Fashion in Economic Reforms: Washington Consensus or Washington Confusion? Paper prepared for the IMF Conference on Second Generation Reforms, Washington, DC, October.

Nash, John, Sebastian Edwards, and Thomas Vinod, eds. 1991. *Best Practices in Trade Policy Reform* (Oxford: Oxford University Press).

Nash, John and Wendy Takacs. 1998. *Trade Policy Reform: Lessons and Implications* (Washington, DC: World Bank Regional and Sectoral Studies).

Nelson, Joan, ed. 1990a. *Economic Crisis and Policy Choice. The Politics of Adjustment in the Third World* (Princeton, NJ: Princeton University Press).

Nelson, Joan, ed. 1990b. The Politics of Adjustment in Small Democracies: Costa Rica, The Dominican Republic, Jamaica. In *Economic Crisis and Policy Choice. The Politics of Adjustment in the Third World*, edited by Joan Nelson (Princeton, NJ: Princeton University Press), 169–214.

Nelson, Joan, ed. 1994. *A Precarious Balance*, vols I and II (San Francisco, CA: International Center for Economic Growth and Overseas Development Council).

Nogues, Julio and Sunil Gulati. 1994. Economic Policies and Performance under Alternative Trade Regimes: Latin America during the 1980s. *World Economy* **17**: 467–96.

Notermans, Ton. 1999. Policy Continuity, Policy Change and the Political Power of Economic Ideas. *Acta Politica* **1**: 22–48.

Obstfeld, Maurice. 1998. The Global Capital Market: Benefactor or Menace. *Journal of Economic Perspectives* **12** (4): 9–30.

Odell, John. S. 1982. *U.S International Monetary Policy: Markets, Power and Ideas as Sources of Change* (Princeton, NJ: Princeton University Press).

O'Donnell, Guillermo. 1994. Delegative Democracy. *Journal of Democracy* **5**: 55–69.

OECD. 1996. *Privatisation in Asia, Europe and Latin America* (Paris: OECD).

Oppenheim, Lois. 1993. *Politics in Chile: Democracy, Authoritarianism and the Search for Development* (Boulder, CO: Westview).

Orenstein, Mitchell A. 2003. Mapping the Diffusion of Pension Innovation. In *Pension Reform in Europe: Process and Progress*, edited by Robert Holzmann, Mitchell A. Orenstein, and Michal Rutkowski (Washington, DC: The World Bank).

Ortiz, Guillermo. 1994. *La Reforma Financiera y la Desincorporación Bancaria* (México, D.F.: Fondo de Cultura Económica).

Parker, David. 1998a. Introduction. In *Privatization in the European Union. Theory and Policy Perspectives*, edited by David Parker (London: Routledge), 1–9.

Parker, David. 1998b. Privatization in the European Union. An Overview. In *Privatization in the European Union. Theory and Policy Perspectives*, edited by David Parker (London: Routledge), 10–46.

Pastor, Manuel. 1987. *The International Monetary Fund and Latin America. Economic Stabilization and Class Conflict* (Boulder, CO: Westview Press).

Pericchi, L. R. n.d. "Análisis De Decisión, Inferencia y Predicción Estadística Bayesiana." Manuscript, CESMA.

Pierson, Paul. 1993. When Effect Becomes Cause. Policy Feedback and Political Change. *World Politics* 45: 595–628.

Pitelis, Christos and Thomas Clarke. 1995. The Political Economy of Privatization. In *The Political Economy of Privatization*, edited by Christos Pitelis and Thomas Clarke (London: Routledge), 1–29.

Popkin, Samuel. 1991. *The Reasoning Voter* (Chicago, IL: University of Chicago Press).

Privatisation Yearbook. 1994, 1995, 1996, 1997, 1998, 1999, 2000 (London: Privatisation International).

Przeworski, Adam. 1991. *Democracy and the Market. Political and Economic Reforms in Eastern Europe and Latin America* (New York, NY: Cambridge University Press).

Przeworski, Adam. 1992. The Neoliberal Fallacy. *Journal of Democracy* 3 (3): 45–59.

Przeworski, Adam. 1999. "Stability and Change of Policy Regimes." Manuscript, New York University.

Przeworski, Adam and James Vreeland. 2000. The Effect of IMF Programs on Economic Growths. *Journal of Development Economics* 62 (2): 385–421.

Przeworski, Adam, Michael Alvarez, José Cheibub, and Fernando Limongi. 2000. *Democracy and Growth* (New York, NY: Cambridge University Press).

Quattrone, George A. and Amos Tversky. 1988. Contrasting Rational and Psychological Analysis of Political Choice. *American Political Science Review* 82 (3): 719–36.

Quinn, Dennis. 1997. The Correlates of Change in International Financial Regulation. *American Political Science Review* 91: 531–51.

Quinn, Dennis and Carla Inclán. 1997. The Origins of Financial Openness: A Study of Current and Capital Account Liberalization. *American Journal of Political Science* 41 (3): 771–813.

Quinn, Dennis and Ana María Toyoda. 2008. Ideology and Voter Sentiment as Determinants of International Financial Liberalization. In *The Global Diffusion of Markets and Democracy*, edited by Beth Simmons, Mark Dobbin, and Geoffrey Garrett (New York, NY: Cambridge University Press), 173–219:

Raiffa, Howard. 1972. *Decision Analysis. Introductory Lectures on Choices under Uncertainty* (Reading: Addison–Wesley).

Ramamurti, Ravi. 1999. Why Haven't Developing Countries Privatized Deeper and Faster? *World Development* 27 (1): 137–55.

Ramírez, Miguel D. 1994. Privatization and the Role of the State in Post–ISI Mexico. In *Privatization in Latin America. New Roles for the Public and the Private Sectors*, edited by Werner Baer and Melissa Birch (London: Praeger), 21–44.

Remmer, Karen. 1986. The Politics of Economic Stabilization: IMF Standby Programs in Latin America 1954–1984. *Comparative Politics* **19** (1): 1–24.

Robinson, James. 1998. Theories of Bad Policy. *Policy Reform* **1**: 1–44.

Rodríguez, Francisco and Dani Rodrik. 1999. Trade Policy and Economic Growth: A Skeptic's Guide to the Cross National Evidence. *NBER Working Paper* 7081.

Rodrik, Dani. 1992. The Rush to Free Trade in the Developing World. *NBER Working Paper* 3947.

Rodríguez, Miguel Angel. 1994. Comment. In *The Political Economy of Policy Reform*, edited by John Williamson (Washington, DC: Institute for International Economics), 376–381.

Rodrik, Dani.1994. The Rush to Free Trade in the Developing World: Why So Late? Why Now? Will It Last? In *Voting For Reform. Democracy, Political Liberalization, and Economic Adjustment*, edited by Stephan Haggard and Steve Webb (Washington, DC: World Bank and Oxford University Press), 61–87.

Rodrik, Dani. 1996. Understanding Economic Policy Reform. *Journal of Economic Literature* **34**: 9–41.

Rodrik, Dani. 1997. *Has Globalization Gone Too Far?* (Washington, DC: Institute for International Economics).

Rodrik, Dani. 1998. Who Needs Capital-Account Convertibility? In *Should the IMF Pursue Capital Account Convertibility? Essays in International Finance 207*, edited by Peter Kenen (Princeton, NJ: Princeton University Press), 55–65.

Rodrik, Dani, ed. 2003. *In Search of Prosperity. Analytic Narratives on Economic Growth* (Princeton, NJ: Princeton University Press).

Rodrik, Dani. 2006. Goodbye Washington Consensus, Hello Washington Confusion? *Journal of Economic Literature*, December: 973–87.

Rodrik, Dani. 2007. *One Economics, Many Recipes. Globalization, Institutions and Economic Growth* (Princeton, NJ: Princeton University Press).

Rogers, Everett M. 2003. *Diffusion of Innovations*, 5th edition (New York, NY: Free Press).

Rogoff, Kenneth. 2003. The IMF Strikes Back. *Foreign Policy* January/February: 39–46.

Rose, Richard. 1991. What Is Lesson-Drawing? *Journal of Public Policy* **2** (1): 3–30.

Rose, Richard. 1993. *Lesson Drawing in Public Policy: A Guide to Learning Across Time and Space* (New Jersey: Chatham House).

Rowthorn, Bob and Ha–Joon Chang. 1994. Public Ownership and the Theory of the State. In *The Political Economy of Privatization*, edited by Christos Pitelis and Thomas Clarke (London: Routledge), 54–69.

Rudra, Nita. 2002. Globalization and the Decline of the Welfare State in Less Developed Countries. *International Organization* **56** (2): 411–45.

Sabatier, Paul A. and Hank C. Jenkins–Smith. 1993. *Policy Change and Learning: An Advocacy Coalition Approach* (Boulder, CO: Westview Press).

Sachs, Jeffrey and Andrew Warner. 1995. Economic Reform and the Process of Global Integration. *Brookings Papers on Economic Activity* **1**: 1–118.

Sachs, Jeffrey, Aaron Tornell, and Andrés Velasco. 1995. The Collapse of the Mexican Peso: What Have We Learned? *NBER Working Paper* 5142.

Salinas de Gortari, Carlos. 2000. *México. Un paso difícil a la Modernidad* (Barcelona: Plaza y Janés Editores).

Santín, Osvaldo. 2001. *The Political Economy of Mexico's Financial Reform* (Aldershot: Ashgate).

Schamis, Hector. 2002. *Re-Forming the State: The Politics of Privatisation in Latin America and Europe* (Ann Arbor, MI: University of Michigan Press).

Schelling, Thomas. 1978. *Micromotives and Macrobehavior* (New York, NY: Norton).

Schneider, Ben Ross. 1990. The Politics of Privatization in Brazil and Mexico: Variations on a Statist Theme. In *The Political Economy of Public Sector Reform*, edited by Ezra Suleiman and John Waterbury (Boulder, CO: Westview Press), 319–45.

Sen, Amartya, Nicholas Stern, and Joseph Stiglitz. 1991. Roundtable Discussion Development Strategies: The roles of the state and the private sector. In *Proceedings of the World Bank. Annual conference on development economics, supplement to the World Bank Economic Review and the World Bank Research Observer* (Washington, DC), 421–33.

Shafaeddin, Mehdi S. 1994. The Impact of Trade Liberalization on Export and GDP Growth in Least Developed Countries. *UNCTAD Discussion Papers* 85 (Geneva).

Shipan, Charles R. and Craig Volden. 2008. The Mechanisms of Policy Diffusion. American Journal of Political Science **53** (4): 840–57.

Sigmund, Paul E. 1990. Chile: Privatization, Reprivatization, Hyperprivatization. In *The Political Economy of Public Sector Reform*, edited by Ezra Suleiman and John Waterbury (Boulder, CO: Westview Press), 346–63.

Sikkink, Katherine. 1991. *Ideas and Institutions: Developmentalism in Brazil and Argentina* (Ithaca, NY; Cornell University Press).

Silva Herzog, Jesús. 2007. *A la Distancia. Recuerdo and Testimonios* (México D.F.: Océano).

Simmons, Beth. 1999. The Internationalization of Capital. In *Continuity and Change in Contemporary Capitalism*, edited by Herbert Kitschelt, Peter Lange, Gary Marks, and Joseph D. Stephens (New York, NY: Cambridge University Press), 36–69.

Simmons, Beth and Zachary Elkins. 2004. The Globalization of Liberalization: Policy Diffusion in the International Political Economy. *American Political Science Review* **98** (1): 171–89.

Simmons, Beth, Frank Dobbin, and Geoffrey Garrett. 2006. Introduction: The International Diffusion of Liberalism. *International Organization* **60** (4): 781–810.

Simon, Herbert. 1956. Rational Choice and the Structure of the Environment. *Psychological Review* **63**: 129–38.

Smith, William, Carlos Acuña, and Eduardo Gamarra. 1994. *Latin American Political Economy in the Age of Neoliberal Reform* (Miami, FL: North–South Center).

Soto, Marcelo. 2000. Capital Flows and Growth in Developing Countries: Recent Empirical Evidence. *Working Paper* 160. (Paris: OECD Development Centre).

Srinivasan, T. N. 2000. The Washington Consensus a Decade Later: Ideology and the Art and Science of Policy Advice. *The World Bank Research Observer* **15** (2): 265–70.

256 References

Stallings, Barbara. 1992. International Influence on Economic Policy: Debt, Stabilization and Structural Reform. In *The Politics of Economic Adjustment*, edited by Stephan Haggard and Robert Kaufman (Princeton, NJ: Princeton University Press), 41–88.

Stark, David and Lazlo Bruszt. 1998. *Postsocialist Pathways* (New York, NY: Cambridge University Press).

Starr, Paul. 1990. The New Life of the Liberal State: Privatization and the Restructuring of State–Society Relations. In *The Political Economy of Public Sector Reform*, edited by Ezra Suleiman and John Waterbury (Boulder, CO: Westview Press), 22–55.

Stiglitz, Joseph. 1998. Knowledge for Development: Economic Science, Economic Policy and Economic Advice. Annual Bank Conference in Development Economics, Washington, DC, April 20–21. Web site http://www.worldbank.org.

Stiglitz, Joseph. 2000. Reflections on the Theory and Practice of Reform. In *Economic Policy Reform*, edited by Anne Krueger (Chicago, IL: Chicago University Press), 551–84.

Stiglitz, Joseph. 2001. Failure of the Fund: Rethinking the IMF Response. *Harvard International Review* **23** (2): 14–18.

Stiglitz, Joseph. 2002. *El Malestar en la Globalización* (Madrid: Taurus).

Stokes, Susan C. 2001a. *Mandates and Democracy. Neoliberalism by Surprise in Latin America* (New York, NY: Cambridge University Press).

Stokes, Susan C. ed. 2001b. *Public Support for Market Reforms in New Democracies* (New York, NY: Cambridge University Press).

Stone, Diane. 1999. Learning Lessons and Transferring Policy across Time, Space and Disciplines. *Politics* **19** (1): 51–59.

Stone, Randall. 2002. *Lending Credibility: The International Monetary Fund and the Post Communist Transition* (Princeton, NJ: Princeton University Press).

Sturm, Jan. E, Helge Berger, and Jakob de Haan. 2005. Which Variables Explain Decisions on IMF Credit? An Extreme Bound Analysis. *Economics and Politics* **17** (2): 177–213.

Sturzenegger, Federico and Mariano Tommasi. 1998. *The Political Economy of Reform* (Cambridge, MA: MIT Press).

Suleiman, Ezra. 1990. The Politics of Privatization in Britain and France. In *The Political Economy of Public Sector Reform*, edited by Ezra Suleiman and John Waterbury. (Boulder, CO: Westview Press). 113–36.

Suleiman, Ezra and John Waterbury. 1990. Introduction: Analyzing Privatization in Industrial and Developing Countries. In *The Political Economy of Public Sector Reform*, edited by Ezra Suleiman and John Waterbury (Boulder, CO: Westview Press), 1–21.

Swank, Duane. 2002. *Global Capital, Political Institutions, and Policy Change in Developed Welfare States* (New York, NY: Cambridge University Press).

Swank, Duane. 2006. Tax Policy in an Era of Internationalization: Explaining the Spread of Neoliberalism. *International Organization* **60**: 847–82.

Swoyer, Chris. 2002. Judgement and Decision Making: Extrapolations and Applications. In *Judgements, Decisions, and Public Policy*, edited by Rajeev Gowda and Jeffrey Fox (New York, NY: Cambridge University Press), 9–45.

Taylor, Lance, ed. 1993. *The Rocky Road to Reform. Adjustment, Income Distribution, and Growth in the Developing World* (Cambridge, MA: MIT Press).

Tetlock, Philip. 2005. *Expert Political Judgement. How Good is It? How Can We Know?* (Princeton, NJ: Princeton University Press).

Thacker, Strom. 1999. The High Politics of IMF Lending. *World Politics* **52** (1): 38–75.

Tinbergen, Jan. 1984. Development Cooperation as a Learning Process. In *Pioneers in Developments*, edited by Gerald M. Meier and Dudley Seers (Oxford: Oxford University Press), 315–31.

Tommasi, Mariano and Andrés Velasco. 1995. "Where Are We in the Political Economy of Reform?" *Working Paper* 95–20.C. V. Starr Center for Applied Economics, New York University.

Tornell, Aaron. 2000. Privatizing the Privatized. In *Economic Policy Reform*, edited by Anne Krueger (Chicago, IL: University of Chicago Press), 157–82.

Toye, John. 1994. Comments to in Search of a Manual for Technopols, in *The Political Economy of Policy Reform*, edited by John Williamson (Washington, DC: Institute for International Economics), 35–43.

Trudel, Robert. 2005. Effects of Exchange Rate Regimes on IMF Program Participation. *Review of Policy Research* **22**: 919–36.

Valdés, Gabriel. 1995. *Pinochet's Economists*: The Chicago School of Economics in Chile (New York, NY: Cambridge University Press).

Valenzuela, Arturo. 1997. The Chilean Miracle: Lesson of South America's Success Story. *Harvard International Review* **19** (4): 24–27.

Van de Walle, Nicholas. 2001. *African Economies and the Politics of Permanent Crisis, 1979–1999* (New York, NY: Cambridge University Press).

Vaubel, Roland. 1991. The Political Economy of the International Monetary Fund: A Public Choice Approach. In *The Political Economy of International Organisations*, edited by Roland Vaubel and Thomas Willett (Boulder, CO: Westview Press), 205–45.

Vickers, John and Vincent Wright, eds.1989. *The Politics of Privatization in Western Europe* (London: Frank Cass).

Villasuso, Juan Manuel 1990. Reflexiones sobre la Nueva Estrategia de Desarrollo Costarricense. In *Crisis Económica y Ajuste Estructural*, edited by Luis P. Vargas (Costa Rica Editorial Universidad Estatal a Distancia), 87–113.

Vreeland, James R. 2002. The Effect of IMF Programs on Labor. *World Development* **30** (1): 121–39.

Vreeland, James R. 2003. *The IMF and Economic Growth* (New York, NY: Cambridge University Press).

Vreeland, James R. 2007. *The International Monetary Fund: Politics of Conditional Lending* (New York, NY: Routledge).

Wacziarg, Romain and Karen H. Welch. 2003. Trade Liberalization and Growth: New Evidence. *NBER Working Paper* 10152.

Wade, Robert. 1990. *Governing the Market: Economic Theory and the Role of Government in East Asian Industrialization* (Princeton, NJ: Princeton University Press).

Wade, Robert. 1992. East Asia's Economic Success. Conflicting Perspectives, Partial Insights, Shaky Evidence. *World Politics* **44**: 270–320.

258 References

Wahba, Jackline and Mahmoud Mohieldin. 1998. Liberalizing Trade in Financial Services: The Uruguay Round and the Arab Countries. *World Development* **26** (7): 1331–48.

Waterbury, John. 1992. The Heart of the Matter? Public Enterprise and the Adjustment Process. In *The Politics of Economic Adjustment*, edited by Stephan Haggard and Robert Kauffman (Princeton, NJ: Princeton University Press), 182–217.

Waterbury, John. 1993. *Exposed to Innumerable Delusions: Public Enterprise and State Power in Egypt, India, Mexico, and Turkey* (New York, NY: Cambridge University Press).

Way, Christopher. 2005. Political Insecurity and the Diffusion of Financial Market Regulation. Special Issue of the *Annals of the American Academy of Social and Political Sciences* **598**: 125–44.

Webb, Richard. 1994. Peru. In *The Political Economy of Policy Reform*, edited by John Williamson (Washington, DC: Institute for International Economics), 355–375.

West, Michael and Jeff P. Harrison. 1997. *Dynamic Bayesian Forecasting and Dynamic Models* (New York, NY: Springer–Verlag).

Western, Bruce. 1998. Causal Heterogeneity in Comparative Research: A Bayesian Hierarchical Modelling Approach. *American Journal of Political Science* **42** (4): 1233–59.

Western, Bruce and Simon Jackman. 1994. Bayesian Inference for Comparative Research. *American Political Science Review* **88** (2): 412–23.

Westphal, Larry E. 1990. Industrial Policy in an Export-Propelled Economy: Lessons from South Korea's Experience. *Journal of Economic Perspectives* **4** (3): 41–59.

Weyland, Kurt. 1996. Risk Taking in Latin America Economic Restructuring: Lessons from Prospect Theory. *International Studies Quarterly* **40**: 185–208.

Weyland, Kurt. 1998. The Political Fate of Market Reform in Latin America, Africa and Eastern Europe. *International Studies Quarterly* **42**: 645–74.

Weyland, Kurt. 2002. *The Politics of Market Reforms in Fragile Democracies* (Princeton, NJ: Princeton University Press).

Weyland, Kurt. 2005, Theories of Policy Diffusion: Lessons from Latin America Pension Reform, *World Politics*, **57** (2): 262–95.

Weyland, Kurt. 2007. *Bounded Rationality and Policy Diffusion. Social Sector Reform in Latin America* (Princeton, NJ: Princeton University Press).

Weyland, Kurt, ed. 2004. *Learning from Foreign Models in Latin American Policy Reform* (Baltimore, MD: Woodrow Wilson Center and Johns Hopkins University).

Williamson, John. 1990. *Latin American Adjustment. How Much Has Happened?* (Washington, DC: Institute for International Economics).

Williamson, John. 1993. Democracy and the 'Washington Consensus.' *World Development* **21** (8): 1329–80.

Williamson, John, ed. 1994. *The Political Economy of Policy Reform* (Washington, DC: Institute for International Economics).

Williamson, John. 2000. What Should the World Bank Think about the Washington Consensus? *The World Bank Research Observer* **15** (2): 251–64.

Williamson, John and Stephan Haggard. 1994. The Political Conditions for Economic Reform. In *The Political Economy of Policy Reform*, edited by John Williamson (Washington, DC: Institute for International Economics), 525–96.

Willner, Johan. 1998. Privatisation in Finland, Sweden and Denmark: Fashion or Necessity. In *Privatisation in the European Union*, edited by David Parker (London: Routledge), 172–91.

Winkler, Robert L. 1972. *An Introduction to Bayesian Inference and Decision* (New York, NY: Holt).

Woods, Ngaire. 1995. Economic Ideas and International Relations: Beyond Rational Neglect. *International Studies Quarterly* **39**: 161–80.

World Bank. 1987. *World Development Report 1987* (Washington, DC: World Bank).

World Bank. 1994a. Trade Policy Reform in Developing Countries since 1985: A Review of the Evidence. *Discussion Paper* (Washington, DC: World Bank).

World Bank. 1994b. *Adjustment in Africa: Reform, Results and the Road Ahead* (Washington, DC: World Bank).

World Bank. 1995. *Bureaucrats in Business. The Economics and Politics of Government Ownership* (Oxford: Oxford University Press).

World Bank. 1998. *World Bank Privatization Data.* www.worldbank.org.

World Bank. 2004. *World Bank Development Indicators.* www.worldbank.org.

World Bank. 2005. *Economic Growth in the 1990s. Learning from a Decade of Reform* (Washington, DC: World Bank).

Wotipka, Christine M. and Francisco Ramírez. 2008. World Society and Human Rights: An Event History Analysis of the Convention on the Elimination of All Forms of Discrimination against Women. In *The Global Diffusion of Markets and Democracy*, edited by Beth Simmons, Frank Dobbin, and Geoffrey Garrett (New York, NY: Cambridge University Press), 303–43.

Wright, Vincent, ed. 1994. *Privatization in Western Europe: Pressures, Problems and Paradoxes* (London: Pinter Publishers).

Yee, Albert. 1996. The Causal Effects of Ideas on Policies. *International Organization* **50** (1): 69–108.

Zellner, Arnold. 1997. *Bayesian Analysis in Econometrics and Statistics: The Zellner View and Papers* (Cheltenham: Edward Elgar Publishing).

Index

Act to Promote Domestic Investment and Regulate Foreign Investment, 158

adaptation: of posterior beliefs, 51–58; rational updating, 46–47

Africa: capital account liberalization in, 151–152; financial liberalization in, 176n31; IMF agreements in, 195n16, 205n24; imposition hypothesis of privatization in, 128; nonlearning behavior in, 233; privatization in, 120; reform successes in, 235–236; trade liberalization in, 21n23, 22n23, 105

Alfonsín, Raúl, 80–81, 232n12, 235n13

Allende, Salvador, 116–117

alternative hypotheses, policy convergence and learning and, 22–29

anchoring heuristic, policy innovation and, 20

Ardito-Barletta, Nicolás, 9–10

Argentina: budget deficits and privatization in, 124; market reforms in, 5–6; privatization in, 118–120; trade liberalization in, 85, 85n18, 86

Arias, Oscar, 50

Arriagada, Genaro, 10

Aspe, Pedro, 22, 80–81, 101–103, 159, 162–163

Austral Plan, 80–81

Austria, public enterprises in, 114

authoritarian regimes: capital account liberalization and, 145–157; market reforms and, 12–13, 65–67; probability of entering and sustaining IMF agreements and, 200; trade liberalization and, 98–103

autonomous states: development strategies and, 79n7; market reforms and, 12–13, 13n14

availability heuristic, policy innovation and, 20

average experience in the world variable, trade liberalization and, 96, 96n28

AVERAGE RESULTS variable, sustainability of capital account liberalization and, 166–167

Azis, Iwan, 10

balance-of-payments problems: history of IMF agreements and, 183; impact of IMF agreements on, 189, 189n10, 193; International Monetary Fund (IMF) role in, 181–183, 187–188; standby IMF agreements and, 193

Balcerowicz, Leszek, 223, 232n12, 235n13

Balladur, Edouard, 120

Bangladesh, trade liberalization in, 105

bank disincorporation, Mexican narrative of learning and financial liberalization and, 157, 159n16, 160n17, 163

Bayesian learning: capital account liberalization and, 150; Costa Rican trade liberalization policy and, 38; market reform and, 8–10; operationalization of, 231n10; prior beliefs and, 40–42; rational updating and, 29–30, 38–39

261

262   *Index*

Bayesian updating, 57n22; posterior beliefs and, 47–58, 68; probit modeling and, 62–64; shock-based learning variable and, 92

beliefs: learning hypothesis and role of, 38n3; posterior beliefs, 43; prior beliefs, 40–42

Bennett, Colin, 14

Biersteker, Thomas, 16

Blasena, Krieger, 85n18

Bod, Peter, 9, 223–224

Bollard, Allan, 12

bottom-up convergence, economic policy and, 23–24

bounded learning, 21n23, 22n23; emulation and, 228–229; market reform and, 17, 17n17, 18n18, 22; trade liberalization and, 105n33

Brazil: import substitution in, 75–76; market reforms in, 5–6, 158; pension system reform in, 21n22, 21n23; privatization in, 118–119; trade liberalization in, 83n16, 83n17, 85, 85n18, 86

Bretton Woods Conference, 148n7, 183

Britain: imposition hypothesis of privatization in, 130; privatization policies in, 127, 232

British Petroleum, 122

Brune, Nancy, 112, 147n6, 148n7, 149–150, 151n10, 169n24

budget deficits: impetus to privatization from, 122–124; predicted probability of signed IMF agreements, 204

Camdessus, Michael, 189

Campos, Roberto, 85n18

capital account liberalization: economic growth and, 152, 152n13, 153n14, 157; imprudent behavior in wake of, 171–172; launching and sustainability probability of, 164; learning hypothesis and, 163–167, 226n6; list of countries with, 154–179; open *vs.* closed capital accounts and variability of economic growth, 153–157; partisan preferences and, 147n6, 148n7; political economy of, 145–157; prior beliefs and, 154–179; proportion of countries with open

capital accounts, 151–152; statistical parameters, 154–179; theoretical case for, 177–178; trade liberalization and, 168n21

capital controls in financial crisis, 162, 162n20, 163; imprudent behavior as catalyst for, 171–172; learning hypothesis and, 168–169

capital mobility: diffusion as factor in, 144–145; globalization and, 142–145; learning hypothesis and, 33–34, 144; political factors in, 142–143; trade liberalization and, 143–144

Carazo, Rodrigo, 49, 65

Cardoso, Fernando H., 5–6, 118–119

Caribbean, IMF agreements in, 195n16

case study model, economic policy analysis, 31

Castillo, Carlos Manuel, 37, 49–50

cause-and-effect relationships, learning and, 14–15

Cavaco Silva, Anibal, 119

Centeno, Miguel, 22

change teams, market reform and, 13–14

Chile: export orientation in, 80; global economic integration by, 2; influence on OECD of, 139; market reforms in, 5–6, 9–12; privatization in, 19–21, 115–117, 120, 122, 127; trade liberalization in, 105, 105n33

Chiluba, Frederick, 8

China: debt crisis in, 172n27; market reform and debt relief in, 235n13, 237n14

Chirac, Jacques, 115–116

Chwieroth, Jeffrey, 147n6, 148n7, 148n8, 149n9

Clark, Mary, 53

closed capital accounts, economic growth and, 153–157

clustering behavior: regional experience and privatization in Latin America and, 138, 138n18; trade liberalization and, 80, 80n11

coercion: capital account liberalization and, 148n8, 149, 149n9; capital mobility and, 144; privatization policies and, 127–137; probability and sustainability of capital account liberalization and, 164; probability of adopting export

Index

263

orientation and, 101–102; trade liberalization and, 105–106

collinearity in learning variables: default-based adoption of export orientation, 103n30; learning models and, 90n21

Collor de Mello, Fernando, 8, 118–119

Colosio, Luis Donaldo, 160

Communism: global integration and fall of, 2; imposition hypothesis of privatization and, 130; imposition hypothesis of privatization and fall of, 129; interventionism and collapse of, 57; in Latin America, privatization and, 133

competition: capital account liberalization and, 148–150; interventionist strategies for financial crisis and, 173–175; policy convergence and, 28n30

conditional distribution of the mean, 42–43

conditionality: failure of, 185n6; imposition hypothesis and, 227–229; International Monetary Fund (IMF) policies and, 181, 181n1, 183–210

confidence intervals: predicted probability of policy adoption and, 221–222; for predicted probability of trade liberalization, 98–100

conjugate priors, 41n7; limitations of, 72n30; posterior beliefs and, 44; sampling techniques for, 69–71

control variables: policy diffusion and, 63–66; trade liberalization and, 101–103

Conway, Patrick, 185n6

Corporación para el Desarrollo de Costa Rica (CODESA), 49

Corbo, Vittorio, 80–81

Costa Rica: adaptation to regional information and import substitution, 52; coercion and persuasion of policy form in, 63–66; economic development history in, 48–50; posterior beliefs and economic policy in, 47–58; rational learning, 38–39; stabilization program in, 65; trade liberalization, 30; trade liberalization in, 37

credibility of IMF agreements, governments' belief in, 192

crisis-based initiation of market reform, 6–9; democratization and, 95–103; government learning, 8–10; interventionist strategies and, 172, 173n28, 175; learning hypothesis and, 167–177, 224–226; Mexican financial liberalization and learning and, 157–163; privatization and, 122–124; trade liberalization and, 88–89

crisis management, International Monetary Fund role in, 185–186

criterion of need, IMF policies and, 186n8

Cruzado Plan, 80–81

currency crises: in Costa Rica, 49; sustainability of capital account liberalization and, 169–171

Cypher, James, 1_7

Czechoslovakia, privatization in, 101–102, 119n3, 121n4

DEBT SERVICE variable: predicted probability of signed IMF agreements, 203–204; probability of entering and sustaining IMF agreements and, 200

debt shock of 1982: economic reform and, 57–58; IMF agreements and, 205–208; IMF participation and, 194; learning hypothesis and, 225–226; as learning variable, 92, 104n32, 105n33; posterior beliefs and, 56–57; probability of entering and remaining under IMF agreements and, 207

decision problems, policy choices and posterior beliefs, 58–59

de la Hoz, Martinez, 85n18

de la Madrid, Miguel, 117, 157–158

democracies, market reform in, 65–67

democratization: capital account liberalization and, 145–157; crisis-based market reforms and, 95–103; economic growth and, 229–231; trade liberalization and, 74, 79, 92–94, 105–106

developing countries: adoption of export orientation in, 94, 95n27; capital account liberalization in, 145–151, 151n10, 151n11, 152, 157; capital mobility and, 143, 143n1, 144, 145n2; democratization and trade liberalization in, 146n5; domestic

Index

developing countries (*cont.*)
politics and economic conditions in,
229–231; economic growth and capital
liberalization and, 145–153, 153n14,
157; financial liberalization in, 171n25;
learning hypothesis and development
strategies in, 81–89; market reform in,
220–234; paradigm shift concerning
market reform in, 237–238; trade
liberalization in, 85–86
development financing, IMF role in,
185
development strategies: debate over ISI *vs.*
EO, 73–74; decisions concerning,
32–33; descriptive statistics for, 76–108;
domestic policies and, 78; export
orientation *vs.* import substitution, 75;
features and policy instruments table,
75; historical experience and adoption
of, 80–81; improvisation and ad hoc
responses and, 77n6; institutional
factors in, 78–79; international system
and, 78; learning hypothesis and,
81–89; list of countries involved in,
76–108; posterior beliefs and learning
and, 89–103; prior beliefs and, 107–108;
regional growth rates and, 86–87;
theoretical description and alternative
theories, 75–81; trade liberalization
and, 74n1
Development Strategies Database, 83–84,
86–88, 90, 94, 101–102, 104
dichotomous indicators: capital account
liberalization and, 150–151; of regime
characteristics, 129n13
dictatorships: development strategies and,
79; probability of entering and
sustaining IMF agreements and, 200
diffusion mechanisms, policy convergence
and, 23–24
disaggregated indicators of openness,
82n15
dogmatism, learning hypothesis and, 234
domestic conditions: economic
development and, 232; IMF agreements
and, 209; learning hypothesis and,
229–231
Drazen, Allan, 6–7, 104n32, 105n33
dynamic probit model, 62, 62n27, 64; of
capital account liberalization, 164;
probability of entering and sustaining

IMF agreements and, 200–202; rational
updating and, 30

East Asia: export orientation and, 75–76;
IMF agreements in, 195n17; Japan as
model for, 103–104; market reforms,
10–11, 11n10, 11n11; trade
liberalization and, 21n23, 22n23, 105
East Central Europe, privatization in,
101–102, 119n3, 121n4
Easterly, William, 104n32, 105n33
Echeverría, Luis, 117
Economic Commission for Latin America
(ECLA), 75–76, 80–81; export
orientation promotion by, 105–106
economic growth: capital account
liberalization and, 148–150, 152,
152n13, 153n14, 157; domestic politics
and, 229–231; growth rates and
imposition hypothesis of privatization,
132–133, 133n17; growth rates and
volatility of IMF agreements and,
191–192; growth rates with and without
privatization, 135–137; impact of IMF
agreements on, 189, 190n11, 193;
International Monetary Fund (IMF)
policies and, 181–183; market reform
and, 3n4; open *vs.* closed capital
accounts and variability of, 153–157;
open *vs.* closed regimes and variability
of, 76–108; privatization as rationale
for, 113–121, 124; rate comparisons for
IMF and non-IMF countries, 195–196;
trade liberalization *vs.* trade
protectionism and, 98–100;
uncertainty, 42–47; volatility of trade
liberalization and, 87–88
economic policy failure, government
learning from, 6–9
Edwards, Sebastián, 57, 80–81
Effective Exchange Rate (EER), export
orientation and, 107–108
Effective Rate of Protection (ERP), 82n14;
export orientation and, 107–108
Eichengreen, Barry, 147n6, 148n7, 167
electoral politics: economic growth and,
229–231; GATT membership and
variable of, 93–94; market reforms and,
17n16; predicted probability of signed
IMF agreements, 204; trade
liberalization and, 93

Index

Elkins, Zachary, 149–151, 168, 168n21, 169n23

embedded autonomy, development strategies and, 79n7

empirical analysis; capital liberalization and, 176; learning and, 14

emulation: adoption of export orientation and, 94; bounded and rational learning and, 228–229; capital account liberalization and, 148–150; global trade liberalization and transition to, 98–100; horizontal policy convergence and, 27, 27n29, 28, 28n29; imposition hypothesis of privatization and, 132–134, 227–229; International Monetary Fund agreements, 93; Japan as model for, 103–104, 104n31, 104n32; learning from others *vs.* learning from shocks variable, 90–95; policy diffusion and, 63–66, 223–224; privatization policies and, 120–121, 127–137; probability and sustainability of capital account liberalization and, 164; probability of adopting export orientation and, 101–102; probability of entering and remaining under IMF agreements, 199–202; shock experience and, 96–98; sustainability of capital account liberalization and, 166–167; trade liberalization and, 96–98, 98n29, 99n29; transition to export orientation and, 94–95

Etheredge, Lloyd, 14–15

European countries: budget deficits and privatization in, 123; Exchange Rate Mechanism (ERM) crisis in, 161; IMF agreements in, 195n16; market reforms in, 9, 11n10, 11n11, 21n23, 22n23; privatization in, 117, 119

European Monetary Union (EMU), 26n27

European Union (EU), imposition hypothesis of privatization and, 128–129, 133–134

Exchange Rate Mechanism (ERM) crisis, 34; in Europe, 161; financial crisis and, 169–171; Mexican narrative of learning and financial liberalization and, 157–163

"exit option," capital account liberalization and, 142

experience: capital account liberalization and, 177–178; East Asian policy change

and impact of, 223; emulation and, 223–224; IMF agreements and role of, 209; learning hypothesis and role of, 216–217; market reforms and role of, 11–12; Mexican narrative of financial liberalization and, 159–160; privatization adoption as result of, 120; risk reduction strategy and, 46n17; sustainability of policy and, 61–64; trade liberalization as result of, 105

explanatory variables, market reforms and, 66–67

export orientation (EO): Asian success of, 75–76; default-based adoption of, 103, 103n30; East Asian success of, 73; growth increase and 86–87; history in Latin America of, 80–81; import substitution industrialization and, 32–33; Latin American growth rates and, 47–48; learning variables and adoption of, 89–103; limitations in Asia of, 76–77; posterior beliefs and, 52–53, 56–57, 89–103; predicted probability of adoption of, 94; probability of adoption of, 90–92, 94; risk aversion and, 105

export-promotion policies, global promotion of, 2

extended model of IMF agreements, 199–205

external imposition, policy diffusion and, 63–66

externalities, market reforms and, 220–234

Figueres, José, 49

financial liberalization: aspects of, 145n4; crises in wake of, 171; developing countries, 171n25; IMF advocacy of, 185; imprudent behavior in wake of, 171–172; Mexican narrative of learning and crisis from, 157–163

first-generation economic reform, analysis of, 31

Fishlow, Albert, 103, 103n30

fixed exchange rates: capital account liberalization and, 147n6, 148n7; Mexican financial liberalization and, 160–161; proportion of countries with, 151n12

foreign direct investment (FDI), trade liberalization and, 96–98

France: privatization in, 115–116, 120; public enterprises in, 114
Free Democratic Party (FDP), 117
Frieden, Geoffrey, 146
Fujimori, Alberto, 8, 118–119, 133

García, Alan, 8, 10–11, 80–81
Garnaut, Ross, 11
Garrett, Geoffrey, 112
General Agreement on Tariffs and Trade (GATT): coercive power of, 105–106; impact of controls on trade liberalization and, 101–103; top-down policy convergence and, 26n27; trade liberalization and, 93
Germany: imposition hypothesis of privatization and unification of, 129n14; learning hypothesis and unification of, 226–227; privatization in, 119n3, 121n4
global convergence: capital mobility, 33–34; privatization policies and, 120–121
globalization, capital mobility and, 142–145
González, Felipe, 5–6, 10–11
government preferences: capital mobility and, 142–143; IMF agreements and, 208–210; learning hypothesis and, 3–4, 232–233; market reforms and, 5–14; Mexican narrative of learning and crisis and, 157–163; policy failures and successes and learning by, 6–9
Graham, Carol, 10
Guisinger, Alexandra, 80, 80n11, 95n27, 147n6, 148n7, 149–150, 151n10, 169n24

Hall, Peter, 14–15, 16n15, 17, 23, 224–226
Harberger, Arnold, 8–9
Hawke, Bob, 5–6, 11
Heckscher–Ohlin theorem, 79n8
Heclo, Hugh, 14–15
Hong Kong: export orientation in, 75–76; global economic integration by, 2
horizontal policy convergence: capital account liberalization and, 148–150; economic policy and, 26–29; mechanisms of, 226–227

Horn–Wacziarg index of trade liberalization, 84
Howlett, Michael, 14
Hungary: market reforms and, 9; privatization in, 119n3, 121n4
hyperinflation: imposition hypothesis of privatization and, 130; as market reform catalyst, 8, 104n32, 105n33
hyperprivatization, Chilean phenomenon of, 116–117

ideological preferences: capital account liberalization and, 148n8, 149n9; imposition hypothesis of privatization and, 130, 130n15, 133–134; market reform and, 5–6, 6n6; predicted probability of privatization and, 134–135; privatization and, 115–121
Iglesias, Enrique, 11–12, 80–81
Ikenberry, John, 127
import substitution industrialization (ISI), 32–33; failure in Latin America of, 75–76; Latin American growth rates and, 47–48; learning from failures of, 73, 103, 103n30; posterior beliefs about, 55–57, 89–103; rate of growth under, 55; volatility as factor in transition to export orientation, 94
imposition hypothesis: emulation and, 227–229; privatization and, 127–137; statistical model of, 130–132
impossible trilogy: capital account liberalization and, 147n6, 148n7; capital mobility and, 142–143
Inclán, Carla, 147n6, 148n7
India, trade liberalization in, 105
Indonesia, market reforms in, 9–10
industrialized countries: capital mobility and, 143n1, 145n2; IMF agenda controlled by, 184, 184n4; privatization in, 33
inflation variables, imposition hypothesis of privatization and, 130n16
information gathering: learning hypothesis and role of, 216–224; rational learning and, 45–46
institutional factors, development strategies and, 78–79
interdependent policymaking, horizontal policy convergence and, 26–29

Index

interest groups, market reform and, 7n8
international comparisons of privatization, 122
international financial institutions (IFIs): capital account liberalization and, 147–148; imposition hypothesis and, 227–229; learning hypothesis and, 220–238; market reforms and, 10–11; Mexican financial liberalization and, 162–163; pressure for privatization from, 127–137; top-down policy convergence in, 24; international forces, impact on privatization, 112
International Monetary Fund (IMF): adoption of export orientation and agreements with, 94; agreements by, 32; baseline model of, 189n10; capital account liberalization and, 147–148, 148n7, 148n8, 149n9, 169; coercive power of, 105–106; consequences of agreements with, 189–193; credibility problem for, 186–187; crisis management by, 185–186; criterion of need for, 186n8; debt shock of 1982 and, 205–208; descriptive statistics on agreements, 181n1, 210; development financing role of, 185; economic growth rate comparisons for IMF and non-IMF countries, 195–196; economic policy making and activities of, 181–183; exchange restrictions and controls, 150–151; export orientation strategy and agreements with, 92; extended model of agreements with, 199–205; Fund Executive Board, 184, 184n4; government trade policies and, 3–4; history of agreements with, 183–189; imposition hypothesis of privatization and, 128–129, 133–134, 228, 229n8, 230n9; learning hypothesis and agreements of, 34–35, 193–205, 220–238; legitimacy and credibility of agreements with, 192; list of countries with agreement, 181n1, 210; policy preferences of, 186–189; predicted probability of signed agreements with, 202–203; prior beliefs and, 181n1, 210; probability of entering and remaining under agreements with, 199–202; probability of entering and remaining

under IMF agreements during debt shock and, 207; probability of open capital accounts and agreements with, 174–176; proportion of countries under, 191–192; responses to financial crisis by, 172n27; sustainability of capital account liberalization and, 166; top-down policy convergence, 25–26
international system, development strategies and, 78
interventionist strategies: adaptation of beliefs and, 52–53; adaptive modeling of, 54–55; export orientation and, 76–77; in financial crisis, 172, 173n28, 175; government posterior beliefs *vs.* observation and, 55; limitations of, 57; market forces and, 77; privatization and, 133; regional information and, 54–55
INVESTMENT variable: predicted probability of signed IMF agreements, 204; probability of entering and sustaining IMF agreements and, 200
inward-oriented industrialization, 1–2

Japan, Asian emulation of, 103–104, 104n31, 104n32
Jervis, 17n17, 18n18
joint learning, imposition hypothesis of privatization and, 132–134
joint posterior distribution, conjugate prior sampling, 69–71

Kahler, Miles, 17, 17n16, 25
Kaunda, Kenneth, 8
Keeler, John, 7
Klaus, Václav, 10, 232n12, 235n13
Kogut, Bruce, 112
Kubota, Keiko, 104n32, 105n33

labor, impact of IMF agreements on, 192, 192n12, 193n13
labor-rich countries, capital account liberalization in, 145, 147n6, 148n7, 157
Lange, David, 5–5
Latin America: budget deficits and privatization in, 122–124; capital account liberalization in, 151–152; economic growth rates in, 47–48; export orientation in, 80–81, 85–86;

268   *Index*

Latin America (*cont.*)
    health reforms in, 19–21; IMF
    agreements in, 195n16; import
    substitution and posterior beliefs in, 51;
    imposition hypothesis of privatization
    and, 130, 132–133; inward-oriented
    industrialization in, 1–2; legacy of
    reform in, 220–238; open capital
    accounts in, 175n30; posterior beliefs
    and economic policy in, 47–58;
    privatization in, 33, 115–120; regional
    experience and privatization in, 138,
    138n18; sustainability of privatization
    in countries of, 126–132; trade
    liberalization in, 21n23, 22n23, 85n18,
    105n33
LEARNING FROM AVERAGE
    EXPERIENCE, OWN variable,
    probability of trade liberalization and,
    96–98, 102–103
LEARNING FROM AVERAGE
    EXPERIENCE, WORLD variable,
    sustainability of capital account
    liberalization and, 166–167
LEARNING FROM EXPERIENCE,
    REGION variable, probability of IMF
    agreements and, 205
LEARNING FROM THE EXPERIENCE
    IN THE WORLD variable, predicted
    probability of signed IMF agreements,
    203–204
LEARNING FROM THE VARIABILITY
    OF RESULTS variable: probability of
    adopting export orientation and,
    101–102; rush to free trade and, 92–94;
    transition to export orientation and,
    89–90
learning hypothesis: capital account
    liberalization and, 163–167; capital
    mobility and, 144; debt shock of 1982,
    92, 104n32, 105n33; development
    strategies and, 81–89; economic shocks
    and, 224–226; financial crisis and,
    167–177; by government, market
    reforms and, 3n3, 5–14; government
    preferences and, 232–233; horizontal
    policy convergence and, 26–29; IMF
    agreements and, 34–35, 189n10,
    193–205; imposition hypothesis of
    privatization and, 127–137;

international financial institutions and,
    220–238; learning from others *vs.*
    learning from shocks, 90–95; legacy of,
    35; lessons about, 216–224; limitations
    of, 29–30; market reform in developing
    countries, 220–234; Mexican financial
    liberalization and crisis and, 157–163;
    neoliberal economic policy and, 3–4;
    policy convergence and alternative
    hypotheses, 22–29; posterior beliefs and
    development strategies in, 89–103;
    privatization and, 33, 111–113,
    121–137; rational and bounded
    learning, 17–22; reform outcomes and,
    232n12, 235n13; social learning, 15–17;
    trade liberalization and, 81–89, 106;
    varieties of, 22
Leblang, David, 147n6, 148n7, 167–168
leftist ideology: capital account
    liberalization and, 147n6, 148n7;
    market reforms and, 5–6
legitimacy of IMF agreements,
    governments' belief in, 192
Levy, Jack S., 14
López Portillo, José, 117, 157
Lora, Eduardo, 104n32, 105n33

macroeconomic environments, capital
    account liberalization and, 163–167
Madagascar, import substitution in,
    83
Malaysia, debt crisis in, 172n27
mandates, market reform and, 7n7
Manzetti, Luigi, 115–116, 120, 135
Maravall, José María, 9
market forces, state interventionism and,
    77
market reform: autonomous states and,
    12–13, 13n14; crisis-based initiation of,
    6–9; in developing countries, 220–234;
    economic growth and, 3n4;
    government learning and, 5–14;
    ideological preferences and, 5–6, 6n6;
    limitations of, 220–234; paradigm shift
    concerning, 236–238; political process
    of, 12n12, 13n13; privatization as part
    of, 128–129; regime characteristics and,
    65–67; social learning, 15–17
Markov Chain Monte Carlo techniques,
    conjugate priors and, 41n7

Index

May, Peter, 14–15
McPherson, Jay Muir, 112
mean distribution, prior beliefs, 71
mean-standard deviation preference function, policy choices and posterior beliefs, 59n24
median voter, economic growth and, 229–231
Menem, Carlos, 5–6, 8, 133
Mexican Stock Exchange, 157
Mexican Treasury Bill (Cetes), 158–160
Mexico: capital mobility in, 34; experience and financial liberalization in, 223; import substitution in, 75–76; inward-oriented industrialization in, 1–2; learning, financial liberalization and crisis in, 157–163; OECD membership of, 122n6; policy innovation in, 22, 22n24; privatization in, 114–117, 120, 122
Mexicobre, 117
Middle East, IMF agreements in, 195n16
Milner, Helen, 104n32, 105n33
Minushkin, Susan, 158
miraculous performance paradigm, policy choices and posterior beliefs and, 60–61
Monge Alvárez, Alberto, 37, 49–50
moral hazard, International Monetary Fund (IMF) policies and, 181–183
multinational corporations (MNCs), capital account liberalization and, 142–145
Mundell–Fleming open economy macroeconomics, capital mobility and, 142

Naim, Moisés, 10–11
nationalization, privatization as replacement for, 137–139
National Liberation Party (Partido de Liberación Nacional) (PLN) (Costa Rica), 37; economic policy of, 49
National Solidarity Program (Mexico), 126
neo-liberal revolution, 2–3
newly industrialized countries (NICs), economic growth in, 73
New Zealand, market reforms in, 12

Nigeria, IMF agreements with, 199n19
non-victims with a program: baseline IMF model and, 198–199; IMF agreements and, 188
normal distribution, conjugate prior sampling, 69–71
normative issues: learning hypothesis and, 35–36; market reform in developing countries and, 220–234
North American Free Trade Agreement (NAFTA), 161
NUMBER OF OTHER COUNTRIES variable: predicted probability of privatization and, 134–135; predicted probability of signed IMF agreements, 203; predicted probability of trade liberalization and, 100–101
NUMBER variable, policy diffusion and, 63–66

Oduber, Daniel, 49
Olszewski, Jan, 114
open capital accounts: economic growth and, 153–157; IMF agreements and probability of, 174–175; in Latin America, 175n30; prior parameters for, 154–179; probability of launching and sustainability, 164, 175–176; sustainability of, 169–171; theoretical case for, 177–178
open trade regime, proportion of countries with, 84
Organization for Economic Co-operation and Development (OECD): budget deficits and privatization in countries of, 122–124; imposition hypothesis of privatization and, 128–133, 137; Latin American influence on privatization by, 139; privatization policies and, 33, 114–116, 122n6; sustainability of privatization in countries of, 126–132
orthodox paradox, 77, 77n5
Ortiz, Guillermo, 22, 159–160
OWN experience variable: predicted probability of signed IMF agreements, 204, 204n23; sustainability of capital account liberalization and, 164–167

Pacto de Solidaridad, 80–81
Panama, market reforms in, 9–10

paradigm shift: learning hypothesis and, 224–226; market reform and, 16, 16n15; mixed record of market reform and, 236–238

Park Chung Hee, 5–6, 76–77

Partido Revolucionario Institucional (PRI) (Mexico), 160

partisan preferences, capital account liberalization and, 147n6, 148n7

par value system, IMF policies and collapse of, 184

Pastor, Manuel, 192

past participation variable, probability of entering and sustaining IMF agreements and, 202n22

per capita income, market reform and, 104n32, 105n33

Pérez, Carlos A., 10–11

Peronist government, 5–6

persuasion, capital account liberalization and, 148n8, 149n9

Peru: market reforms in, 11; privatization in, 118–119

peso crisis, 160–161; Mexican narrative of learning and financial liberalization and, 157, 161n19, 163

Pinochet, Augusto: economic reforms of, 5–6; privatization under, 115–117, 120, 133

point estimation: Bayesian rational updating and, 40n4; posterior distribution and, 43n11

Poland: privatization in, 119n3, 121n4; shock therapy stabilization in, 223

policy change: dynamic probit and, 62–64; International Monetary Fund (IMF) role in, 181–183; learning operationalization and, 58; predicted probability of adopting and sustaining, 219–222; sustainability of, 61–64

policy choice: convergence on, 217–219; learning hypothesis and, 58–67, 217

policy convergence: capital mobility and, 144–145; competition and, 28n30; Latin American trade liberalization and, 81–89; learning and alternative hypotheses and, 22–29; policy choices and, 217–219; privatization and, 127–139

policy diffusion: capital mobility and, 144–145; dynamic probit model and, 62–64; privatization and, 112

policy innovation, 21n21; bounded learning and, 19, 19n20, 21; diffusion of, 112–113; experience as factor in, 222; regional experience and privatization in Latin America and, 138, 138n18

policy makers, rational and bounded learning and, 18–19, 19n19

policy switches, Bayesian updating and rational decision making and, 53

political economy, of capital account liberalization, 145–157

political factors: capital account liberalization and, 142–143; economic success and, 232, 232n11; in financial crises, 171n26; in IMF policies, 187–188; imposition hypothesis of privatization and, 133–134; learning hypothesis and, 226–227; market reforms and government preferences, 5, 7–8; Mexican financial liberalization and, 160–161; policy choices and posterior beliefs and, 60–61; policy diffusion and, 63–66; prior beliefs, 40n6; in privatization, 115–116; in privatization policy, 122–124; probability of entering and sustaining IMF agreements and, 200, 202n21; regime characteristics and policy choices, 65–67; sustainability of privatization and, 126–132

politics, economic growth and, 229, 230n9, 231

populist ideology: market reforms and, 5–6; paradigm shift concerning market reform in, 238

Portugal: IMF agreement, 198; influence of Latin America on, 139; privatization, 119; privatization in, 118

posterior beliefs: equations for, 44–45; learning and development strategies and, 89–103; learning hypothesis and role of, 216–224; parameters for, 43–44; policy choices and, 58–68; predicted probability of trade liberalization, 98–100; privatization and, 125–137; probit modeling and, 62–64;

production of, 43; summary statistics, 71–72; updating process, 47–58

POSTERIOR BELIEFS ABOUT AVERAGE GROWTH, REGION, predicted probability of privatization and, 134–135

POSTERIOR BELIEFS ABOUT OWN GROWTH variable, trade liberalization vs. trade protectionism and, 99–100

posterior distribution, point estimates, 43n11

power distribution, policy preferences and, 65

pragmatism, privatization policy and, 115–124

principal-agent theory, privatization and, 114

prior beliefs: development strategies and, 107–108; economic policy and, 40–42; International Monetary Fund agreements and, 181n1, 204, 210; open capital accounts and, 154–179; parametrization of, 71; policy innovation and, 113; privatization and, 125, 125n10, 137, 140; trade liberalization and, 76–108

prior sum of squares, 44n15, 45n15

private capital, IMF policies and rise of, 184

privatization: basic principles of, 113–121; benefits of, 124, 124n9; descriptive statistics on, 140; in East Central Europe, 119n3, 121n4; economic development and, 77n4, 124; economic growth and, 32; emulation and coercion and, 127–137; in Europe, 117, 119; international forces and adoption of, 112; international proportion privatizers, 122; in Latin America, 116–119; learning hypothesis and, 33, 111–113, 121–137; list of countries adopting, 140; Mexican narrative of learning and financial liberalization and, 158, 159n16, 160, 160n17; miscellaneous motivations for, 115n2; policy diffusion and, 112; political rationales for, 115–116; pragmatic and political factors in, 122–124; predicted probability of, 134–135; prior beliefs and, 125, 125n10, 137, 140; probability

of launching and sustaining, 126–132; regional variations, 111, 111n1, 115n2, 121n4

Privatization around the World, 121–122

Privatization Yearbooks, 121–122

probit modeling, 40n4; probability of entering and sustaining IMF agreements and, 202n22; sustainability of policy and dynamic probit, 62–64

psychological factors in decision-making, market reforms and, 7–8, 11–12

public sector: economic development and, 77n4; horizontal policy convergence and, 27n28; privatization and streamlining of, 113–121

Quinn, Dennis, 147n6, 148n7, 149–151

Ramamurti, Ravi, 120

rates of growth, 44–45, 45n16; import substitution and, 55

rational learning, 21n23, 22n23; economic policy reform and, 38–39; emulation and, 228–229; imposition hypothesis of privatization and, 137; information sources and, 216–217; legacy on policy change of, 224; market reform and, 17, 17n17, 18n18, 22; policy innovation and, 112–113; privatization and, 125–137; successful decision making using, 67–68, 68n29

rational updating: learning hypothesis and, 29–30; regional classifications, 28n30, 31n32

Reagan, Ronald, market reforms under, 5–6

regime characteristics: development strategies and, 79; dichotomous indicators of, 129n13; electoral politics and, 92–93; EMULATION variable and, 90–92; global trade liberalization and policy change, 98–100; imposition hypothesis of privatization and; as learning variable, 92–94; market reform and, 65–67; for predicted probability of trade liberalization and, 98–100; probability of entering and sustaining IMF agreements and, 200; trade liberalization and, 96–98; World Bank

272 *Index*

regime characteristics (*cont.*)
Development Report classification, 107–108
regional experience: capital account liberalization and, 151–152; development strategies and, 86–87; emulation and, 223–224; import substitution and export orientation and, 52; intervention and adaptation, debt shock of 1982, 54–55; policy change and, 223; predicted probability of signed IMF agreements, 204; prior beliefs and IMF agreements, 205; privatization and, 111, 111n1, 115n2, 121n4; trade liberalization and, 105
religious preferences, capital account liberalization and sharing of, 149, 168
rent-seeking behavior, privatization and, 114
Report in Issues and Developments in International Trade Policy, 82
representativeness heuristic, policy innovation and, 20
re-privatization, Chilean phenomenon of, 116–117, 122
RESERVES indicators: baseline model of IMF and, 198n18; predicted probability of signed IMF agreements, 203–204; probability of entering and sustaining IMF agreements and, 200
reverse causality, capital account liberalization and, 147n6, 148n7
Ricardo–Viner specific factor model, capital account liberalization and, 146–147
rightist governments: capital account liberalization and, 147n6, 148n7; imposition hypothesis of privatization and, 129–130; market reform and, 5–6
risk aversion: import substitution and, 94–95; policy choices and posterior beliefs and, 60–61, 61n25; privatization and, 125–137; risk reduction strategy, 46n17; trade liberalization and, 105
risk-prone behavior, sustainability of capital account liberalization, 164–167
Robinson, James, 11–12, 103–104
Rodríguez, Miguel A., 11

Rodrik, Dani, 6, 11n10, 102–103
Rose, Richard, 14–15
Ruiz Massieu, José Francisco, 160
Russia, privatization in, 114

Sachs–Warner trade liberalization measure, 48–49, 74n1, 84
Salinas de Gortari, Carlos: learning hypothesis and policies of, 80–81, 101–103; Mexican narrative of learning and financial liberalization and, 158–160; privatization efforts of, 115–117, 126–132
Santín, Osvaldo, 158
Sarney, José, 80–81
satisficing, bounded learning and, 17n17
Schamis, Hector, 120
second-generation reforms, policy analysis, 31, 31n33
sectoral interests, development strategies and, 78
security issues, IMF policies and, 186–187
shared beliefs: rational and bounded learning and, 18–19; social learning and, 17
shock modeling: learning from others *vs.* learning from shocks, 90–95; learning hypothesis and, 224–226; of posterior beliefs, 47–58; posterior beliefs and, 56–57
short-term debts, financial liberalization and, 171
Silva-Herzog, Jesús, 161n19
Simmons, Beth, 149–151, 168, 168n21, 169n23
Singapore: export orientation in, 75–76; global economic integration by, 2
SIZE coefficients: controls on trade liberalization and, 101–103; trade liberalization policies, 93–94
size variables, trade liberalization and, 93–94
social interests, capital account liberalization and, 147n6, 148n7
socialism, market reforms and, 5–6
social learning, market reforms and, 15–17, 17n16
South Asia: export orientation in, 89n20, 90n21; IMF agreements in, 195n16; trade liberalization and, 21n23, 22n23

South Korea: export orientation in, 75–76; global economic integration by, 2; limits of export orientation in, 76–77; market reforms in, 5–6, 11n10; public enterprises in, 114

sovereignty costs: IMF agreements and, 188, 209; probability of entering and sustaining IMF agreements and, 202–203

Spain: influence of Latin America on, 139; privatization in, 122

spatial lagged variables analysis, trade liberalization and capital account liberalization, 168n21

Srinivasan, T. N., 11n10, 11n11

Standby IMF agreements, learning hypothesis and, 193, 193n13

state-owned enterprises (SOEs): in Chile, 116–117; in Latin America, 118–119; Mexican narrative of learning and financial liberalization and, 157–163; in Mexico, 126; in Spain, 117

statist economic development: in Costa Rica, 49; export orientation and, 76–77; future role of, 236–238; marketization as replacement for, 137–139; policy debates concerning, 73–74; privatization and, 133

statistical parameters: capital account liberalization and, 154–179; descriptive statistics on privatization, 140; economic growth measurement and, 42–47; International Monetary Fund agreements and, 181n1, 210

status quo bias against market reform, 8

Stiglitz, Joseph, 3n4

Stolper–Samuelson theorem, 79n8; capital account liberalization and, 146

Stone, Randall, 185n6

sustainability: of capital account liberalization, 164–167, 169–171; of economic policies, 61, 63n28, 64; of open capital accounts, 175–176; predicted probability of policy adoption and, 219–222; of privatization policies, 126–132

Taiwan: global economic integration by, 2; market reforms in, 11n10; public enterprises in, 114

tariff reforms: adoption of export orientation and, 95n27; in Costa Rica, 50, 50n19

technocratic alignment: successful decision making and, 67–68, 68n29; top-down policy convergence, 25, 25n26

Telmex, 117

Thailand, privatization in, 101–102

Thatcher, Margaret, 5–6, 12, 111, 115–116, 120

third-order change, market reform and, 15–17

Tomassi, Mariano, 8–10

top-down policy convergence; Mexican liberalization crisis and, 162–163; privatization and absence of, 138

Toyoda, Ana María, 149–150

trade liberalization: capital account liberalization and, 167–168, 168n21; capital mobility and, 143–144; Costa Rican example of, 37; definitions of, 81n13, 82n13; democratization and, 74, 79, 92–94; development strategies and, 74n1; experience as basis for, 105; growth rates and volatility of results, 87–88; IMF policies in support of, 186; international comparisons, 37–38, 80; learning hypothesis and, 81–89, 226n6; list of countries involved in, 76–108; measurements of, 82–83, 83n16, 83n17; prior beliefs and, 76–108; probability of, 96–98; variability of economic growth and, 76–108

Trade Liberalization Database, 83n16, 83n17, 87–88, 90, 96–98

Trade Policy Reform in Developing Countries since 1985, 83

trade protectionism, economic growth and, 76–100, 108

transitional probabilities: developmental strategies, posterior beliefs and, 89–103; policy sustainability and, 63n28

t-Student distribution: conditional distribution of the mean, 42n9; conjugate prior sampling, 69–71

uncertainty, 38n3; adaptation of beliefs and, 52–53; economic growth and, 42–47; government posterior beliefs vs.

274 *Index*

uncertainty (*cont.*)
observation and, 55; in IMF
agreements, 206n25, 208; prior beliefs
and, 40–42; rational and bounded
learning and, 18–19, 38–39
unemployment, success of economic
reform linked to, 61n25
United States, domination of International
Monetary Fund, 184, 184n4, 186
universal convergence, 1
Uruguay, IMF agreement with, 198
utility criterion, policy choices and
posterior beliefs, 59

VARIABILITY OF RESULTS, OWN,
sustainability of capital account
liberalization and, 166–167
variance of mean, prior beliefs, 71
variance of results: learning and
developmental strategies and, 89–90;
trade liberalization and, 96, 96n28,
98n29, 99n29
VARIABILITY OF RESULTS, WORLD:
probability of trade liberalization and,
96–98, 102–103; shock experience and,
96–98
Velasco, Andrés, 8–10
Venezuela, debt crisis in, 172n27
veto players model, probability of entering
and sustaining IMF agreements and,
202n21
"victims without a program," IMF
agreements and, 188
Villegas, Alejandro, 85n18
Vreeland, James R., 192, 192n12, 193n13,
199–202, 202n21

Vreeland's criterion of need, 186n8, 188

Wade, Robert, 103–104, 104n31, 104n32
Washington Consensus, 1, 1n1, 1n2;
capital account liberalization and,
147–148; International Monetary Fund
(IMF) policies and, 181n1, 185, 210;
legacy of, 236; market reform proposals
of, 11n10; rightist defenses of, 5–6;
top-down policy convergence, 24
Webb, Richard, 11
Weyland, Kurt, 7–8, 17n16, 19–21,
80n11
Williamson, John, 9, 11
World Bank: capital account liberalization
and, 149n9; market reform data from,
235; privatization data, 124; regime
classification criteria, 107–108
World Bank Development Report, 82
World Bank Privatization Database, 121
World Development Indicators:
probability of entering and sustaining
IMF agreements and, 200; trade
liberalization and, 96–98
World Trade Organization (WTO):
coercive power of, 105–106; impact of
controls on trade liberalization and,
101–103; top-down policy convergence
and, 26n27

YEARS UNDER variable, probability of
entering and remaining under IMF
agreements, 199–202

Zapatista rebellion, 160
Zedillo, Ernesto, 160–161